Changing Schools from the Inside Out

Changing Schools from the Inside Out

Small Wins in Hard Times

Third Edition

Robert L. Larson

ROWMAN & LITTLEFIELD EDUCATION

A division of

ROWMAN & LITTLEFIELD PUBLISHERS, INC.
Lanham • New York • Toronto • Plymouth, UK

KH

Published by Rowman & Littlefield Education
A division of Rowman & Littlefield Publishers, Inc.
A wholly owned subsidary of The Rowman & Littlefield Publishing Group, Inc.
4501 Forbes Boulevard, Suite 200, Lanham, Maryland 20706
http://www.rowmaneducation.com

Estover Road, Plymouth PL6 7PY, United Kingdom

British Library Cataloguing in Publication Information Available

Library of Congress Cataloging-in-Publication Data

Larson, Robert L.
  Changing schools from the inside out : small wins in hard times / Robert L. Larson. — 3rd ed.
      p. cm.
  Includes bibliographical references and index.
  ISBN 978-1-60709-527-9 (cloth : alk. paper) — ISBN 978-1-60709-528-6 (pbk. : alk. paper) — ISBN 978-1-60709-529-3 (electronic)
  1. Education, Secondary—Aims and objectives—United States. 2. School improvement programs—United States. I. Title.
  LA222.L37 2010
  373.73—dc22   2011004177

♾ ™ The paper used in this publication meets the minimum requirements of American National Standard for Information Sciences—Permanence of Paper for Printed Library Materials, ANSI/NISO Z39.48-1992.

Printed in the United States of America

8/23/12

To Kenneth D. Benne (1908–1992), Matthew B. Miles (1926–1996), and J. Lloyd Trump (1908–1985), three educators whom I had the good fortune and privilege to know personally and to work with and who influenced my professional life and career in several important ways

Contents

Acknowledgments

An essential way to gain understanding about change and innovation in schools is for researchers to probe their dynamics in the real world of public education—to "muck around" in life in schools against the backdrop of theories of what ought to be. This book examines the realities of those dynamics in the Fairhaven Union High School and the Hazen Union School, both in Vermont. The findings enabled other national research to be connected to the field studies so that the outcomes demonstrated applicability beyond the Vermont context.

I am indebted to the principals, superintendents, teachers, and staff who provided the foundational data for half the chapters. They demonstrated a high degree of professionalism in supporting the project, in offering their unqualified cooperation and help, and in being candid and thoughtful research subjects.

In addition to my indebtedness to those professionals, so too am I for this edition to Kevin Turner, principal of the Harwich (MA) High School, Terry Russell, retired principal of the Barnstable Middle School, and Thomas Johnson, educational consultant and former associate superintendent for Human Resource Management and Development for the Broward County (FL) Public Schools. Each read the second edition and urged me to update it because the content was more relevant than ever to what has been happening in and to public education since 1999.

Terry also read some chapter drafts and provided ideas for figures relative to the role of teachers and principals.

Another word about Kevin: he always found a spot in his packed calendar for me to drop by to check something out, to discuss an issue, or to clarify current practice. His generosity with his time, plus his insights and feedback helped greatly to ensure that this edition would be relevant to professionals in schools today.

Second, I thank Carolyn Cragin, superintendent of the Harwich Schools and Carla Blanchard, director of curriculum, for their advice and sharing of materials.

Third, the sections on technology could not have been added without the help of some Harwich faculty, namely Jim Birchfield, instructional technology specialist, and teachers John Anderson, Jill Eastman, Elizabeth Hoff, and Rebecca Stang. Each allowed me to observe their classes and talk with their students, and each sat for more than one interview.

Fourth, I thank Joel Peterson for his meticulous updating of the bibliography by deleting passé entries and adding new ones from my scrawled legal pad notes. Joel also used his computer expertise to create several new figures from my hand-drawn sketches.

Fifth, I express deep gratitude to my wife, Karin, and to my friend, George Voland. Karin read every chapter draft before it was sent to George, who again put the manuscript under his editorial microscope from his perspective as a retired high school English teacher. George also went beyond pure editing to prod my thinking along the rewriting route and provided critical ideas and commentary along the way.

Finally, this third edition would not have been written without the enthusiastic proposal support and then approval of Tom Koerner, vice president and editorial director, Education Division, Rowman & Littlefield.

Foreword

Perhaps you help run schools from a state department of education or in a school district as a superintendent, assistant superintendent, director of instruction, or board member.

Perhaps you work in school administration as a principal, assistant principal, department chair, coordinator of special education, or head of guidance.

Perhaps you work directly with students each day in the classroom as a teacher, special educator, or teacher's aide.

Or maybe you are a parent, a media reporter, an education analyst, or a textbook writer.

All of you, both inside and outside the classroom, have had experiences with top-down, mandated reforms aimed at improving public education. If you are the creator of a mandated change in education, you know how it feels to have gone through the stages of reform, from its inception to its adoption. You have invested yourself in this mandated change, and you are excited to see it produce the anticipated outcomes. If you're a concerned outsider, you, too, look forward to seeing students get the benefit of the reform.

If you serve students as a public educator, though, one who works directly with students in the classroom, special education services, guidance office, or administrative offices, you know, in a very different way, how it feels when your school faces yet another top-down reform. You don't feel excited because you have been through this exercise many times already. However, you chose to become and remain a public educator so you can serve students, so you will obviously work positively with this latest mandate, just as you have in the past and as you do with whatever enters the helping environment of your classroom.

Whether you are a school insider or outsider, you will quickly know that Bob Larson knows well both how and why top-down education reformers do what they do. And he has a rare understanding as well for how and why public school educators feel as they do about mandated change.

He knows because he has spent his life as an educator, first as a high school teacher and then as a respected professor, researcher, and consultant for three decades at the University of Vermont. And most important for all those who care about improving public education, he has done the academic and field research you have always hoped would be done to either validate or negate what you have known all along from anecdotal evidence. Even the most well-intended top-down initiatives rarely meet their intended goals, and some violate what should also be a change agent's oath: "First do no harm."

Perhaps this third edition of *Changing School from the Inside Out* may be the third-time-is-the-charm edition that helps all of us see the relative fruitlessness of top-down, mandated change in education. Perhaps we will instead see, with convincing historical clarity, how inexorably mandated changes have moved in and out of classrooms. Perhaps we will see that they do bring with them some benefits, but at a large price to educators and students because they also bring with them unnecessary disruption and even outright damage to students and educators and, thus, to the institutional psyche of public education.

What has Larson uncovered that can help all who want the changing of public schools to work for good rather than ill?

At the very least, widespread knowledge of Larson's findings could make it more evident to all of us who wield political power over public education that we need to wake up to the reality presented here in *Changing Schools from the Inside Out: Small Wins in Hard Times* That reality tells us: "No matter how well-intentioned you are, if you continue to use your power to force reform on schools, you will be exhibiting symptoms of insanity defined as 'doing the same thing over and over again but expecting different results.'"

At the most, the ideas in this book will renew our hope that we can and will discover anew and use effectively an approach to changing education that steadily improves public education. As Larson shows us in the following pages, we can realize the promise of real progress in education, even in harsh economic times—perhaps especially in such times—if we awaken to the wealth of human resources that already reside in our schools.

It seems quite clear to me—as a high school educator for thirty three years, as well as the fortunate editor who has parsed, from the inside out, every work and idea in this book, just as I did with the first two editions—that the time has come for all of us to alter how we view and effect change in education. As Larson says of this effective approach to educational reform, ". . . there is no magic in it. It is incremental and evolutionary, requiring the support and industry of all the parties that have an investment in public education in America."

No pithy classroom sound bites, no media-birthed "reality" education show, no *No Child Left Behind*, no White Knight heroics. Simply hard, dedicated, deeply rewarding work daily with learners, the kind of sustained effective effort that we see in thousands of classrooms that make up schools—like the "Bromley" and "Mansfield" you will read about in Larson's case studies—where administrators, teachers, counselors, and other staff commit themselves to trust one another and their students and to use the most effective practices available in order to help their students learn and grow to their full potential.

Sustained, sustainable, evolving change in education works just like change in any other dynamic endeavor that involves human relationships. We can and must embrace it now so we can work together in the best way possible to produce the kind of informed electorate that a democracy requires if it hopes to flourish.

George Voland

Preface

When I revised this book in 1999, I noted that public school educators faced a time of great challenge. Then it contrasted sharply to the context of the first edition in 1992.

Since 1999, the challenge has become even greater. Yet, now as then, educators still strive to graduate young citizens who will bring competence, caring, and responsibility to their roles in society. They still aim to achieve nothing less than the historic goal public education was designed to achieve for all citizens in the United States: to ensure an informed electorate for the health and viability of a democratic society.

But the attacks on public education of a decade ago seem tame compared to what educators have already faced during the first part of this new millennium. Some politicians and special interest groups have stepped up their assaults, and educators have seen already inadequate resources diverted from schools toward alternative organizations within the school system and to private forms in the community.

Then, while the public school system tries to advance toward its goal of producing an informed electorate, it finds itself harried by severe budget cuts or level-funded budgets; uncooperative children, youth, and parents; antagonistic and unsupportive communities; the testing requirements of *No Child Left Behind* plus those of states; and ever-increasing expectations heaped on the organization in response to a myriad of social needs,

No wonder educators struggle to find the time, resources, and energy they need if they hope to help their students by increasing the quality and relevance of curricula and instruction.

Seldom do we hear words of praise for our schools from the political establishment or the press—or, at the very least, words of understanding about the obstacles that block the path to real improvement. Indeed, those hostile to the public schools are better organized and better supported financially than they were in 1999.

The "accountability squeeze" (described in Chapter 1) has led, for example, to publicly labeling schools as "pass or fail" and to fledgling moves to grade teacher performance similarly; to having wide success at implementing charter schools and schools of choice in every state; to having private companies manage schools; and to making "turnaround schools" the latest addition to the accountability lexicon imported from the private sector.

Efforts such as these seem aimed at weakening schools so that talented youngsters will be siphoned off to charters or schools of choice or, ultimately, to private schools (with voucher support). As a result, public schools will be serving the less motivated and less academically capable students who will be harder to educate and easier to write off as the residue of educator failure. Hence, why should schools continue to get the support they have enjoyed? Therefore, reduce their budgets to match their failure.

But thankfully, there is still a solid base of community support for our schools, and that base provides the impetus for successful innovation and admirable accomplishments despite the number and difficulty of the challenges. You cannot stifle the steady movement toward improved learning and the closing of the achievement gap brought about by committed and skilled educators and their supporters in communities and legislatures.

The eight chapters that follow are written so that they can be read separately, depending on one's time and interests, put aside, and returned to easily. Highlights are:

- the effect of the nation's current social, cultural, economic, and political context on school improvement
- the ways that technology affects teaching and learning
- the major secondary school improvement projects that have been implemented during the last four decades
- the way some business practices can be useful to schools
- the effect that social-psychological features of schools and classrooms have on school improvement
- the critical roles principals and teachers play in bringing about change in education
- a clear and plausible theory base for realistic, achievable change through a strategy of small wins, drawing on two case studies of schools to illustrate how the process works

- real school examples that illustrate the concepts of garbage can decision-making, loose coupling, organized anarchies, and classrooms as busy kitchens
- real school examples of the application of the Concerns-Based Adoption Model
- a concluding chapter that depicts how several concrete, practical "levers" and "footings" for change can be used in any school
- an extensive, up-to-date bibliography

Despite the threatening context faced by educators, they have a great responsibility—and the great ability—to seek new opportunities to improve education and seek new ideas for doing so. The job will be tougher than ever, but those who believe in public education have no choice but to meet the challenge. Change is not an option. My goal in writing and revising this book is to help them succeed, for today's public educators must succeed for the sake of the future of our young people and the society in which they live.

Introduction

In the new era of school reform, change is approached on an incremental basis.

—Marzano, 2003, p. 159

Given the relative stability of organizations, one might expect that innovation would be very rare. On the contrary, innovation is going on all the time in almost every organization.

—Rogers, 1983, p. 349

At a time when it seems that everyone from the president to the parent is demanding change in the way we educate our children, we are going to focus on change that works: small-scale, incremental change in high schools, those 20,620 7–12 or 9–12 organizations out of 98,916 public elementary and secondary schools (Keaton, personal communication, February 4, 2010). Marzano, who reviewed the school improvement literature for the last thirty years, concluded that this approach has the greatest chance for success. Elmore (2004) says: "To succeed, school reform has to happen from the inside out" (p. 3).

Not only does small-scale, incremental change work in education, it also provides a viable route to improvement in the private sector. Senge, in his best-selling business-oriented book, *The Fifth Discipline,* states: "Small changes can produce big results, but the areas of highest leverage are often the least obvious" (2006).

Changing Schools from the Inside Out: Small Wins in Hard Times examines this approach in good schools to see how it works to effect evolutionary improvement. What works in these schools should also, in most cases, apply to elementary- and middle-level organizations in a rural, suburban, or urban

1

setting. The "inside out" approach, however, has been neglected or downplayed by innovation advocates, and, hence, there has been no substantive research base for it.

My professional experiences over forty one years, plus my good fortune to be able to observe schools during twelve retirement years, have convinced me of the validity of Marzano's, Rogers', and Senge's observations. I am impressed by the inventiveness of educators in changing practice from the inside out and in adapting to practices foisted on them.

Their organizations adopt, develop, and drop innovations within the context of recurring cycles of societal expectations and support for schools. Fitting here is the "innovativeness" discussed by Fullan in the fourth edition of his classic synthesis of the change literature (2007), the capacity to engage in continuous improvement (p. 11).

But this is not to deny that there are too many schools, which, for a multitude of reasons, have achieved the dubious label of "turnaround schools." Some 5,000 such schools are the ". . . nation's worst performing schools" (*Education Week*, August 12, 2009, pp. 1; 18). And no one is certain how many others are close to this categorization across our fifty states.

For some school critics, however, dismay about the "performance" of schools goes beyond this current grouping of 5,000. To them, the overall organization is stuck in the status quo. Yet, despite severe resource limitations, "Schools are being asked by elected officials-policy leaders, if you will, to do things they are largely unequipped to do" (Elmore, 2004, p. 43). As we shall see in the next chapter, such expectations are increasing. "Do more with less" is the current exhortation!

Such reformers usually have learned few lessons from the history of the change research. Thus, they tend to place the blame for resistance to change primarily at the doorstep of school personnel, a conclusion similar to a major finding from Goodlad's landmark study of 38 schools and 1,016 classrooms: "We refuse to face the realities of what it takes to change such complex social/ political institutions as schools (Tye & Tye, 1984, p. 319). As we shall see in the next chapter, more recent reform efforts still demonstrate, in too many instances, the sad and distressing tendency to skip the findings from research and practice and instead launch another new program.

However, parents, students, and educators in thousands of communities express satisfaction with the quality and form of curriculum and instruction offered by their schools. These "satisfying" schools, as Goodlad describes them, ". . . are at a stage of greater readiness for more fundamental improvement" (1984, p. 270).

Such schools, several of which were high schools, share similarities with those described by Lightfoot in her book about "good" high schools (1983) (see also Ogden & Germinario, 1995). *U.S. News & World* Report annually surveys virtually all high schools to find the top 100 that were preparing students for college, schools from affluent as well as less affluent communities (Terrell, 2010, p. 65). In addition, the magazine also selected another 100 Silver Medal Schools.

Boston Magazine conducts an annual analysis of "best public and private high schools" in the greater Boston area. Out of the pool of schools, it selects twenty of the best based on student/teacher ratios, state test scores, SAT scores, and graduation rates (De Gersdorff, 2009). These communities (and many others) are highly pleased with the quality of education offered by their organizations.

All of these observations are in line with the annual Phi Delta Kappa/Gallup Poll about schools. The 2010 poll found that 50 percent of Americans surveyed awarded a grade of A or B to schools in their community, and 77 percent of parents assigned a grade of A or B to schools attended by their oldest child, two points above the 2009 survey (Bushaw & Lopez, 2010, pp.12–13). These parental judgments were based on criteria broader than preparation for college.

In addition, an award-winning examination of a century of reform efforts by Tyack and Cuban led them to conclude that" . . . the nearer the observer is to the schools, the better they look; and confidence in schools is higher than in other institutions" (1995, p. 30).

We cannot overlook the fact that many schools in our nation find themselves in a critical condition due to their inability to meet either state or federal "accountability" measures, nor can we avoid the fact that others suffer from chronic "health" issues due to dire financial straits, lack of community support, being overwhelmed by the nature of their student bodies, an underperforming staff, poor leadership, or some combination of them all. However, we will instead focus on those organizations that have managed to do better despite delimiting conditions.

What can we learn about the dynamics of change in these secondary schools that will allow us to take our schools to another level of effectiveness, regardless of the setting? How can already good schools or those who fall short become better by building on their current success?

What we can learn will help us meet the need for low-cost strategies for school improvement, strategies that the local school initiates, not strategies that begin with mandated, across-the-board innovations at the district or school levels, external incentives to change through various grant programs, or planned, top-down, comprehensive change across an organization or system. Most of the time, as we shall see from the research, these approaches do not work as intended, have minimal impact on learning, and do not become institutionalized.

HOW THIS BOOK WILL BE OF HELP TO YOU

You will become more conversational with the knowledge base about recurring small-scale change in the site-managed building—"small wins" to use Weick's term (1984). "Small victories attract constituents, create momentum, get people to remain on the path" (Kouzes & Posner, 2007, p. 198). This commonplace type of innovation traditionally has been slighted in studies of societies and organizations (Barnett, 1953) with more recent studies (to be cited in chapters to come) demonstrating that this 1953 observation is highly relevant today.

However, this slighting of smallness is not as true in the private sector. Senge, in his popular treatise on the learning organization, concludes: "For system thinking also shows that small, well-focused actions can sometimes produce significant, enduring improvements, if they're in the right place. Systems thinkers refer to this principle as 'leverage'" (2006, pp. 63–64). Kouzes and Posner, in their managerial research spanning twenty five years, devote several pages to achieving small wins (2007, pp. 188–199).

In the public sector, support for this "inside out" approach to change comes from education historians Tyack and Cuban: "We favor attempts to bring about such improvements by working from the inside out, especially by enlisting the support and skills of teachers as key actors in reform" (1995. p. 10). And more recent support comes from Marzano's research (2003, p. 159).

Unfortunately, this form of change has received short shrift in most of the literature that focuses on educational administration. Some have seen it as "tinkering" in the negative sense—fiddling around without accomplishing much of importance—as opposed to tinkering as a ". . . commonsense remedy for everyday problems" (Tyack & Cuban, p. 4).

Hence, the fact is that the bulk of the school change literature focuses on prescribed, ambitious, system-wide, or, at least, subsystem innovation. Even though research clearly shows that such an approach seldom succeeds in meeting its goals, you will see many references to it in the chapters that follow because it is important to understand this history.

Clearly, educators need more knowledge and strategies that can help them to appreciate, understand, and implement smaller-scale innovations because such innovation has proven that it can be a successful avenue to school improvement.

You will find simple operational concepts and practical techniques that will enable you to become better at effecting and managing change within the hectic, pressured environment of schools. I have learned from my experiences in education the wisdom of the admonition, "Keep It Simple, Stupid!"—KISS for short—that was a major theme in the best-selling, *In Search of Excellence:*

Lesson's From America's Best-Run Companies (Peters & Waterman, 1982, p. 63). KISS and effective change go hand-in-hand.

This is not to say that becoming better at school improvement through more "simple," singular strategies is a non-theoretical enterprise. Indeed theory provides the foundation for these strategies. In today's fast-moving organizational worlds, the old dictum "There is nothing so practical as good theory" holds more truth than ever. We must develop our ability to conceptualize and understand the processes associated with, in this case, small-scale change while engaged in the daily demands of delivering curriculum and instruction.

So count on this book to help you develop or refine your *theory of changing* as advocated by Fullan (1991, pp. 107–113) and Sarason (1996, p. 63). Such a theory will integrate concepts, technical knowledge, human relations skills, and knowledge of the social psychology of the workplace. Such knowledge integration will give you a better chance of understanding change and change situations from the perspective of those experiencing it rather than from the perspective of those initiating and pressing for it.

As you proceed through this book, you will see that new perspectives of organizational dynamics dispel the image that there is any *one change process* as asserted by Fullan who says, "This chapter and the next one contains a description of *the* (my emphasis) educational change process and an explanation of why it works as it does" (2007, p. 64). In 2009, he reiterated that assertion (p. 11), which seems to conflict with his stress on a theory of changing. This image is common in the larger organizational literature. For me focusing a search on the "right" process can engender considerable frustration and dismay as such a search is futile.

A theory of changing allows one to get beyond the surface meaning of the innovation and more fully understand its subtle meanings to others in the workplace. One has a greater chance to understand why those affected by the change might resist the change or at least not be initially enthused about it. One has a greater chance to understand why conflict might arise in what seems to be the most innocuous of situations. Hence, it is unproductive to search for that "one" process. Because most change situations involve so many interacting variables, it is impossible to try to identify and work with each in isolation. Instead, a way of thinking about change and perceiving its overt and subtle dynamics offers busy practitioners the kind of assistance they need to meet with more success in change situations (Fullan, 1991).

A theory of changing is in contrast to a *theory of change,* which focuses on the elements of process, or the characteristics of the innovation and what *should* change and how the process *should* work because it is all so rational

(Fullan, 1991). In later chapters, you will see examples of educators involved in change situations who are guided by one or the other of these "theories." You will find some new applications of old theory and some new applications of new theory.

And you proceed through the following pages, you will also find that this book has more of an organizational/sociological rather than a psychological bent. That is because educators are reared on pre-service programs that focus primarily on psychological rather than on organizational/sociological principles. This is understandable; beginning educators must concentrate their learning on the students they will instruct, on how to establish relationships with them, on how to manage the classroom, on how to deliver the curriculum they are assigned to teach, on how to assess learning, and on how to handle data and data analysis. The focus on these elements leaves virtually no space in undergraduate programs to deal with equally crucial organizational issues.

Consider the extensive preparation in organizational/sociological principles that undergraduates receive in a school of business. Compare such a background with that of school administrators, usually promoted teachers, who assume leadership roles with master's degree training that too often provides a modicum of academic knowledge about organizational processes like power, conflict, leadership, communications, and change because so much else must be learned as well.

But they are expected to lead and manage a cadre of professionals, interacting with a complex external environment, who know equally little about these processes and about the social psychology of living and working in an organization.

To add to your understanding of change processes in the schools, you will find that forthcoming chapters will connect several themes to organizational literature:

- Organizations are always changing, but they usually change through a routine, fairly unnoticed process rather than in dramatic, grand ways.
- Change is usually effected by ordinary people doing ordinary things in a competent way.
- Routine organizational processes are often key levers for improvement.
- Change is often unpredictable and not well understood.
- Organizational adaptation is an interplay of rationality and foolishness, of cognition and affect.
- Small wins can set in motion a process for continued small wins, a process that strengthens organizational capacity and ability to solve larger-scale problems.

Schools can change, they do change, and they will change, but often the ways in which effective organizations change for the better are relatively imperceptible and far from headline-grabbing. Yet you will see them more clearly as you read on, and you will learn how to use the effective tools that administrators, teachers, other school personnel, and board members need as they strive, against great odds, to educate our children and our youth.

Chapter 1

The Current Context for School Improvement

What gives us confidence that schools are able to make the shift to a student-centric approach? A primer on the theory of disruptive innovation reveals that schools in the United States have in fact constantly improved. Society just keeps moving the goalposts on schools by changing the definition of quality and asking schools to take on new jobs. Even in these new landscapes, where most successful organizations fail, schools have adapted remarkably well.

—Christensen, Horn, & Johnson, 2008, p. 11

Times have changed and so must the promise of public education. Today, our schools must ensure that our high school graduates know and are capable of much more than ever before.

—Massachusetts Department of Education, 2008, p. 2

SOCIAL FORCES IMPACTING SCHOOLS

As we enter this second decade of the 21st century, we are immersed in a period of turbulence and challenge on the national and international scenes, a period that is testing, as never before, our ability to deliver quality education to *all* learners. In one form or another, we Americans, and others in the global community, are experiencing the phenomenon of future shock, defined by Toffler in his seminal 1970 book as ". . . the shattering stress and disorientation that we induce in individuals by subjecting them to too much change in too short a time" (p. 4).

What elements of future shock have jolted American society in just the past two years, either by their "newness" or by the pace of their impact? Here is a sample list: Cyberbullying; electronic books; the underwear bomber; the anal bomber; social networking such as MySpace and Facebook; "friend-ing"; sexting; apps; digital dirt; reputation manager; grazing; deep dive; sex addiction clinics; same-sex marriage; pharma parties; melting polar ice caps; investment bank collapses; video store closings; laser scalpels; nanotubes; and cost-effective medicine.

In addition, America's economy is now mired in a recession. Stability of societal institutions seems to be a thing of the past. Ferment seems the norm. Ask someone you know who is in a profession such as education, law, medicine, theology, or business, whether he would urge his chil-dren to enter the same line of work. I have, and rarely do I get a positive response.

Keeping up with this onslaught of change in America is often frustrating and nerve-racking. Add to it the changes internationally that shout at us from the television, Internet, and newspaper headlines. No wonder our minds are numbed by change and boggled by how to sort it all out and make some sense of what often seems to be a double future-shocked landscape.

Toffler (1980) depicted three "waves" of societal change. The first was the agricultural that dominated until the mid-18th century. The second was the industrial that dominated until the mid-20th century. The third was variously labeled the post-industrial, the super-industrial, or the information age—all still applicable today (pp. 9–16).

Now, within just five decades, we are entering another age, one that Friedman calls Globalization 3.0, the shrinking of the world, the leveling of the national competitive playing field, and the empowerment of the individual due to rapid technological change (2005, pp. 10–11).

Pink sees the emergence of the "Conceptual Age," characterized by a sub-tle, gradual shift from the dominance of left-brain logical, linear thinking, to right-brain, more dynamic thinking, dominated by emotional intelligence, creativity, problem-solving, empathy, and spiritual fulfillment (2006).

"When a society is struck by two or more giant waves of change, and none is yet clearly dominant, the image of the future is fractured" (Toffler, 1980, p. 15). It is today for America. We struggle to find a viable path forward through daunting impermanence. We are unsure where we are headed and often feel apprehensive as our politics become more polarized as a result. This polarization makes it at least difficult, and sometimes impossible, to reach agreement on critical legislation. The evidence of this condition is all around us within our states and nation and made vivid by the election results from November 2010.

Eventually, out of this cauldron of change, trends emerge that have a profound impact on schools and particularly on the secondary school. Here are three relatively recent ones at the top of my impact list that are less obvious than others relating to economics, society, technology, or politics, already discussed extensively in the media.

DIGITAL OVERLOAD

In their insightful book, *Born Digital,* Palfrey and Gasser (2008) look closely at students currently in schools, the first generation, born after 1980 to have lived all their lives in the digital age. The authors call them "Digital Natives," young people who are totally comfortable and facile with all forms of technology around them and us. They have known only a digital world.

They study, write, talk, process information, and interact with peers and others in ways that are very different from their predecessors because they have been immersed in ". . . the most rapid period of technological transformation ever, at least when it comes to information" (p. 3).

In addition, new technologies invade the marketplace seemingly overnight (e.g., Twitter) and the Digital Natives can adapt to them swiftly and easily, seeing immediately how to use them in their lives. Witness such adaptation even among kindergarteners!

Also referred to as the "net generation" (Wagner, 2008), its members have a compulsion for connectivity. The average member spends an average of seven and one half hours a day engaged with some form of electronic device (e.g., computer, smartphone, TV, iPod, and video games) compared to six hours five years ago according to a Kaiser Family Foundation study (Lewin, 2010). Teenagers alone send an average of 2,000 text messages a month according to a Pew Internet and American Life Project. Such messages are rapidly replacing cell phone calls (Yen, 2009, p. A5).

This net generation is ". . . coming of age tethered to the Internet, as well as to a host of instant communication devices that were unimaginable twenty years ago (Wagner, p. 170). These devices encourage isolation rather than face-to-face group interaction. The days of the pickup team on the vacant lot, which tested and honed social skills of give and take, have disappeared.

"Breakfast Can Wait. The Day's First Stop Is Online" headlined an article confirming this trend toward individualism (Stone, 2009). The new routine to start the day is for all family members (if they can afford it) to first check a cell phone, a laptop, or a smartphone before eating breakfast. As real times together disappear, family time declines sharply, as shown in a 2000 study by the Annenberg Center for the Digital Future in which survey respondents reported spending an average of twenty six hours per month in interaction with family members. By 2008, that figure had dropped to eighteen hours, a 30 percent decline (Ortutay, 2009, p. A4).

Two Public Broadcasting System programs, "Growing Up Online" (2008) and "Digital Nation" (2010) portray this dynamic vividly. So does anecdotal evidence. The other day, a friend of mine described how he could not get his teen granddaughter to talk with him during a two-hour drive because she was chained to text messaging.

The identity of Digital Natives is profoundly shaped by the technology they use. The forming of a "self" takes place especially during this time of life when we are most vulnerable. Who do we hope to become? Who are the role models we admire most? What aspects of their lifestyles would we like to incorporate into ours?

It used to be that formation of the self largely evolved in "effortless and unconscious" ways, patterned after one's forebears and peers in a "post-figurative" culture that was stable and relatively unchanging (Mead, 1970, p. 18). Think of the agriculture age. "The past is the road by which we have arrived at where we are" (p. 93).

Until the mid-19th century, then, individuals and social institutions like the family, church, and school, generally adapted incrementally, almost imperceptibly, to new technology and cultural changes. Evolutionary change was the norm.

Over time, usually spurred by technology, society evolves into a co-figurative culture ". . . in which the prevailing model for societal members is the behavior of their contemporaries" (p. 32). The older generation still holds much sway and sets the general boundaries within which the younger act. There is little questioning of established ways of being and doing, but the pace of technological development increases as in pre-television America.

The third stage that Mead depicts is the "pre-figurative" in which ". . . it will be the child and not the parent or grandparent that represents what is to come" (p. 88). This third stage invites a pervasive feeling of uneasiness because little from the past and present seems meaningful and workable. Such "dis-ease" now characterizes America and other economically advanced nations.

With uncertainty as the climate, parents are unsure how to influence and discipline their children during this critical phase in child and adolescent development. They are losing control. Old tenets are challenged and ignored. "Today's children have grown up in a world their elders never knew, but few adults knew that this would be so" (Mead, p. 64).

Today, the identities of young people can be manipulated, reformed, remixed, and morphed by others through countless software applications.

"The nature of identity is changing in the 21st century" (Palfrey & Gasser, 2008, p. 36). Through social network sites or through text messages, images and works can be conveyed in a flash to one's peers or strangers who can learn quickly who that person is (or supposedly is). The need to stay connected means that one is bound to these images whether they are complimentary or destructive. Because they are there, one is drawn to "check them out." Hence the power of the Internet trumps the power of family and relatives.

Sexuality, physical appearance, ethnicity, race, and habits, all are fair game for those who engage in what amounts to identity theft. Digitally driven creation and manipulation of identity can lead to great psychological turmoil. The gravity of the issue is such that Palfrey and Gasser make it the first chapter of *Born Digital.*

In addition, "The online world is full of every sort of image, story, and encounter that the human mind can come up with" (Palfrey & Gasser, 2008, p. 86). In less than a decade, it has become virtually impossible for anyone to prevent even those of the middle school years from being exposed to images and information that they are not ready to see, hear, or read. All this is so new that we can only speculate on the way the direct or indirect effects of digital overload will play themselves out in the adult years of today's students.

CYBERBULLYING

One immediate effect of digital technology is a new form of bullying. I remember, sixty four years ago, my first experience with the old form of bullying. Francis pushed me around during playground time. When I cried at home that evening, my father said, "Hit 'em back, Robert!" How simple a solution! Now the Internet and its remix and editing tools and applications has promoted the warp-speed emergence of complex cyberbullying. Identity theft now leads to suicides with a recent case in Massachusetts gaining nationwide attention. A fifteen-year-old girl, subject to endless taunts and insults via Facebook and text messaging, hung herself (McCabe, 2010, pp. B 1; 4).

As with traditional bullying, this new phenomenon is the intentional act of irritating, harassing, or doing harm to someone. But no longer does it involve a face-to-face incident with a Francis. Instead, the harm can take place anonymously through the Internet. It can begin quite innocently with simple "kidding around" and teasing, but can quickly careen out of control with digital speed fueled by darker motivations.

Educators are not immune from the practice. Recently, a teacher sued a student for harassment carried out via Facebook. The case is proceeding in the courts revolving around the issue of First Amendment rights and complicated by its digital overtones. What rights apply to one's right to "express opinions or ideas?" (*Cape Cod Times,* 2010, p. A4).

This "modern" form of bullying is now diverting valuable time from educator schedules because of the need to develop new policies. Traditional harassment policies are being updated to reflect cyberbullying, the bullying of gay and lesbian children and youth, and the bullying of children and youth from diverse families. The overall goal of such policies is to teach tolerance and understanding. But that goal, in some communities, is colliding with local norms that disapprove of homosexuality and alternative lifestyles. The result is conflict and turmoil (Eckholm, 2010), again illustrating how tenuous the school/community relationship can be.

DEFINING DEVIANCY DOWN

This is the title of an oft-cited article written in 1993 by former U.S. Senator Daniel Patrick Moynihan. Its central thesis is that, as deviant behavior increases in a society, society is faced with the decision of enforcing the rules, laws, or norms against it through public disapproval (the stocks) or some kind of penalty (fines or incarceration). If the behavior becomes too prevalent, the society is faced with either increasing resources for enforcing the rules or laws (more stocks, more police, or more prisons) or ignoring the behavior or redefining what is now acceptable (lines 40–56).

Right now, there is a shift in societal attitudes toward accepting marijuana use for medical purposes. There is a shift toward lesser penalties for the use of cocaine powder versus crack cocaine. There is a shift toward changing "three strikes, you're out" laws for certain infractions such as minor drug use. There is a shift toward acceptance of medically assisted suicide. There is a shift toward the acceptance of "public" violence with more and more states passing legislation to permit "ultimate fighting" or "human cockfighting" in a cage.

Schools have always been faced with the dilemma of what is and what is not acceptable behavior and what rules to enforce. In his forerunning analysis of the sociopsychological attributes and penchants of the school as a social institution, Willard Waller depicts the "crowd and mob psychology" that permeates the organization (1965, pp. 160–175 but written in 1932).

Most of the time, students act as a crowd whether in a classroom, study hall, or cafeteria. Student control can be tenuous and can easily spin in a disorderly direction. Many crowd situations contain combustible ingredients. "Teachers know well that certain behavior, once started, tends to go through the entire school, passing from one room to another with little loss of time and none of intensity" (p. 173).

Today, traditional behavior is changing rapidly with the barrage of images and messages crossing our children's screens. This barrage is one that adults find next to impossible to hinder, no less stop. Just reducing the flow seems to be an unachievable goal. We live in an X-rated environment that slams us through music, fashion, film, music videos, video games, cable networks, and talk radio. Sexting is no longer an unusual event. "Dirty dancing" (the name of an old, hugely popular film) is an enforcement tribulation for administrators: Is "grinding" all right in place of the two-step?

Language is changing fast in terms of what is acceptable at home, in one's peer group, at home, at school, and in the public arena. "Bitch," "friggin'," "kick-ass," and "pissed off" are samples of formerly banned words from the print and visual media that are rapidly moving into the mainstream press, other media, and schools. Educators could not give enough detentions nor would there be enough room in the detention hall to enforce the norms for "acceptable" language. Today, protecting children and youth from ". . . all contaminating contact with the world" (Waller, 1965, p. 36) is an unrealizable objective.

Style of dress also invites a recurring tussle between parents, their children, and educators. Obscene T-shirt slogans, plunging necklines, crotch-high shorts, and butt-clinging pants, all are evident when one visits any high school. What clothing and behavior could be deemed unacceptable if they manifest themselves so blatantly every day?

Recently, I visited a school where at the passing bell it was not uncommon for those who were "items" to kiss good-bye as they parted to attend separate classes. This is a far cry from school in the 1960s when I stood at the cafeteria door to inspect for boots that marked the polished floors and for dresses that were creeping beyond the knees!

IMPLICATIONS FOR EDUCATION

What does all of the above mean for schools and learning? Consider these observations and questions based on my fifty two years working in, with, and observing public schools, the information gathered for this work, and talking with dozens of practicing educators.

- Watching rather than reading dominates students' lives. Reading requires discipline and focus. Watching does not.
- Reading engages the whole brain because it unfolds in a linear fashion but requires students to imagine, invites them to proceed at their own pace, and encourages recursive thinking. Watching contains none of these elements,

all of which are crucial components of the writing process. If reading and writing make up two sides of valuable coins and if learning to write is learning to think, then watching is, by comparison, a worthless currency.

- Reading enables one to focus on content; it requires screening out distractions. The digital environment is filled with auditory and visual distractions that require little or no concentration. They are there at a mouse click, a keystroke, or a button pushed.
- "The amount of information on the Web is staggering and potentially debilitating (Palfrey and Gasser, 2008, p. 186). But in addition to the Web, there are the gadgets and devices, described earlier, that provide additional diversions to the thinking process.
- What is truth? What is fiction? In this copy-and-paste milieu, it is easy to move information in and out of one's compositions. The line between one's own work and that of others gets blurred in the digital age. We live in a Facebook (approaching 500 million subscribers) and Wikipedia world where an individual can supposedly create new knowledge and share it with hundreds or thousands of people. If "consumed" by them, does that then give it the stamp of "truth"? Is Wikipedia as reliable a source of data, information, and knowledge as the *Encyclopedia Brittanica*?
- How do teachers find the time to monitor what is authentic from students and what is plagiarized? It takes a few minutes to have to call up on the Web "Fact Check" or "Urban Legends." With twenty five students in a class, those minutes add up rapidly!
- Information comes to students in "snippets," in one- or two-minute bursts, or in sound bites. How do they make sense of it and put it into meaningful, coherent form? Are they really learning? Is learning being redefined in not well understood ways?
- Everything is interactive, quick, and in an informal/shorthand style. Linear thinking is not the norm. With their digital, popular media upbringing, students expect to be "entertained" in the classroom. Engaging the Digital Native is a great challenge for teachers. As one teacher said to me the other day, "We started to lose them with *Sesame Street!*"
- Spelling and writing are being affected negatively in an abbreviated world of fingertip tapping. Again, the same teacher: "I tell them, your paper is interesting, but I have to be able to read it" This teacher finds it necessary to teach students how to uses spell-check.
- "Cursive, foiled again" was the headline of a *Boston Globe* article on writing (Mehegan, 2009). The typed or tapped composition is replacing the historic skill of handwriting. Take note of the way many young people grasp a pencil or pen. They grip them not between the thumb and trigger finger, but in some awkward, twisted fashion that impedes writing. And

there is anecdotal evidence that many young people have trouble reading handwriting (just as some can only read a digital clock).

- The statistics on time spent on Internet-related activities cited earlier show that it has a very direct, visible effect on the sleep habits of students. The hours in a day are finite, but the extracurricular activities that can pull a student off task are infinite. Staying socially connected on the Internet or phone becomes a dominant goal. "Are the teens texting because they can't sleep or are they staying awake because they are texting?" (Burrell, 2009, p. C2).

- How do schools adapt to the fact that not all students can afford to possess all the technology that others have for carrying school work home? How is homework assigned? Not all students have computers, and, if they do, they may not have high-speed Internet access that is critical today for just doing homework. The "digital divide" is increasing every day as the technology is on a fast track of planned obsolescence, thus compelling the continued purchase of replacement upgrades.

- How do these new classroom realities affect the academic focus of teachers who everyday are confronted with these new learners? Will preoccupation with this "new" or at least more commonplace language and behavior affect teacher effectiveness? Are teachers being psychologically distracted by errant behavior that is increasingly the norm?

- What are the positives emerging from this immersion in the digital world? Palfrey and Gasser devote a chapter to the topic. They say, "Just because Digital Natives are learning differently from the way parents did when they were growing up doesn't mean that Digital Natives are not learning" (2008, p. 240). Creativity, artistry, scanning for relevancy, digesting lots of information, integrating, and reforming it, finding how to integrate symbol configurations and language, connecting to one's peers, and establishing new relationships are just some of the "pluses" that are easy to overlook in the dynamics of this high-tech age.

- What kind of staff development is required to assist teachers in becoming proficient with the beneficial aspects of digital media? And where will they find the time to acquire this new knowledge and skills?

- How do teachers part the curtain of negatives so that they can draw on the positives in maintaining and perhaps creating a new kind of classroom? How do teachers adapt to these new ways that students are learning? How do they adapt to integrate this new technology into their teaching?

- And how will educators bridge this emerging communications gap with the children and youth they educate? When television crept onto the scene in the late 1940s, there was plenty of time for adults to adjust to families watching Milton Berle and the Ed Sullivan together; TV viewing was a common cultural experience.

- When I began to teach high school in 1958, my "culture" and that of my students were sides of the same coin. We talked the same cultural language. Now breakfast with one's own electronic companion is typical, a companion that allows one to enter his own private world where little is shared with parents or peers. And the devices keep bursting into the marketplace so adults are literally left in the digital dust.
- In sum, Mead's pre-figurative culture is here in full force. How does education adapt to it? In 1967, in a prescient little volume, McLuhan and Fiore observed that "Innumerable confusions and a profound feeling of despair invariably emerge in periods of great technological and cultural transformation" (p. 8). We are now sorting all this out.

EDUCATION AND SOCIETAL EXPECTATIONS

Educators in communities, in addition to being enmeshed in this thicket of complexities and perplexities thrust on them at the school and classroom levels, also find themselves buffeted about in a wave of national educational reform that began in 1983 with the publication of *A Nation at Risk.* That document galvanized the attention of the nation because it sharply criticized the condition of public education and used charged rhetoric about the threat to our economic future posed by that condition. A sample: "We have in effect," the Commission said, "been committing an act of unthinking, unilateral disarmament" (p. 3).

Political response to these concerns was swift and sweeping. For example, during the "first wave" of reform that began in 1983 (Hawley, 1988), state legislatures generated more educational rules and regulations than they had enacted in the previous twenty years and, between 1984 and 1986, passed more than 700 statutes affecting directly or indirectly some dimension of public schooling (Timar & Kirp, 1989).

Most of these statutes fell into four categories: higher academic standards and increased academic requirements for students; recognition of the importance of the role of the teacher; ways to reward teachers for superior work; and higher standards for entrance to the profession (Passow, 1989).

These changes fit the category of what Cuban labeled "first-order" changes, changes that help improve the effectiveness of what schools *do now.* They are not aimed at bringing about "second-order" reform—reforms that will inject new goals or perhaps alter the fundamental goals of education. Second-order reforms will alter the ways in which schools are organized; they alter the ways in which traditional roles are performed within the organization (1988a, pp. 341–344).

Cuban's conceptualization of change captures the central, age-old tension that confronts schools and educators, the role of the organization as an agent of change or as a pillar of the status quo, (Witness the issues over harassment policies.) Is it true, as the anthropologist Jules Henry contended, that "Throughout most of his historical course, homo sapiens has wanted from his children acquiescence, not originality. It is natural that this should be so, for where every man is unique there is no society, and where there is no society there is no man" (1963, p. 286).

President Johnson envisioned schools as agents of change. In his education message to Congress in 1965, recommending the passage of the first iteration of the "Elementary and Secondary Education Act," Johnson said:

> We are now embarked on another venture to put the American dream to work meeting the new demands for a new day. Once again we must start where men who would improve their society have always known they must begin—with an education system restudied, reinforced, and revitalized (*The New York Times*, January 13, 1965, p. 20).

At that time, millions of dollars were appropriated to enable educators and other agents of government to take on the tasks of societal improvement. During the 1960s, the federal government was supporting the broad goals of achieving excellence and equity. In contrast, President George H.W. Bush's vision of reform, spelled out at the 1989 "Education Summit" with the nation's governors (the first of such gatherings focused on education), revolved around "competitiveness, improving the learning environment, accountability, flexibility, tougher standards, and a result-oriented system" (Cohen, 1989, p. 18).

These goals resulted in *America 2000: An Education Strategy* (U.S. Department of Education, 1991) that focused on six national goals, which were first-order and rooted in themes of efficiency and effectiveness.

A reading of the goals statement subsequently adopted by the National Governor's Association (but never enacted into federal law) demonstrates that the six goals, although very important, reflect more of a present than a futures perspective because they did not address matters of societal reform. The goals address children's readiness for elementary school; an increase in the high school graduation rate; increased competency in basic curricular subjects with a focus on science and mathematics; adult literacy; and drug and violence free schools.

"These goals are about excellence" (National Governors Association, 1990, p. 16). It enlisted the assistance of the states and corporations to fund school reform *without* additional federal monies.

Soon thereafter, there began to emerge what Hawley has labeled a "second wave" of reform, a wave that did not catch the public's eye as much as many of the first wave reforms, but one that is very connected to it. Major emphases of this wave included: (1) Increasing the standards for entry into teacher education programs; (2) increasing the rigor of teacher education programs; (3) improving the working conditions of teachers; (4) and restructuring schools through delegating to the local school more site managed authority, at least, over curriculum, personnel, and budgeting (Hawley, 1988; Passow, 1989).

In March 1994, Congress passed the *Goals 2000: Educate America Act,* which built upon the *America 2000* strategy by continuing a national focus on the six goals of *America 2000* but added goals relating to teacher education, professional development, and parental participation. The centerpiece of *Goals 2000* was initially $400 million in federal money a year in grants to states and districts that adopted reform plans (Pitsch, 1994). This legislation was followed by the five-year reauthorization, in October 1994, of the *Elementary and Secondary Education Act,* which authorized about $11 billion in fiscal 1995 for most federal K-12 education programs (*Education Week,* 1994).

But although these federal monies may seem significant, federal support of elementary and secondary education, in fact, came to about 7 percent of total expenditures. Today, it is about 10 percent (*Digest of Educational Statistics,* 2010).

In the mid-90s, we began to ride a third wave of reform, pushed by the 2000 reports and others from various organizations. This wave included antidotes for the main areas of need that Hawley (1988, p. 417) observed as weaknesses in the first two waves. Third-wave reformers proposed raising expectations and standards for *all* learners: placing emphasis on learning for understanding and higher-order thinking; integrating learning; and focusing on the processes of problem solving, inquiry, and teamwork. To these, Hargreaves would add ingenuity, invention, and the ability to initiate and cope with change (2003, pp. 1–34).

While this wave has been suppressed considerably since the enactment of *No Child Left Behind* (2002), there is reemerging recognition by business and policy leaders that these so-called "soft" or "applied" skills and knowledge must get more attention (Gewertz, 2007, pp. 25–27). "In an increasingly global, technological economy, they say, it isn't enough to be academically strong" (p. 25).

Three important new books develop this theme. In *The Race Between Education and Technology,* Goldin and Katz trace in great depth the connection between our standard of living and the level of education of our citizenry. "A greater level of education results in higher labor productivity. Moreover, a greater level of education in the entire nation tends to foster a higher rate of aggregate growth" (2008. p. 2).

They show how our high school graduation rate has remained stagnant over the last twenty five years and so has college enrollment. Until the 1970s, the gap between the rich and the poor had been closing, but, in recent years, income inequality has risen. Real wage growth for the middle and lower classes has slowed dramatically (see also Philips, 2002), and we no longer lead the world in the education of young adults.

In *A Whole New Mind,* Pink examines how the changes brought by global-ization and technology will require schools to pay more attention to the right brain (more creative) rather than left brain (more linear) thinking patterns He introduces the "six senses" of design, story, symphony, empathy, play, and meaning.

Third is Wagner's *The Global Achievement Gap* (2008), an important work that focuses on high schools and affirms the concerns of Goldin and Katz. Wagner's extensive national interviews with educators and business leaders, combined with classroom observations, enabled him to build a provocative case for "seven survival skills for teens today." They range from critical think-ing and problem solving to curiosity and imagination.

"In today's highly competitive global 'knowledge economy,' all students need new skills for college, careers, and citizenship" (Wagner, p. xi). These are the same themes that *Education Week* identified in its national study, *Diplomas Count* (2007) and that are used by the Federal Department of Education. The conclusions all fit within the newest educational buzzphrase, "21st-century skills" (Gerwertz, 2008).

STATE-LEVEL ACCOUNTABILITY

In the context of this emerging movement toward the "soft skills," the theme of accountability now dominates discourse in all fifty states, and they have set standards that are course- or grade-specific and measurable by assessments (*Quality Counts,* 2010, pp. 39–40).

But a radical new thrust for a federal system has also emerged, even though the responsibility for such matters has always been with the states. Estab-lished at the national level would be "common core standards" in English and mathematics. A national panel has made such a proposal, and it is supported by the Obama administration. As of this writing, two-thirds of the states have adopted these grade-level expectations (Sawchuk, 2010c). It is an amazing about-face considering the hostile reaction to setting such standards during the Clinton administration.

Hence, the focus on academic skills is a formidable barrier to bringing more of the "new" skills into the curriculum or giving them the attention they should be getting if they are already in the curriculum. And a huge impediment is the 180-day-plus school year, which allows little extra space for other content.

Massachusetts is an example of a state in this situation. In 1993, it passed the *Education Reform Act*. It identified a common core of learning (broad goals for what students should know and be able to do), curriculum frameworks in virtually all subject fields connected to the core, standards, benchmarks, and a comprehensive assessment system. The common core was an integration of "hard" and "soft" learning outcomes.

Also incorporated into the act are several accountability measures, including an annual school report card—to be published for every school in a district—portraying test results in terms of proficiency levels in reading, mathematics, English language arts, and science. Then a complex state formula kicks in to determine if, after three years of underachievement by a school or district, certain "corrective actions" are needed.

All schools must develop an annual school improvement plan through a building-level school improvement council. If corrective actions are taken after three years, a school must build into its plan tutoring for underachieving students, and, after four, the improvement plan must lead to significant changes in curriculum, instruction, or staffing. After five years, a failing school might be restructured or taken over by the state (see MA DESE).

The plan is a combination of top-down and bottom-up processes, a combination that Fullan (2007) had concluded is the most effective way to achieve systemic change whether at the building or district level (p. 262). Combining the two increases the capacity of the system.

Massachusetts was making progress in delivering this balanced curriculum until the enactment of the federal *No Child Left Behind* law in 2002, another iteration of the *Elementary and Secondary Education Act* (1965). "The revised law is designed to close achievement gaps and bring all students to the 'proficient' level on state tests by 2013–14 . . ." (Olson, 2004, S1).

A planned schedule of standards-based tests in English, mathematics, and science is required beginning in grade 3 and running through grade 10. Data must be disaggregated by subgroups such as income levels, limited English proficiency, disabilities, and racial and ethnic minority backgrounds. Targets are established for Annual Yearly Progress (AYP) as measured by test score gains. These scores are based on a scoring formula relating to state assessments. The goal is for these targets to keep rising so that 100 percent of students are proficient in reading or English language arts, mathematics, and science by 2013–14 (Linn, 2009, p. 165).

The U.S. Department of Education gives final approval to each state's testing program. If annual test results are not acceptable, the U.S.D.E. requires states to penalize schools receiving Title I funds. Missing AYP targets two years in a row leads to designating an organization as needing "school improvement," which makes it eligible for technical assistance that might include supplemental services for children.

If still no improvement, sanctions can be applied. They can range from: (1) replacing the curriculum; (2) lengthening the school day or year; (3) restructuring that can mean closing the school and reopening it as a charter school or replacing the principal and staff; or (4) state takeover (Olson, 2004).

"The cornerstone of NCLB is more testing for students and a strict accountability system of sanctions associated with schools' failure to make progress in meeting student outcomes" (Wells, 2009, p. 31). The philosophy represents a radical shift from the ESEA of 1965 with its emphasis on equity and resource inputs and absence of testing to the new emphasis on excellence and outputs.

To make an understatement, NCLB has been controversial from its inception and continues to be. Debates about it rage in professional journals, at conferences, and in the press. Those debates will no doubt continue when it is reauthorized, possibly in 2011.

But before that happens, the Obama administration has set aside $4 billion in federal economic stimulus funds, passed by Congress in February 2009, for grants to states that compete for *Race to the Top* awards. Grants are based largely on three criteria: (1) a persuasive local reform agenda; (2) willingness to expand charter schools; and (3) a plan to factor student performance into the evaluation of principals and teachers.

The 500-point grant application grading scale gives special emphasis to plans for a state's reform agenda and its capacity to carry it out (McNeal, November 2009).

In addition, the secretary of education plans to demand that, if some 5,000 of the nation's "worst performing" schools want to complete for grants from another $3.5 billion in school improvement aid, they would have to adopt one of four rigorous intervention models. They are: (1) turnaround, including the replacement of the principal and at least half of the teaching staff; (2) school closure; (3) restart, where a closed school would be reopened as a charter school; and (4) transformational, including new leadership and staff, extended day, and implementing new instructional strategies (McNeal, September 2009a).

In this day of a shortage of qualified candidates for principal, teacher, and superintendent, one has to wonder what magic formula policymakers have concocted to inject into a struggling school so that personnel changes will "turn around" the organization within the short time frame expected, often one year. Kentucky received money from the first round of state competition and already has imposed one-year expectations on some of its schools (Maxwell, L.A., 2010). These questionable expectations also apply to proposals to evaluate teachers more on a *performance* basis (primarily test scores) when there are widespread reductions in supervisory personnel.

In this severe economic downturn ". . . states are desperate for the money. They don't want to leave it on the table" (Williams, 2009). Hence the squeeze is on to apply more harsh accountability practices to underperforming schools (and implicitly to all schools). Districts and schools find that their discretionary decision-making is more and more curtailed.

In January, the governor of Massachusetts signed a sweeping education bill that gives districts the authority to expand charter schools, factors student performance into teacher evaluation, and gives superintendents increased power to overhaul failing schools, including the dismissal of principals and staff. A prime motive to pass the bill was to make the state eligible for about $250 million in federal *Race to the Top* money (MacQuarrie, 2010a). That objective was met in August when the state received that sum from the second round of awards, receiving 471 points out of the possible 500 (Vaznis & Levenson, 2010). However, the message is there for *all* schools.

"Money talks" goes the old admonition. States like Massachusetts that had capped the number of charter schools or that had not linked teacher pay to student performance have now been forced to alter those stances because of the economic crisis.

Thus educators are confronted with an *Alice in Wonderland* world of seeming incompatible events and policies in a sea of reform waves (Darling-Hammond, 1993, p. 756). They try to make sense of their environment for themselves and their students so they can make the best decisions for a 21st-century program while meeting the expectations that they can do more with less. They try to decode the messages to be more professional while being treated more and more, in too many districts, like technocrats. Distressingly, seldom does a reform advocate indicate that he is even aware of the counterproductive ethos he might have created.

EDUCATION AND THE ECONOMY

There is little debate that America (and the world) is in the throes of the Great Recession, the worst since the Great Depression of the 1930s. Despite the official pronouncement of the Federal Reserve chairman, Ben Bernanke, in late 2009 that it is "very likely over" (Lebaton, 2009), developments over the last few months strongly indicate that it will not be for a few years. Consumer confidence and spending has slipped again, personal saving rates are up because purchasing is down, the housing market is the worst in decades, foreclosure rates remain too high, job growth is stagnant, the stock market is sluggish and often volatile, and loans are still difficult to obtain.

Recently the Federal Reserve policy committee stated that the economy "was not expected to improve anytime soon" (*New York Times,* August 12, 2010). And the political gridlock in Washington, reinforced by the November 2010 election outcomes, prevents further federal spending equivalent to the 2009 stimulus bill, so any recovery is largely dependent on the private sector as weak as it is (Gavin 2010).

Kuttner summarized conditions succinctly:

> The economy is in a self-reinforcing trap. Consumer purchasing power is down due to high unemployment and falling earnings. Businesses are reluctant to invest because they don't see customers. Risk-averse banks won't lend except to the most reliable borrowers. Depressed housing prices and a foreclosure epidemic are a drag both on household net worth and on bank balance sheets (2010).

The states are now being hammered by the national recession, too. An extensive analysis of the economic condition of the fifty states by *Time* magazine led the author to conclude: "From Hartford to Honolulu, once sturdy state governments are approaching the brink of financial calamity as the crash of 2008 and its persistent aftermath have led to the reckoning of 2010" (Von Drehle, 2010, p. 22). Sales, income, and corporate taxes, the prime sources of state income, are declining significantly and show no signs of imminent recovery. In 2011, there will be an estimated collective gap of $55 billion between states' income and obligations.

A headline from the *Boston Globe* captured the situation vividly for public education: "Outlook is grim for the public schools" (Chea, 2010). I agree. Not only is the trend to level fund budgets but also to cut them, in essence a double cut when factoring in inflation.

Consider the following indicators that reinforce this pessimistic outlook. (All have appeared in the last year or so in the *Boston Globe, U.S. News and World Report, New York Times, Education Week, Wall Street Journal, and Cape Cod Times.*) The list is exemplary rather than exhaustive.

- State revenue shortfalls for the next decade are predicted to be in the area of $350 billion.
- Flat or plummeting revenues from sales, income, capital gains, and corporate taxes are causing cities and towns to become more and more reliant

on the property tax, the most regressive of taxes. Hence, there is more and more resistance to increasing property taxes to support public services and particularly schools.

- Unemployment, currently hovering just below 10 percent, is not predicted to fall much below that figure for at least the next couple of years. And if one factors in the underemployed (those carrying two or three jobs) to that figure, the unemployment rate is calculated to be anywhere from 17 to 20 percent. There are six workers, on average, competing for one job.
- Employment increased only 0.5 percent since 2000. Private sector jobs declined. There has been no net job creation in the private sector since December 1999, yet the labor force in the last decade has grown by 12 million workers.
- Middle-class income has stagnated since the early 1970s, barely keeping up with inflation. Purchasing power has declined, which affects the consumer spending needed to fuel an economic recovery. Thrift is now "in" again with consumers saving extra income to pay off personal debt rather than spending it on goods and services to fuel the economy. And when new jobs become available, they are often in the service sector, which pays lower wages.
- The total federal debt is over $12 trillion with an annual interest payment in the vicinity of $400 billion (and projected to grow rapidly), thus depriving public services of crucially needed funding increases and even leading to cutting existing budgets.
- The new national health care legislation (Patient Protection and Affordable Care Act) will divert more resources from education.
- Homeland security and drug enforcement costs are skyrocketing and draining resources from other public sector needs. Add to that the funding of two wars.
- There is a dramatic need to increase infrastructure spending. As an example of infrastructure needs, a recent EPA study estimates that it would take over $350 billion just to maintain our tap water systems in coming decades. Upgrading our electrical system is estimated to require roughly $12 billion.

A national survey of all fifty states by *Education Week* in 1997 revealed that ". . . educators in virtually every state worry about getting enough money to do the job. That is especially true for many thousands of inner-city and poor rural schools" (p. 54). One could repeat that statement in 2010 as other studies show that the percentage of gross domestic product (GDP) committed to K-12 education in 2006 was 4.1, less than in 1975 (Peterson, 2010, p. 153). As Krugman puts it, we have "the return of Depression-era economics" (2009).

UNDERFUNDED AND UNFUNDED MANDATES

Two federal laws illustrate the unfair and unethical practice of underfunded mandates. Perhaps more than ever before, states and communities must take responsibility for policy implementation with their own or partially their own funding. This "devolution" of responsibility to the states and local communities began in the Reagan years and has now accelerated as the federal government confronts the national economic crisis. In turn, states are increasingly engaged in the same financial handoff game with local communities.

This philosophy of "close to constituents" government, which has ebbed and flowed throughout American history, fits well with those critics who preach an anti-Washington doctrine and wish to "defund" it of its ability to meet many national needs. Today the "Tea Party" exemplifies this movement. In the present polarized political environment, devolution is here to stay regardless of the community's ability to pay.

The 1975 PL 94–142, now the *Individuals with Disabilities Education Act,* included the pledge that, by 1982, 40 percent of local costs would be assumed by the federal government. Currently, 17 percent of those costs are assumed (Shinn, personal communication, February 10, 2010). In my community of 1,330 students, with 225 eligible for special education services, 40 percent funding would bring in another $500,000. In addition, as disability diagnosis becomes more sophisticated, eligibility numbers increase every year as they do in every community. In certain cases, it costs over $200,000 to educate one child.

$500,000 would eliminate the need for a possible town meeting override vote (permitting an increase in the property tax rate) in my community for about the same amount to stem reduction in professional and support staff plus loss of programs and increased class sizes. What would 40 percent mean to cities and towns all across the country? And throughout Massachusetts, communities are faced with state special education funding reductions as well.

No Child Left Behind ". . . has been underfunded since the year it was passed, meaning that such inequalities in the educational system are not being offset by federal funding targeted toward poor students" (Wells, 2009, p. 31). Neill came to the same conclusion a year after the law was originally enacted (2003, p. 226).

Critics say that the underfunding is approximately $6 billion to $7 billion short of Congress' authorized level. An in-depth cost-indexing study of NCLB in Texas concluded:

> The costs of achieving the student performance goals established by NCLB are substantially higher than the amount of additional federal funds that have been

provided over the past two years and larger than any additional federal education funds that are likely to be provided in future years (National Tax Journal,
2004, p. 8).

In addition, $500 million was authorized per year for school improvement
purposes, but, for the first five years, no money was appropriated (Packer,
2007, p. 267). But Chester Finn, former assistant secretary of education in
the Reagan administration, disagrees adamantly with the charge that NCLB
funding is off the mark. He contends that the costs to local districts to comply
with the law "are actually very modest" (2008).

There is also the matter of unfunded mandates. Here are examples from
Massachusetts. The new bullying law (to be discussed in chapter 3) carries
no funding with it. Districts, in the midst of a statewide budget crisis, are
expected to "find" a few thousand dollars to mount a staff training program.
Monitoring homeschooling and documenting educational plans is a local
expense. So too are most of the costs of giving, monitoring, and processing
state accountability tests.

As we have seen, the financial needs of the federal government and the
states are dire. Current forms of taxation will not solve the problem, nor will
massive reductions in government programs without devastating effects on
our social fabric. The only solution is to enact a different *national* tax that
would be small and broad-based but would raise huge sums. One solution is
the VAT or value-added tax, which is a sales tax common around the world in
developed countries (Montgomery, 2009).

Another such effective way to raise significant monies for public needs is
the financial transactions tax. A tiny, perhaps 0.25 percent fee, would be added
to the sale or transfer of stocks, bonds, and "exotic instruments" like deriva-
tives (Herbert, 2009). Monies from such sources would then be distributed
to the states and local communities, as was done with the Revenue Sharing
program begun under President Nixon in 1971 (Message to Congress). He
said, "Let us share our resources to rescue the states and localities from the
brink of financial crisis."

In 1972, he spoke about revenue sharing in more detail, stressing that
heavy reliance on property taxes for funding local education was endangering
the health of the institution.

[property taxes] . . . have become one of the most oppressive and discriminatory
of all taxes, hitting most cruelly at the elderly and the retired, and they threaten
schools as hard pressed voters understandably reject new bond issues at the polls
(Message to Congress).

From that date until 1988, when the program was killed by President Reagan, some $83 billion went to the states and local municipalities. Recently, that was the estimated yearly cost of the war in Iraq. Think of what that kind of assistance would mean today to states and municipalities! Would it not be refreshing to hear some political leaders speak out like this? Would it not be refreshing to hear actual creative proposals like Nixon's? Would it not be refreshing to feel that there is at least national recognition of the crisis we face at the state and local levels, a crisis that is eroding the quality of public education?

But, sad to say, the chances of serious movement in a direction like this seem remote at best. The Republican party is vehemently opposed to any new taxes even to reduce our total debt. Cutting services and taxes are its answer to addressing our grave resource needs (Calmes, 2010). Increased class size is perfectly all right to save tax dollars; the impact on learning is unimportant. The *cult of efficiency* permeating public education, described by Callahan in his compelling study (1962), is alive and well. Business and industrial values and practices are still seen by some as the silver bullets that are the key to improving schools.

THE ACCOUNTABILITY SQUEEZE

When I began to teach high school in Massachusetts in 1958, it was unheard of for a school budget to be voted down. There were no teacher unions, and I had the textbook for curriculum guidance. The state provided nothing to the school and me except a listing, of courses, that must be taught (e.g., U.S. history and problems of democracy). Textbooks were the framework for course content. I had total autonomy to teach that content in any way I wished as long as a reasonable number of students passed my courses.

The good news was that this autonomy was highly motivating to a young teacher. The bad news is that, without some top-down guidelines and supervision, I could have wandered considerably from the content I was supposed to deliver. I recall a teacher or two who did. Certainly, some well-financed, suburban communities provided such guidance, but they were the exception, not the rule.

Contrast the autonomy of that era to the current level of teacher autonomy under the Massachusetts *Reform Act of 1993* as depicted in Figure 1.1 (for teachers of English language arts and mathematics). Keep in mind that teachers who teach high-stakes testing subjects such as these must operate under more stringent constraints than those applied to teachers in subjects like art, music, or

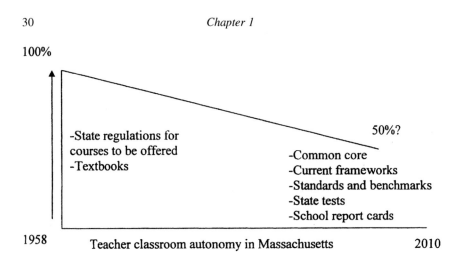

100%

-State regulations for
courses to be offered
-Textbooks

50%?

-Common core
-Current frameworks
-Standards and benchmarks
-State tests
-School report cards

1958   Teacher classroom autonomy in Massachusetts   2010

Figure 1.1. The Accountability Squeeze

social studies. In Massachusetts, science is also part of the testing mix. Teachers of all subjects in schools judged as failing, however, share the increased constraints on autonomy that standardized testing forces on the curriculum.

Government sanctioned accountability rules, regulations, and measures are here to stay. Personal professional accountability has always been with us, but, in today's highly charged political environment, it is largely ignored as the chorus of school doubters—and yes, even haters—drowns out that fact. Finn, for example, said recently, in response to the new Diane Ravitch book, "She's more inclined to trust the traditional school structure, and I'm more inclined to blow it up" (cited in Viadero, 2010).

The accountability movement was launched in 1970 by Leon Lessinger with his provocative book, *Every Kid a Winner*. It was packed with ideas such as performance contracting (with an outside firm for a fee); external educational audits; more standardized testing; vouchers; and the overall concept of educational engineering. His book was aimed at improving student achievement in low-performing schools, particularly in large cities. Almost simultaneously, in March of that year, President Nixon sent a special message to Congress focused on education and accountability, the first president to speak to the concept applied to public education (p. 109).

Lessinger was a champion for experimenting with nw methods to make schools operate more effectively and efficiently. Cost-effectiveness began to enter the educational vocabulary. Competition for students was a good thing As he put it, schools ". . . must define their output no longer as teaching done, but as learning proven" (p. 9).

So was laid the foundation for NCLB and Race to the Top and the accountability mania that is everywhere today. The latest nostrum to gain a foothold that relates to such "output" is to factor student achievement into evaluating teacher performance, a key expectation for states applying for *Race to the Top* funds.

And "exploding nationwide," according to Dillon, is "value-added modeling," where student scores on state tests at the end of third grade are used as a base to assess achievement at each grade level. If a student gains the next year, it is seen as the value the fourth-grade teacher added to the child's education. And so it will go through the grade levels (2010a). The statistical methods required to ensure validity, reliability, and fairness to teachers are boggling. In this economic climate, where will districts and schools find the money to implement such a system?

But right now, the advocates for value-added are not bothering to address these concerns or to consider the numerous variables that affect student achievement that are beyond a teacher's control such as family situation, student characteristics, and enrollment mobility factors. (Many of these plus others will be discussed in chapter 3.) But despite substantive considerations, the *Los Angeles Times*, this summer, published the names of 6,000 elementary teachers and rated their performance, least to most effective, based on test scores for their classes (Lovett, 2010).

Permeating these movements is a new word, "metric." It is fast becoming the "in" word as the accountability proponents push hard to further Lessinger's ideas.

Finally, the U.S. Department of Education's own research arm warned that value-added estimates "are subject to a considerable degree of random error." Yet the U.S.D.E through the *Race to the Top* competition, is telling states that they have to factor test score results into the evaluation of teachers if they wish to be competitive for grant money (Dillon, 2010a).

It is not much of a stretch to appreciate the impact of this latest accountability nostrum on the morale and motivation of school staff who are confronted daily with the societal changes described earlier in this chapter as well as with the "organized anarchy" and "busy kitchen" characteristics of the profession to be discussed in chapter 3. Again, politics trumps reason and research.

What will be the impact of the current iteration of the accountability movement—again focusing on private sector practices and terminology—on public education? Will schools become more effective in the short and long runs, or will they become shackled to standardized tests and fail to address the "soft" learning advocated by Pink and Wagner? Will teachers adapt to these new forces in their professional lives and become better educators, or will they become more like technicians?

Ravitch, a noted historian of American public education, has done a U-turn in her thinking about these matters since her days supporting the development and implementation of NCLB. In her analysis of public education since 2002, she expresses deep concern about the impact of the accountability movement, particularly with regard to charter schools and testing (2010).

DOING BETTER WITH WHAT YOU HAVE

J. Lloyd Trump, the inventor of the "Trump Plan" to significantly change patterns of curriculum and instruction and the overall structure of the secondary school (described in chapter 2) had a favorite slogan, "Doing better with what you have" (Trump & Georgiades, 1970, p. 106). For the foreseeable future, this will need to be the placard on every educator's desk.

The situation today will tax and challenge our creativity, patience, and energy for we will have to learn, as Michael Kirst suggests, "How to improve schools without spending more money" (1982, pp. 6–8). He contends that elementary and secondary education has improved considerably during hard times, but it has tended to be of the simple and not eye-catching sort. For example, the introduction of the arguable and "low cost" Carnegie unit of instruction in the early 1900s has had a tremendous impact on curriculum and instruction and so have small-scale innovations at the classroom level.

Kirst emphasizes "alterable variables"—time, curriculum content, instructional methods and materials, and teacher quality—as the focus for improvement. Bloom similarly places more emphasis on such factors, particularly those relating to learners and learning. He contends that we are at a juncture in educational history where we can have a great impact on the quality of education by focusing more of our efforts on using what we know from research about these variables (1980, pp. 382–384). His observation continues to have great validity.

Kirst and Bloom identify some of the basic changes that educators know will improve schools. But they are evolutionary, not revolutionary in nature. They do not square with the more ambitious expectations for change through the reform-through-policy strategy that has been the focus at the federal level since the mid-1960s. As has been noted, this policy route has had two thrusts: to create more equity in public education and to stimulate excellence.

Elmore and McLaughlin, in the Rand Corporation study of those reform efforts, state that this approach is grounded in two assumptions: (1) There are some basic defects in the overall system of education that can be corrected by implementing some specific policies; and (2) these policies will result in better classroom practices that will have more national uniformity that, in turn, will be supported and maintained by administrators and organizational structures (1988, pp. 12–13). Clearly, these assumptions apply today.

But, as the authors state, "In reality, reform is more like the process of introducing changes into a language. Language is independent of our efforts to change it" (p. 13). Gradually, as more and more words are added to a language, fairly dramatic differences become apparent, as can be illustrated by the contrasts between Elizabethan and modern American English. However, English is still English, just as a school is still a school.

While today's educational reformers use accountability policies and practices and declines in funding to force changes in education, they are bucking a strong historic trend as noted in the Rand Study. "School systems respond to external pressure for change, not by highly visible, well-specified, sequential actions, but by subtle shifts over time" (p. 13).

To date, this evolutionary pattern is an explanation for the oft-cited maxim, "The more things change, the more they stay the same." From the perspective of most citizens, the schools from which they graduated are "the same" as they were years ago (and most approve of their local schools, as was demonstrated by the earlier mentioned PDK/Gallup poll).

Although a similar observation could be made about any social institution, schools face a particularly unique situation; virtually all citizens have been members of the organization for a significant portion of their lives. By the time they finish high school, they have observed well over 13,000 hours of classroom teaching, a powerful experience that shapes their lifetime image of schooling (Lortie, 1975, p. 61).

Hence, the first-order changes that have occurred and that continue to be implemented in good schools remain virtually invisible to the layperson, the legislator, and the would-be reformer because they are gradual and incremental (Tyack & Cuban, 1995, p. 5).

The school critics, who see the organization as fixed on the status quo, remember the ineffective and unapproachable tenured teachers rather than the effective and caring ones, and they remember a top-heavy administrative hierarchy and a cadre of unimaginative, change-killing educators (Sarason, 1983, pp. 13–14). This is often the point of view of the reformers described by Elmore and McLaughlin. Such reformers usually have learned few lessons from the history of prior reform efforts. Instead, these critics tend to place the blame for resistance to change at the doorstep of school personnel.

On the other hand, many other critics see things quite differently. To them, schools tend to be mindlessly faddish, jumping regularly on the latest innovation bandwagon. Educators are viewed as passive, malleable people, all too inclined to adopt the latest promoted panacea. From this perspective, rather than not changing enough, the more important problem facing schools is their tendency to change too much (Sarason, 1983, pp. 15–16).

Every veteran educator can recite a list of what, at the time, were innovations in curriculum, instruction, or management practices that suddenly appeared, swooping seemingly out of nowhere, to capture the attention of practitioners. I can begin to compile my list. Behavioral objectives, Management by Objectives, Total Quality Management, career education, Madeline Hunter's Mastery Teaching, open classrooms, Effective Schools, non-graded schools, and Outcomes-Based Education, each promoted widely in journals, at conventions, and by staff development programs. Each was well intentioned, and but most have gradually disappeared from our schools, or, at least, if still utilized, one hears little about them.

There may be traces of some left in some districts, melded with other related practices, but their long-term impact has dissipated. But this "bandwagon" history leaves a residue of skepticism and sometimes cynicism toward the next new innovation. It is an important impediment to change.

Tyack and Cuban capture these poles of perception nicely. "While some lament that educational reform is an institutional Bermuda Triangle into which intrepid change agents sail, never to appear again, others argue that public education is too trendy, that entirely too many foolish notions circulate through the system at high velocity" (1995, p. 4).

ORGANIZATIONAL DILEMMAS

As with most perspectives, there is an element of truth in each of these perceptions. Some organizations appear static; others appear adaptable. "Nothing happens there," some observers say about some schools. "That's a 'with it' place," they say about another.

In some schools, such as the 5,000 now categorized by the federal Department of Education as "worst-performing" schools (McNeal, September 2, 2009b), conditions have deteriorated so much within the organization because of a preponderance of social/economically impacted students and parents, severe underfunding, lack of community support, a questionable mix of staff talent and motivation, and an overall maintenance orientation to education that it takes concerted, external action and support to get improvements.

These organizations have not found ways to deal with the basic organizational tensions and dilemmas that confront all social institutions. They have been unable to establish processes that address the issue of when and how much to change (Miles, 1981, p. 104–110; Katz & Kahn, 1978, pp. 770–771). They have been unable to marshal and focus their resources and energies on their prime educational tasks rather than on bureaucratic needs and political survival. They have been unable to figure out how dependent they should be on their immediate external environment for clues to new directions (Miles, 1981, pp. 57–82).

However, whether or not they resolve their dilemmas, they will nevertheless change. Every organization changes. Accompanying change are issues relating to the extent that change is intentional on the part of the organization or thrust upon it by other forces; types of innovations; their shape and size; whether they are adopted or developed; and the degree to which they connect to one another and to the mission of the organization. (We will look at these issues in chapters 4–7.)

ACTION WITHIN AND AROUND THE CONSTRAINTS

Professional educators must be knowledgeable about the larger context within which schools function, the current forces within the institution that cause or impede change, and the ongoing dilemmas they face regarding improvement. Unarmed with such knowledge, they will be less effective when confronted by critics, angry parents, resistant school boards, and unbending politicians. And they will not be as effective as they could be working with their staffs on the ongoing task of school improvement. "Mum" is not the watchword!

Although the discussion thus far has focused on the broad societal level regarding schools, in a very real way, the concepts apply directly to local buildings because each operates within a social context and is confronted with challenges relating to change.

A school can decide by intent or by default to be a passive structure allowing the context, forces, and dilemmas to work their will, carrying the organization in some unintended direction. As poorly as it might perform, historically, it has survived. But the new accountability policies described earlier have upended that long-standing guarantee. Schools are being closed.

Conversely, the school can decide to act on the context, forces, and dilemmas within the narrow window of action available to it. Numerous "good" schools have done so. According to Cuban, who conducted an extensive study of how high school teachers have taught since 1890, that window of action is the classroom. "The most promising place to begin is precisely where the resources should be concentrated: the classroom teacher" (Cuban, 1982, p. 117).

A century of reform efforts show that where change counts the most is in the daily interactions of teachers and students (Tyack & Cuban, 1995, p. 10). For veteran educators, this conclusion is far from startling. It reaffirms what we have always known to be the key to school improvement, an excellent curriculum delivered effectively by the teacher in the classroom. Fullan says, "Educational change depends on what teachers do and think—it's as simple and complex as that" (2007, p. 129).

However, policymakers and critics continue to ignore this "bottom line" to reform (Cuban, 1984, p. 260). In the face of intense political and economic pressures, most of them are unwilling to defend schools and to explain why there is no "Quick Fix for Bad Schools," as proclaimed in a recent headline in *Time* (Cruz, 2010). Instead, they continue to turn to the "personnel fixes" discussed earlier. Therefore we, as educators, must be defenders whenever we have the opportunity! Classrooms, of course, are not isolated entities. High school classrooms—the focus of this book—are nested within the structure of the school itself, and high schools continue to be the focus of reform efforts, just as they were in the 1960s when Trump and his associates were writing about and implementing new designs for it (Trump, 1959; Trump & Baynham, 1961; Trump, 1977) and James Bryant Conant was reporting on his studies of the same organization (Conant, 1959; 1967). For years, Goodlad has pointed to the school as the unit for educational change (1984, pp. 31; 271–279).

Glickman, who has worked extensively in the field on school improvement projects, asserts, "The only reforms that mean much are *local reforms in local schools and communities* (emphasis in the original) (1993, p. 152). Fullan's fourth edition of his comprehensive treatise on change devotes ten of fifteen chapters to the school itself (2007).

Educators have tried various approaches to effect needed changes in education, both at the school and at the district level. A body of valuable literature has emerged from those efforts. You will find an overview of much of it in chapter 2, and you will see details from it sprinkled throughout the other chapters.

Chapter 2

What Research and Practice
Teach Us about Change

Improvement seldom, if ever, occurs on a straight trajectory; it typically involves bumps and slides, as well as gratifying leaps.

—Elmore, 2004, p. 56

School improvement is a messy, rich process full of coercion and shared struggle, indifference and heavy involvement, uncertain results, and real payoff.

—Huberman & Miles, 1984, p. 1

Formal study of change processes—and the factors that affect them in public schools—began in the late 1930s with Mort and Cornell's groundbreaking analyses of the spread of innovations in Pennsylvania school districts. Those innovations included kindergarten, extracurricular activities, supplementary reading, and a reorganized high school (Ross, 1958, pp. 31–51). These kinds of innovations were grand in size and scope in that they were seen as being adopted across entire schools or school systems.

From these influential studies emerged the "lag theory"; most schools are slow to adopt substantive innovations, taking an average of fifty years to do so after the practices have been employed by the first users (i.e., "lighthouse" schools). This "theory" created a powerful image of lumbering organizations that were highly resistant to change.

But Mort and his associates found that increased financial support could reduce that time frame considerably. Such support produced quicker results because schools could more deliberately assess their needs and make themselves knowledgeable about new practices to meet those needs; they could hire a staff of well-prepared, capable teachers, including teachers who might become "spark plugs" for the innovation, and they could hire administrators who valued innovation, knew how to work with a staff to bring it about, and did not allow the management dimensions of the job to co-opt responsibilities for effecting change (pp. 407–496).

As we shall see, these factors are similar to many of those that current research tells us are critical to successful change.

In addition, the Mort group identified a general process of adopting innovations. Briefly, it encompassed these steps: recognize a need and articulate it; propose a solution; arouse interest in it; have a trial demonstration; increase support for it, and officially recognize the innovation and obtain financial support for its implementation (p. 83). These steps were a precursor to many rationalistic change processes that were developed in the years following Sputnik in 1957.

Aside from three decades of valuable field studies and the dissemination of several monographs connected to the initial work of Mort and Cornell, no publication of note about change in schools emerged until Miles' *Innovation in Education.* This 1964 book examined various change processes and innovative practices in the late 1950s and early 1960s. Since Miles' work, the pace of publications has increased steadily so that today there is available to us a voluminous and instructive body of literature.

We now have detailed knowledge about *planned* change and innovation at the level of the school district and school. Fullan's ongoing, synthesizing work (2007) is invaluable in these regards. The problem for practitioners is to read it, make sense of it, and use it in their situations, a challenging assignment given the heaping plate of daily tasks facing all school personnel.

In the chapters that follow, many of these findings will be referenced, but a total review of this literature is unnecessary given the work of Fullan and others and is beyond the purpose of this book. Readers interested in it are encouraged to pursue cited sources to enlarge their knowledge base. Indeed, we will focus on some broad themes, concepts, and issues particularly relevant to your understanding of small-scale, incremental change.

CHANGE AND INNOVATION

Although the terms "change" and "innovation" are used virtually synonymously in the literature, they have distinct meanings that are important to note.

Change may occur whether willed or not, whether planned or not, due to forces within and outside the organization. Change may be welcomed or unwelcomed. It may be "accidental." It may lead to improvement, and it may not, depending on one's perspective about "improvement." Change can range in magnitude from simple alteration or substitution of practices, to the levels of restructuring ideas and systems and adopting new values.

Innovation, on the other hand, is typically thought of as an intentional act introducing something new or novel into a situation to make it better. Deliberateness is usually at the heart of innovation, but in a groundbreaking book in 1958, March and Simon observed, "Some innovations will result from accidental encounters with opportunities" (p. 183). An innovation is always a change, but a change is not always an innovation.

Beyond mere definition, however, is the fact that, while persons who introduce an innovation may perceive it as novel and unique in that situation, the innovation may not be new to the realm of practice or to someone in a different setting. This notion that innovation is very situation-defined is common to the literature (e.g., Hall & Hord, 1987, p. 9).

But rather than getting ensnared in a definitional tug-of-war, most researchers tend to use these terms interchangeably. Following the advice of Rogers and Rogers (1976, p. 153), I will also do so in this book because the patterns and processes connected to each are so similar.

ADAPTABILITY

Adaptability in education is ". . . the capacity of a school to take on newer and more appropriate educational practices" (Mort cited in Ross, 1958, p. 26). To Schmuck and Runkel, it means ". . . that the organization constructively manages change, that it does not merely adjust or acquiesce to externally imposed change" (1994, p. 23). The concept was integral to the early research on school improvement.

Adaptability might seem to imply simply reacting to events, adjusting accordingly, which is necessary for all organizations to survive. Unpredicted events are a constant input. But its use in the organizational literature means to act before the organization is buffeted about more than ordinarily by the myriad of forces that swirl around every social institution. Intentionality sets direction rather than crises. Failure to adapt would deprive the school of the influence it should have over its future, and its programs would become increasingly outmoded in relation to the needs of its clientele.

Although many other organizational theorists have contended that adaptability is central to any organization's long-term health and effectiveness (e.g., Miles, 1973, p. 441; Schein, 1980, p. 35), the concept has not received much explicit attention in education during the last three decades of research on schools. It is not mentioned in Marzano's review of that literature (2003), nor is it by Fullan, but certainly the idea is implicit in their writings. So, too, is it implied in Goodlad's well-received national study of 1,016 classrooms (1984).

Given external pressures for schools to change quickly, it is likely that adaptability has not gained headlines because it is an incremental route to improvement, and that route bumps up against the impatience of policy-makers, the media, and many laypeople. Media hype promotes unrealistic, "overnight" expectations such as the *Time* headline, "How to Fix America's Schools" (Ripley, December 8, 2008). This kind of prescriptive remedy conveys to a critic that the organization is stonewalling change. Thus educators find themselves herded onto the latest bandwagon.

Since the publication of the Peters and Waterman book in 1982, however, adaptability in the private sector has become noticed and respectable again as a key characteristic of a healthy and effective organization. That volume catapulted innovation to the top of corporate America's agenda. Researchers began to recognize that ongoing change, sometimes on a very small-scale and often imperceptible level, was crucial to the survival of a business in today's turbulent marketplace. Change in corporate organizations comes to be viewed as expected; it becomes the norm rather than the exception because failure to do so can literally mean going out of business.

Innovation, through adaptability, does not have to be splashy or sweeping in order to be important. That is a theme in a subsequent book by Waterman (1987) and the work by Kouzes and Posner (2007) and Senge (2006) describing the components and characteristics of adaptability in the business world, although they do not use the word. This literature will be described further in upcoming chapters.

FORMS OF CHANGE

All healthy organizations strive to channel and even control change. But despite this voluntary, proactive approach, schools cannot avoid the impetus to change that comes from osmotic and policy forces. Although I separate three forms of change—osmotic, policy, and voluntary—for academic purposes, some readers may find the distinctions difficult when deciding exactly which one was the primary stimulus for a particular innovation. Thus, some may find it helpful to be able to recognize the three broad forms of educational change portrayed in Figure 2.1.

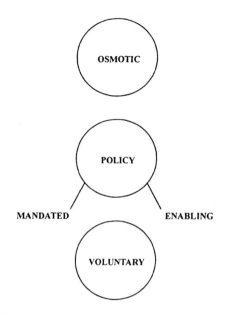

Figure 2.1. Forms of Change

Osmotic

Like osmosis in the natural world, many times, change seems to simply happen or move into an organization. Often, it is unclear who was responsible for initiating it or where it came from. The osmotic process demonstrates how permeable the school is to the evolutionary forces of the larger society; osmotic pressures often give educators little choice but to adopt, develop, or jettison past practices. Schools and other organizations often change in spite of themselves, and schools exist in a kettle of particularly powerful forces as we saw in Chapter 1.

An example of such a process is the rapid alteration in medical care that began in the 1980s on a small scale, but has accelerated at a dizzying pace since then. Technological innovation and increasing financial realities drive change in medical care, and, as we shall see in chapters that follow, the power of technology has also had a significant impact on practice in public education. Many hospitals and doctors have been forced to change their ways of providing care and dealing with the business side of their practices. They have been swept up in a vortex of social, economic, and political forces vividly illustrated with the passage of the first national health care law.

In education, student attire and deportment are considerably different today than they were in 1958 when I began to teach high school. Strict codes began to give way as a societal shift began in the mid-1960s and dress codes disappeared, with the assistance of the courts. My school and others found themselves powerless to resist the change. Currently, dress codes enjoy a revival in some locales as society pressures schools to establish more order in the face of an increased number of unruly students and public criticism about the lack of internal control. School uniforms are acceptable again.

Another example of the osmotic process is the swing between "back to basics," "open education and humanizing the school," "back to basics," and now "standards and assessment." Right after Sputnik in 1957, for example, we witnessed an emphasis on basic education as well as on more advanced subjects. Then, in reaction to Vietnam, our racial upheavals, and a general feeling that schools were placing too much emphasis on traditional knowledge at the expense of attitudes, values, and feelings, humanistic education became the focus. Then society returned to the basics in the mid-1970s in reaction to the perceived excesses of humanistic and open education.

Subsequently, since the early 1990s, a new wave (as discussed in the last chapter) of societal concern has washed over the schools. It contains problem-solving, inquiry, research, and group processes knowledge and skills, all bumping up against the mandates of "standards and assessment."

Clearly societal changes of all kinds cause "innovative" responses in schools. If you had clipped newspaper and magazine articles and columns from the 1950s to the present relating to education (as I have), you would have filled more than one large box. But usually these pieces are just reports; distressingly rarely does an in-depth treatment of issues appear. Thumb through the clippings, and you will see the seemingly endless demands on schools clashing with proposals for a more focused curriculum and standards-based instruction. Society continues to pile expectations onto schools and expects educators to make room for them in the curriculum.

In terms of the regular curriculum, here are some examples of the osmotic process at work. In response to the problem of homeless, schools at all levels may be required to provide instruction about the problem and how to relate to the homeless. In response to environmental issues, a "fourth R," recycling, infuses into the curriculum. In response to the danger of guns in homes, some schools implement "gun awareness" units, ironically seen by gun advocates as a way to encourage eventual gun ownership. In response to drug and alcohol problems, more material on these subjects enters the curriculum at all levels.

In response to a stressful environment at home and at school, some organizations develop "stress management" courses and provide increased mental health counseling. In response to the increase in bullying, schools instruct students in the dangers and immorality of such actions. Voluntary student forums show up as add-ons to the curriculum in order to give students a place to discuss their religious views.

In response to efforts to reduce the dropout rate, schools forge new relationships with business and industry that lead to work/study programs. In another approach to the dropout problem, school districts create alternative schools.

In response to "No pass, no play" policies in districts or at the state level, athletes get help through special tutoring programs. In response to disruptive or distressing home situations, many schools create new counseling programs and support groups for students and parents. In response to health care needs, social service agencies offer services in the building. In response to the schedules of working parents, some schools append early morning and late afternoon study hall/recreational programs. In order to respond to the needs of working teenagers, schools alter homework practices. It is often next to impossible to sort out what has become part of the regular curriculum and what is part of the "services curriculum" that primarily relates to the social and psychological services provided to students (Powell, Farrar, & Cohen, 1985, pp. 33–39). All levels of school are expected to respond to these needs, and the intensity of osmotic change often transforms high schools into "shopping malls" for academic and non-academic experiences.

Rarely will politicians or state department of education officials express any caution before pushing these expectations onto the schools or allowing them to evolve. Ironically, these same policymakers magnify the accountability squeeze while failing to add financial resources.

This process of continuing to add layers of social services onto schools reflects Wells' analysis of how America traditionally handles social welfare needs in a complex federalist system stressed by regional differences. There is a tug-of-war between the philosophy of providing people with a "hand up" to better their lives (via schools) versus a "handout" (via social agencies). Wells contends that we place ". . . an enormous burden on the public schools to solve almost all of our social problems" (p. 3). I concur.

In addition to all of the proceeding intrusions on the regular curriculum, the onrush of technology undercuts schools in unintended ways, eroding skills such as handwriting and spelling while favoring word processing and text messaging (described in chapter 1). Parents and teachers observe that children segue right from printing to the computer. If complaints escalate about terrible handwriting, the Rinehart method of teaching handwriting might again be back in the curriculum and hailed as an innovation!

Other outside forces also have an impact on the academic curriculum in other ways. For example, physical education and recess have been cut or reduced in some schools due to the pressure of testing programs. At the same time, the Internet drives young people into a more sedentary lifestyle, and obesity rises. As a consequence, schools are being pressed to restore PE and install weight loss programs. As a result of the struggling economy, schools face pressure to bring back instruction in economics. And as civic decorum and knowledge decline, schools may find themselves compelled to restore what used to be called "civics."

Currently, the accountability movement has led to a reduction in the use of "authentic assessments" in place of traditional tests. Authentic assessments, which include portfolios, exhibits, and presentations, blossomed in the 1990s. Then Stiggins pointed out that we have ". . . become as obsessed with this methodology in the 1990s as others were with the multiple-choice test from the 1940s through the 1980s" (1995, p. 240).

Some of the critics who questioned the cost of implementation and the accuracy of the results of these assessments helped make the "hard-data" *No Child Left Behind* approach the law of the land. Now there are many people inside and outside of education who realize that the NCLB environment has narrowed the curriculum considerably and who now push for more "soft" content and the authentic means to assess learning.

The dynamics of this osmotic process on an organizational level have been described in depth in three volumes written by Smith, Dwyer, Prunty, and Kleine (1986; 1987; 1988). They examine the evolving Milford School District over sixty-five years. They noted the ways in which the changing community affected innovation in the Kensington Elementary School over a fifteen-year period. At one point in their study, they conclude:

> Furthermore, we find that that many of these changes are not Milford or Kensington innovations, that is, planned, creative changes initiated by the District of the School. Rather they are reactions and responses to factors originating in these multiple, external contexts (1988, p. 266).

In a decade and a half, Kensington went from being one of the most innovative to being one of the most traditional organizations in the district, proof of the power of the surrounding environment to affect education.

Grant (1988) examined the transformation of "Hamilton High" from 1953–1985. At its inception, Hamilton served an upper-middle class, primarily white population and had a curriculum that was oriented heavily toward the college bound track. But in the 1980s, the city was desegregated racially, and a new group of students, some with disabilities, had become more prominent. Special education programs, English as a Second Language, and an accompanying drug subculture emerged and significantly altered instructional emphases, the curriculum, and patterns of interaction between educators and students.

Finally, in a unique and revealing examination into "Educational Change Over Time" in three American (northern New York) and five Canadian (southern Ontario) high schools over three decades, Hargreaves, Goodson, and Giles identified five forces that caused major shifts in curricular and instructional practices (2006). The forces were state or province policies, changes in leadership, changing demographics within the teaching ranks, changing community and therefore student demographics, and patterns of school relations within districts.

This sample of eight high schools in urban and suburban settings was comprised of traditional, innovative (strongly grounded in the concept of professional learning communities), magnet, and alternative schools. One hundred eighty-six teachers and principals were interviewed over three decades, a most unusual longitudinal research project. Data revealed how potent the five forces were in steering the organizations in directions they ordinarily would not have chosen to go—even to the extent that innovative schools regressed to being traditional (Giles & Hargreaves, 2006; Hargreaves, 2003).

As Cuban observed, after an analysis of the recurring waves of school reform, change in schools is very much limited by the constituencies they serve (1990b).

Society evolves, writers write, politicians propose policies, commissions issue reports, commentators talk, and parents raise questions (sometimes). Educators then react, either trying to fend off the changes they see and feel, adapting to them, or reshaping them to fit better with their organizations. If one is ahistorical or lacking in understanding about the school as a social institution, this osmotic process may be greeted with considerable cynicism, reinforcing the image that most educators will jump mindlessly on the latest curricular or instructional bandwagon.

On the other hand, if one places the process in context, these oscillations are understandable, "normal," and to be expected as the school tries to fulfill its twin roles as an agent of cultural transmission and of societal improvement. To the astute educator, what worked yesterday, but was then discontinued, may work again today in a different situation with a new group of students and staff. What may appear to be a fad may be a good solution to tomorrow's new/old problem. The societal pendulum swings, and schools move to its rhythm.

Policy

In contrast to the osmotic process, policymakers impose changes on schools through mandate, or schools are induced to change through enabling monies. Such "mandated" and "enabling" approaches stem from policies enacted at the federal, state, and local levels or from funds made available from private organizations (adapted from McDonnell and Elmore, 1987). In the latter case, "enablers" might come from foundations that further the goals of certain policies.

Mandated Change

Mandated changes require that schools comply with laws, regulations, and court decisions. "Their power derives from the sanctions that will be imposed if local educators do not comply" (Firestone & Corbett, 1988, p. 325). Those mandating contend that the mandate was necessary because the organization was not doing something that it was supposed to do. Mandates stir lots of emotional and value reactions that can lead to endless debates about the need for the directive and its positive or negative impact on the intended outcome.

When I began teaching in 1958, the only possible sanction on my high school would have been a mild corrective from the regional accrediting agency. There was little "cost" involved except potential but very remote loss of accreditation.

Mandates that have "punch" rely on the inherent power of the policymaker to exert sheer coercive power. Persons or the organization will pay in some way if they fail to comply (Hersey, Blanchard, & Johnson, 2001, p. 236), and that unpleasant consequence has a strong stage presence as it lurks in the wings.

As was discussed in the first chapter, *No Child Left Behind* is the prime example of a current federal mandate that has stirred strong reactions. So, too, are the accountability laws in all fifty states with the *Massachusetts Education Reform Law of 1993* a prime example of one. Since 1983, states enacted more rules and regulations about education at the local level than they had in the previous twenty years and, between 1984 and 1986 alone, passed close to 700 statutes (Timar and Kirp, 1989). Those statutes, combined with the current ones, create the *Alice in Wonderland* world of compliance discussed previously.

Politicians, feeling the pressures of policy stakeholders, often enact laws in haste and with superficiality rather than slowly with deliberation. The 24/7 mass media world, combined with instantaneous personal digital communication, thus ensures that quick and facile change trumps the deliberate, in-depth kind.

Typically, the policy stakeholders control revenue to states and local communities; funding becomes the prime lever for implementing a law. The more a system depends on another for its survival or at least viability on outside funding, the more compelled it is to comply—as is the case with Title I where the fear of loss of funds gives government a potent federal stick

(Elmore, 2009, pp. 231–241). It is this powerful accountability tool that has brought significant change to schools throughout the nation because of the sanctions attached to the law. This coercive process is increasingly replicated by states.

Compliance is achieved through the threat of regulatory enforcement. "If you don't measure up, we'll take over your school or force it to close." But how can federal or state policymakers enforce compliance if they have a lack of personnel capability to enforce regulations on site? Testing! "Testing is relatively cheap as an instrument of regulatory control" (Elmore, 2009, p. 236). With sanctions to test outcome success and the closing of a "failing" school the ultimate punishment, compliance becomes more possible.

But effective compliance finally depends on the capacity of the local system to respond with knowledge and skill in a manner that will address the need (Elmore, p. 231). In the case of NCLB, we have fifty levels of capacity to respond that have been well publicized in the media. Failure to adequately (at best) respond can then lead to more official and public disenchantment with under-performing schools, which will lead to more calls for charter schools, vouchers, and the like so that students can "opt out" of the system.

"Lack of capacity is the Achilles heel of accountability" (Elmore, 2004. p. 118). The sharp shrinkage in funding for schools makes that tendon ache more every day.

An old but still useful example of radical, mandated change is "Public Law 94–142, the Education for All Handicapped Children Act." From the day it was enacted in 1975, it has had a significant influence on curriculum, instruction, values, and finances. But, as we saw in chapter 1, the now retitled "Individuals with Disabilities Education Act" has never received sufficient funding.

A standard form of mandate is the high school accreditation report or the state education department assessment of local schools. Schools must address the recommendations made through these assessments or incur a penalty, the ultimate being loss of accreditation. But such reports can push a school in new directions or toward more emphasis on certain topics. For example, the most recent report for my local high school strongly recommends more of a focus in all areas on "higher order thinking skills" and more "project-based teaching." Such conclusions are being used as "levers for change" by the principal and department chairs (as will be discussed in chapter 8).

Fundamental to mandated change is "rationalization," the assumption that there is a clear and direct connection between means and ends, between the laws, regulations, and policies on one hand and certain goals on the other. The managerial processes of organizing, directing, and evaluating (to list a few) are central to rationalization. Of those enacting mandates, Ravitch observes, "One need not know anything about children or education" (2010, p. 11).

Sometimes, the link between means and the ends seems clear. But, as Wise contends in an incisive analysis of policymaking (by federal and state governments, the courts, and the executive branches), we are in an era where ". . . we are witnessing the phenomenon of hyper-rationalization, that is, an effort to rationalize beyond the bounds of knowledge" (1979, p. 65). This approach often leads to outcomes such as excessive prescription, procedural complexity, and the application of inappropriate solutions to problems. NCLB fits this description well.

Revisiting the phenomenon of hyper-rationalization almost a decade later but pre-dating NCLB, Wise still saw strong evidence of these effects, the result of subsequent state efforts to gain more control over the schools (Wise, 1988). Twenty-two years later, the accountability trend continues, but, as Elmore concludes, today " . . . accountability systems, as they are currently constructed, do little or nothing to support the learning that is critical to their success" (2004, p. 249).

Rarely are adequate resources delivered to the systems that need to improve. After a careful analysis of local costs to implement federal grants-in-aid, he concluded that NCLB is meeting only a fraction of "capacity costs" to fulfill accountability requirements (p. 255).

"This is an accountability system that is designed to do many things, the least of which is to improve schools" (p. 257). At this moment in 2010, we can only hope that the reauthorization process will begin to finally attend to the real business of education.

Outcomes such as these, combined with the complex nature of the school as an organization (to be discussed in chapter 3), lead to a long history of ineffective policy implementation. Combined with the societal shifts discussed earlier, this process regresses to prior solutions (sometimes in modified form) that previously had worked or not worked (Cuban, 1988b).

"Enabling" Change

This form of policy or private monies uses the metaphorical carrot (usually money) to induce change. Its aim is to improve schools by providing additional resources that will, in turn, increase the innovative capacity of the organization. Enabling policy fits well with the idea of adaptability or the self-renewing school. But, in addition, resources might come from foundations or other private sources to supplement public monies.

The 1950s, 1960s, and early 1970s were the heyday of federal and philanthropic funding to stimulate change. National Science Foundation monies flowed to support projects in developing new content in most subject fields, along with new approaches to delivering that content. Federal dollars were also available to support the reeducation of teachers. Title III provided grants to local districts to develop innovative practices, and later Title IV-C allowed state education departments to allocate monies to schools to stimulate change. Mixed with these sources were impressive sums from private foundations such as Carnegie, Danforth, and Ford.

But today, the climate for enabling funding has changed. The tight financial situation across the country has caused a stark reduction in funds that could induce innovation at the local level. As we saw in chapter 1, in most states, "The money just isn't there." To get it, we now have the current *Race to the Top* federal program, which is forcing states, who hope to qualify for desperately needed funding, to swallow hard and go against long-standing policies on limiting charter schools and not factoring student performance into teacher evaluation in order to qualify for a grant.

But even making those changes may not be enough, as Massachusetts found in the spring of 2010 when it was not awarded a first grant for school improvement. In order to be more competitive in the next round, the state reworked the proposal to signal a willingness to adopt national "Common Core" curriculum standards in certain fields rather than continue to rely on its nationally recognized standards that have been a model for other states.

It also was more specific in how student performance would be factored in to teacher evaluation. "Success" as the state was awarded a $250-million grant (Vaznis & Levensen, 2010). Other states, too, must weigh how much they want to alter their policies in order to win this funding (Dillon, 2010).

Other examples of strings-attached federal grants include Reading First, where recipients agree to use specific reading curricula; teacher incentives that support pay-for-performance programs; expansion of charter schools; and Safe and Drug-Free Schools.

Added to the complex environment for federal grants, Congress must revise and reauthorize the Elementary and Secondary Education Act.

In sharp contrast to the initial authorization in 1965, the anticipated revisions will likely be a vivid reminder just how powerfully the federal government can affect local practice through education policy (as with the IDEA). Secretary of Education, Arne Duncan, stated in an interview with *Education Week* that the coming reauthorization aims to ". . . build on the emphasis on teacher quality, data, standards, and support of low performing schools that is at the heart of the education portion of the economic stimulus law" (Klein, 2009).

Given the financial condition of the states, there are now few local grants available to districts and schools. If there are any, applicants face keen competition that requires endless hours of preparation before they can submit documents. Few principals or superintendents have such time, and the increase in budget reductions has eliminated staff grant writer positions or other staff positions or have diluted grant seeking by adding grant writing to current job responsibilities. Even to seek *Race to the Top* funds for local schools in a small state like Vermont would very likely require the dedication of 2,000 state department of education staff hours (*Burlington Free Press*, April 20, 2010).

Finally, what about the private sector as a source of enabling funds? A 2009 survey of 140 "education grant-makers" that included private and family foundations and corporate philanthropies showed a projected 59 percent drop for the year ahead, 25 percent staying the same, and 14 percent projecting an increase (with 2 percent unrecorded) (Robelen, 2010). So that source is more competitive than ever.

But there are still some private funding options where the philanthropy has not been harmed significantly by the recession. However, in certain cases, the money carries a recipient "price tag."

Until 2002, statistics showed that the top foundations supporting elementary and secondary education (30 percent of all monies given by the fifty largest donors) were Annenberg, Lilly, Packard, and Kellogg. But that year, the Gates and Walton Foundations increased their presence and provided 25 percent of the fifty largest donors. Soon, the Broad Foundation joined the two, and the three came to be known as "venture capitalists" as they ". . . targeted investments in education reform" (Ravitch, 2010, p. 199). This was an important shift in traditional giving as these three now expected certain results from their investments.

Undergirding the grants from Broad, Gates, and Walton are business emphases on competition, choice, deregulation, and incentives. Thus the Broad emphasizes support for charter schools and the more effective and efficient management of districts through training programs for administrators and board members with a focus on urban settings. The Gates emphasis (until 2008) was the creation of small high schools within large schools in urban areas with the overall goal of increasing graduation and college entry rates. The Walton emphasizes support for charter schools, school choice, and voucher-advocating organizations (Ravitch, 2010, pp. 202–222).

So "enabling" funds have evolved from pure no-strings-attached grants to some grants with stipulations that support a specific political agenda or other needs to some grants with stipulations for measurable outcomes. Ravitch contends that, in the case of the Broad Foundation, for example, considerable evidence shows that it selects districts based on the political leanings of school boards that will further the goals of the foundation (pp. 213–217). Hence grant applicants must proceed with some caution; financial needs may be dire, but what expectations come along with the funds?

In her examination of these foundations, Ravitch raises important questions about accountability. To whom are Broad, Gates, and Walton accountable if the programs they support do not result in expected outcomes? And is it democratically responsible to allow such private entities to have such large-scale influence over local schools when they seem to be beyond the reach of the communities and their respective boards of education (pp. 200–201)?

Voluntary Change

While policy change either directs or induces change from outside, voluntary change emerges from within the organization. The school or district decides to initiate the change or decides to participate in it. In some cases, the organization may adapt something forced onto it; it may adopt an innovation and then adapt it; or it may develop its own practices or processes. If adopted, to what extent is fidelity to the innovation essential? Some innovations allow for considerable flexibility in the way educators implement them, whereas others require educators to remain faithful to the design they expect to succeed.

Adoption, Adaptation, and Development

One major criterion of a healthy organization is its adaptability, as described in previous pages. The hallmark of adaptability is the organization's ability to initiate change, to innovate. When we examine Bromley and Mansfield high schools in the next chapters, we will look closely at the dynamics of this process. But adoption and development are important related concepts.

Currently, the *What Works Clearinghouse* of the U.S. Department of Education is a major source of evaluated programs for adoption and possible adaptation and even further development. It was established in 2002 as a successor to the *National Diffusion Network*, and it also offers to educators a menu of vetted, validated innovations at the federal level. The WWC promotes itself as ". . . a central and trusted source of scientific evidence for what works in education" (2010).

Here one can find intervention programs that relate to curriculum and instruction, student behavior, student incentives, school organization and governance, teacher development, and alternative education programs. Educators can also get "practice guides" for instruction. Each is rated on the basis of "consistent with WWC evidence standards."

Slowly, the pendulum is moving away from intervention types based on "scientifically based research"—via mainly experimental studies—and toward the Obama administration's stress on development and innovation for attaining more credible knowledge to improve student achievement. Old fashioned, practical know-how may be acceptable again (Viadero, 2009), evidence that shows that "what goes around comes around" a recurring cycle that veteran educators have come to expect.

In addition to the WWC, textbook publishers offer many "packaged" innovative programs that often align with state standards. But, as a local superintendent said recently, "It is a nightmare to sort out all these national resources and to tease out what's relevant to us." Additionally there is the need to sort out what has to be adopted "as is" from what can be adapted without affecting the effectiveness of the innovation.

Publishers also provide online versions of their books (stipulating that a district purchases the hard copy). For a small fee (perhaps $10 per student), students have access to the text Web site and additional materials, such as games, related to the subject. The same holds for teachers for whom a wealth of other material is available. But educators often have to pass up such resources because they lack the time to find them, assess them, decide where they fit, and finally integrate them in the curriculum.

With this material is a blizzard of other online resources, many of them free from companies like Google and Microsoft. Google Earth, Google Apps, and MS Dream Spark are but three examples of applications that are basically free to schools. Last year, my local high school (400 students, 9–12) received the equivalent of $100,000 in software from Google and $50,000 from MS.

For teachers, software-like apps includes word processing, spreadsheets, Web site construction, and slide and video production. Imaging in various forms is integral to these applications for manipulating and reassembling data. In the words of a high school teacher, "How do we teachers adapt to all this technology?" Another put it this way, "One must embrace the technology in order to be comfortable with it." The learning curve is steep now as the Digital Natives are expecting teachers to use technology. If they do not, they will find it increasingly difficult to engage students.

The overhead projector and video tape recorder were the big technological innovations to which I had to adapt during my forty one years of teaching in public schools and at a university. Compare that with the seemingly exponential rate of change faced by current teachers. The other day a science teacher said to me, "I couldn't find my overhead projector if you paid me." For professional viability in the 21st century, teachers must adapt or become antiquated in the classroom.

Many times, adapting an adopted innovation is the best route, given the local context and today's financial constraints. The Rand study of federal programs supporting change (outlined further in chapter 4) showed that when schools engage in a process of "mutual adaptation"—modifying the innovation to fit the realities of the institutional setting—they are more likely to succeed. Such "learning-by-doing" takes time, much participation and patience, and effective leadership on the part of those directing the effort (Berman and McLaughlin, 1978, p. 28).

Keep in mind that the earlier programs studied by the Rand researchers (e.g., bilingual education, vocational/career education, and reading) initially lacked precise definition compared to WWC programs, and, therefore, they required adaptation if they were to be implemented well and continued rather than discarded.

However, research demonstrates the difficulty schools have in institutionalizing adopted/adapted innovations, whether highly defined or open to modification. In this regard, Supovitz and Weinbaum (2008), examined five types of innovations at the high school level and enlarged the category of "mutual adaptation" by deriving the concept of "iterative refraction." When innovations go through iterative refraction, they are modified regularly as they work their way through an organization or one of its subsystems (pp. 151–169). Various forces (to be described in the next chapter) virtually ensure that variability in implementation will be the rule rather than the exception (p. 7).

LESSONS ABOUT CHANGE FROM PROGRAMS AND PROJECTS

Consider now examples of some major projects, mostly focused on high schools, that contain instructive lessons for those embarking on an improvement journey, be it through adoption, adaptation, or development.

The first example is the Model Schools Project of the National Association of Secondary School Principals. This 1969 project, conceived by the late J. Lloyd Trump and funded by the Ford Foundation, was then the most ambitious, "whole-school," and innovative attempt to bring about comprehensive change in secondary schools. It was based on a decade of research and thought before its application in the field (Trump 1959; Trump and Baynham, 1961) at a time when educators had no instructive studies about effecting educational change as that research was in its infancy.

"The Trump Plan" became widely known and was a popular topic on education convention program in the 1970s. The thirty four participating junior and senior high schools committed themselves to installing a radically different organization-wide model of improvement to reach all students, one that would "restructure" them (but that concept was not in the educational or business vocabulary at that time). The model included team teaching; differentiated staffing; flexible scheduling; learning activity packages; new roles for administrators, teachers, and counselors; and various methods to individualize instruction.

These components of the model, although defined fairly specifically, could be joined together and implemented in ways deemed best by the local school. "Mutual adaptation" was the accepted process. When the project officially ended in 1975, research indicated a checkered pattern of success in the organizations involved (Trump and Georgiades, 1977; *NASSP Bulletin*, November 1977).

Major reasons for lack of consistent success included frequent turnover of leadership; the resistance of unions to changing teacher roles; the lack of ongoing local financial aid once foundational funding ran out; and the decline in community support, particularly among parents of college-bound students.

In 2005, Keefe and Amenta reflected on the impact of the MSP on secondary education. They concluded that overall ". . . much that is good in contemporary schooling can be traced to the influence of the Model Schools Project" (2005, p. 543). Trump ideas and practices are infused in secondary schools throughout the country, and the subsequent Coalition of Essential Schools (CES) owes much to the project.

The CES project was initiated in 1984 by Theodore Sizer, former dean of the Harvard Graduate School of Education and late professor of education at Brown University. The project is grounded in three highly popular books at the time that emerged from a five-year, national study of high schools: *Horace's Compromise, Horace's School,* and *Horace's Hope (*Horace being a fictional teacher).

The involved schools, drawing on ten "common principles" rather than any "model" of change or of a future school, work on giving a more academic focus to their curricula; to have school goals and standards apply to all learners; to personalize learning; to stress the metaphor of the student-as-worker and the teacher-as-coach; and to place the teacher at the heart of the improvement process. But the CES offers no prescription as to how to apply these principles for reform. Each school interprets them within its own context for implementation (Muncey and McQuillan, 1996, p. 8). Again, mutual adaptation and iterative refraction are at work.

The Coalition has grown from 12 charter members in 1985 to 150 dues-paying members today. Hundreds more are loosely linked to the

Coalition via regional "centers" that publicize events and organize a national annual Fall Forum (Viadero, 2009). The CES does not prescribe any set methods for attaining local school goals, and it is this pluralistic and flexible approach to improvement that has made it difficult to evaluate project outcomes (Wikipedia, 2009).

Muncey and McQuillan, educators and anthropologists, published an insightful, forthright book about the Coalition, centered on eight of the original charter member schools. Their five-year study portrays schools that have an uneven record of success in implementing reforms using the CES principles as a template.

Other reports about the Coalition echo similar findings (Viadero, 1995; Cohen, 1995; Wagner, 1994). The schools that changed the most were those with the most severe problems with discipline, attendance, and dropouts. Schools that changed the least had few of those problems and were more traditional, well run, and well supported suburban-type "college prep" schools. Parents in the suburban locales were most resistant to many changes. This factor is similar to one from the MSP research that explained the lack of success in some communities.

Outcomes-Based Education (OBE) is perhaps the most well-conceived attempt to totally change the nature of high school curriculum and instruction. Developed by Bill Spady with a careful, research-based approach over a decade beginning in 1973, the program came to the attention of educators in 1983. From then until 1993, it became nationally known through convention programs, articles in professional journals, consulting services, and demonstration projects in several districts and schools in several states.

Sites that had implemented the program lured a steady stream of visitors. Spady called the program the Future Empowerment Paradigm (1997). The story of its demise is disheartening.

OBE was grounded in the work of Benjamin Bloom and his taxonomies of the cognitive and affective domains of learning and the work of James Block on mastery learning. Central to Spady's work was the assertion that schools needed to make learning the constant and time the variable rather than the reverse premise that permeates public education. In so doing, he developed curriculum and instructional models that framed the ideas that aimed at bringing more meaning and relevance to the learning process.

The basic model conceptualized the evolution of education as a progression from the broad notions of the agrarian age to our current Conceptual Age or Globalization 3.0, as discussed in chapter 1.

With these concepts as the foundation, Spady provided detailed and convincing models of broad new curricula content constructed around the dimensions of creative and critical imagination; personal and cultural relationships;

personal growth and identity; contribution to human well-being; and functional and productive competence.

Depending on the nature of each state's curricula, most of Spady's
approach was congruent with new curricula emphases that, by 1993, were
increasingly becoming integral to new state curriculum standards. By that
date, four states—Florida, Minnesota, Oregon, and Pennsylvania—were
close to modifying state requirements for the calendar year and school day.
These are ". . . undisputed definers of schooling, curriculum, and credit"
(Spady, 1997, p. 42).

The Carnegie unit, focused on 120 hours of course classroom time during
an academic year, was being seriously challenged. Would the "seat time"
of the Carnegie unit or would student performance become the major criterion for graduation? This question is still alive and well and far from being
resolved, as seen in the issues bubbling out of NCLB. OBE, in tandem with
other reform movement of the times such as the CES, Effective Schools, and
Success for All, made the early 1990s into a heyday of important change,
even restructuring, in American secondary education.

But in 1992 in Pennsylvania, a countermovement began that, by the
summer of 1994, effectively killed OBE. In a stunning series of events,
the conservative right objected to elements of the Empowerment Paradigm
being proposed at the state level that it labeled "secular humanism, New
Age lifestyles, federal government tyranny, and world government." The key
learning outcome that generated the reaction was the proposed statement,
"Each student shall gain knowledge of various cultures and lifestyles in order
to foster an appreciation of the dignity, worth, contributions, and equal rights
of all people" (p. 45).

Co-opting that statement, a national anti-OBE political strategy evolved
that built into a tornado and blew away OBE lay supporters and educators.
Today, there is hardly a trace of OBE in any district or school across the nation.
Decades of development work ". . . was lost as a driving force in school reform
on a national scale in less than two years" (p. 53).

The pattern resembles the uproar that arose in the mid-1970s over *Man:
A Course of Study,"* an NSF-funded anthropological curriculum for upper
elementary grades. Inflammatory subjects like evolution, infanticide, wife-
sharing, and communal living led to congressional hearings and a nosedive in
program sales (Ravitch, 1983, p. 264).

If you want to know more about these events, volumes authored by Spady
are listed in this book's bibliography. Although written several years ago, they
are filled with relevant, insightful, and instructive lessons about attempting to
effect large-scale, well-defined, systematic improvement in today's polarized
political environment. One can detect the germination of the accelerating

accountability movement described in chapter 1, culminating in the passage of NCLB in 2002. Also relevant is Ravitch's broader examination, 1960s– 1980, of "Reformers, Radicals, and Romantics" (1983, pp. 228–266).

During the 1980s, a popular route to school improvement that had a program focus was the National Diffusion Network mentioned earlier. Miles and Huberman (1984) conducted a detailed research study that uncovered numerous implementation factors involved in NDN-type innovations. Using case study methodology, they conducted field studies of twelve sites that had implemented innovations (some internally developed) with support from Title IV-C federal monies or adopted NDN innovations. (For anyone interested in multi-site field research, the book contains instructive information about such methodology.)

Seven sites were high schools and included innovations relating to social studies; science courses with an interdisciplinary bent; a career education work experience program; an in-house alternative school for potential dropouts; an individualized program to assess student needs, interests, and career intentions; a new 9–12 reading curriculum; and on-the-job experiences relating to vocational education (pp. 18–31).

Miles and Huberman discovered that: most sites, the processes of adoption, adaptation, and development were at work; opportunistic reasons for adoption were more common than a noticeable planning process; "Large-scale, change-bearing innovations lived or died by the amount of assistance that their users received once the change process was under way" (p. 273); strong professional commitment (teacher and administrator) was key to success; and it was possible to enhance student performance and attitudes (pp. 271–281).

A well-publicized current project is one relating to the New American Schools Development Corporation and its varied New American Schools Designs (NAS). Proposed in 1991 by President Bush in his "America 2000: An Education Strategy," the Corporation was founded and funded by business and foundation leaders in order to test innovative designs for transforming schools. The project introduced "whole-school reform" to the educational dictionary.

Its original five-year life span included design/development, a two-year testing phase, and a two-year "scale-up" phase, meaning that successfully implemented innovations could be adopted or adapted by other organizations. "The intention is not for the designs to be 'replicated' but to offer a focus and a set of broad guiding principles for reform" (Stringfield and Smith, 1996, p. 12). After five years, it was decided to continue fine-tuning implementation.

Stringfield and Smith describe the designs of seven NAS projects that, by 1999, involved over 1,000 schools. These designs include a K-12 comprehensive plan, rooted in community support and participation that promotes authentic teaching and high levels of student achievement; innovative curricular designs for K-12 education; and a "total systems" approach that involves district offices and state departments of education that work in cooperation with local schools and their communities.

In 2001, the Rand Corporation conducted an evaluation of the first decade of NAS. It found, for example, that whole-school design adoption was difficult under common conditions; that strong external, consistent assistance along with supplementary resources were essential for success; and that a strong supportive district/school environment was instrumental for positive outcomes. In sum, the project has had "modest" effects in relationship to its goals (Berends, Bodilly, and Kirby, 2002).

Supovitz, Weinbaum, and Associates (2008) produced the most helpful recent research for school practitioners relating to whole-school and program kinds of innovations. Using fifteen high schools, they examined, over two years, implementation of: a whole-school "High Schools That Work" focused on a comprehensive approach to student achievement; a whole-school "First Things First" focused on improving relationships among students, staff, and parents and improving instructional practices; programs focused on instructional strategies for teaching literacy; and a program "SchoolNet" focused on staff use of data to increase student achievement.

Each innovation was developed elsewhere and adopted for local use. The concept of "mutual adaptation" (outlined in a previous section of this chapter) was highly evident as schools tried to stay "true" to the adopted innovations. How "faithful" should any adopter be to the original intent and parameters of a program? They concluded, "Regardless of the conceptual debate, in the messy real world, programs and policies are highly susceptible to adjustments and adaptations throughout the implementation process" (p. 5). In fact, variability was the rule rather than the exception. The study is valuable also because it examined various types of innovations.

From this research emerged the additional adaption concept of "iterative refraction," which shows how innovations are "adjusted repeatedly" as they are implemented and filtered through the normal organizational layers of district, school, department, and classroom (pp. 151–172).

Linked conceptually to the work of Supovitz and Weinbaum is a case study of one alternative high school as it developed over three years. The "Met," as it is called, is a state-supported high school in Rhode Island that was part of the Big Picture network of (in 2008) sixty three other such schools in sixteen states and the District of Columbia. The network has had considerable support from the Gates Foundation to provide curricula and instructional designs, staff development, and other assistance to organizations that are attempting to "scale-up" innovative programs and practices following the NAS approach (McDonald, Klein, and Riordan, 2009).

From this study, McDonald, Klein, and Riordan identified eight instructive "challenges" facing implementers of a whole-school design. They are: fidelity; teaching; ownership; communication; feedback; resource; political; and mind-set. Related specifically to this section of this book is the observation, "Ignore fidelity and what will you take to scale? Ignore adaptation and your design will crack. This is more than just a challenge. It is a dilemma. It can only be managed, never resolved" (2009, p. 19).

The last and most recent national project focused on high schools is the Small Learning Communities (SLC), underwritten by the Gates Foundation. It ran from 2000–2008 and disseminated $2 billion to some forty high schools in seventeen urban locations across the country to support the creation of new small schools (400 or so students) or to redesign existing schools into SLC of about that size. The new schools typically were charter schools. (The material for this section of the chapter is drawn from American Institutes for Research, 2006, Fouts & Associates, 2006, and Gates, 2009. Gates sponsored extensive evaluation of the project.)

Foundation goals aimed at reducing truancy and dropout rates, particularly among low-income and minority students (every year, a million teenagers drop out of school), increasing attendance, changing attitudes among these students about the value of a diploma, and increasing college readiness among these groups.

For existing schools that housed more than 400 students, the goal was to create within the SLC an environment that would facilitate more personal relations between students and staff; enable staff to attend to student needs more effectively; increase student engagement; and facilitate more individualized instruction. Primarily, funds supported curriculum development, teacher reeducation, and assisting in implementing new schools or redesigning existing ones into SLC.

Decades earlier, two influential and relevant-to-Gates reports on the "comprehensive high school" were authored by James Bryant Conant (1959; 1967), then president of Harvard University. They were stimulated by the launch of Sputnik in 1957 that led to much consternation as to why America had not beaten Russia into space. Conant conducted a survey study of 103 schools in 26 states and personally visited 55 organizations where he interviewed administrators and teachers and collected on-site information about courses and programs of study (1959, pp. 97–101).

The goals of the project were to evaluate the degree to which these schools provided a general education for all students; offered a solid elective program for those aiming to acquire work skills upon graduation; and offered programs to ensure success for those entering a college or university. Both books contain detailed information about high school curricula. They captured the attention of the educational community and the public and galvanized them to achieve quality of this level of public education.

One major conclusion of the Conant research was that too many schools were too small, fewer than 500 students and fewer than 100 in a graduating class. Forty-five percent of the 15,000 high schools reporting were of that size or less (1967, p. 7). According to the study, schools that size could not effectively meet, on a cost-effective basis, the programs that would effectively meet the three dimensions of education mentioned above. These reports triggered the regional high school movement, stimulated the building of larger schools (especially in the cities) of 2,000, 3,000, or even 4,000 students, and led to the closing of thousands of small high schools across the country.

Thirty-five years after the last Conant report, the Gates Foundation concluded instead that small high schools of preferably 400 or fewer students would best meet the particular needs of disadvantaged and minority students who attend large urban high schools. The Gates report noted the fact that such students lived amid social conditions that led to their alienation and thus educational underperformance and that SLCs would help greatly to counter this alienation. In Conant's time, by contrast, researchers paid scant attention to these sociopsychological factors.

Hence in the case of Conant and the case of Gates, outside-the-school events, not inside-the-school decisions, provided stimuli for recommendations for improving high school education. *A Nation at Risk* of 1993, discussed in chapter 1, emerged because of an external prod for change.

From project evaluations, Gates himself concluded that many of the small schools did not improve achievement in any significant way, that basic school culture did not change, and that reformers realized less success when they worked to change existing schools rather than creating new ones (Gates, 2009, p. 4).

External evaluators identified several reasons for less-than-positive project outcomes. One was that high schools, especially ones in urban settings, are complex organizations that are difficult to change in terms of culture, staff behavior, instructional practices, and curriculum. "Foundation officials stress the difficulty and complexity of school improvement in under-performing school districts" (American Institutes for Research, p. 69). This arduous task placed great pressure on school staff whose small size meant even more role expectations on their plates than normal. The result was administrator and teacher fatigue and eventual burnout.

In addition, the challenging students often had special needs and often qualified for special services because of their status as English Language

Learners. Meeting their needs was extremely "labor-intensive" work that took its toll on an overextended staff. When initial grant funding ran out, most districts did not have the financial resources to continue the level of staff support promised, especially in the areas of class size and teaching load. Therefore, participating schools could not meet the unrealistic expectation that they must demonstrate clear positive outcomes in two or three years. (A challenge similar to NCLB anticipated outcomes.)

Budget reductions meant that many teachers had to "travel" from one SLC to another. They had to relinquish the common planning time needed for staff to consult about addressing student needs by adjusting curricula and instructional strategies and by adjusting student schedules to meet their shifting academic and personal needs. In some buildings, even grant-writing demanded teacher time. Most of these logistical challenges fell on the desks of administrators who had to spend valuable time away from matters of curriculum and instruction as they "moved money around" to save or boost programs.

Also, the focus on testing to assess basic learning became counterproductive when students began to rebel against it. The curriculum narrowed and lost its ability to engage students whose attrition grew. Teachers, too, became disillusioned with this focus, a similar negative fallout to that which accompanied the implementation of NCLB.

Additionally, the small schools disappointed students because they could not offer the breath and depth of curriculum and co-curricular offerings that students wanted. They then lost motivation and sometimes switched to a "regular" high school. Conant's three general purposes of a secondary school became impossible to meet largely due to small organizational size.

The SLC also found it difficult to recruit and retain mathematics teachers, thus severely undercutting math instruction, which was to have been a cornerstone for attaining project goals. Inadequate funds for staff development and coaching added another layer of negative effects on teachers in this specialty. A 30 percent staff turnover after three years became a major problem in the new foundation supported schools (AIR, p. 57). Turnover impacts program effectiveness, diverts resources to reeducating new staff, and interrupts instructional continuity.

As a result of these staff issues, many teachers found themselves having to teach elective courses for which they felt ill qualified, or they had to give up teaching a favorite elective for something else. Some staff who offered college preparatory courses found that students often could not handle the material; these teachers either had to adjust courses or drop them altogether, not an easy loss for teachers who find these elective or upper-level courses highly motivating because most students who choose them want to learn. Teachers facing such instructional challenges began to feel that their career paths or even tenure were threatened by the uncertainty of assignments.

The challenged posed by inadequate funding for many new or redesigned schools resulted in less-than-ready curriculum and incomplete instructional modifications. Without such basics in place before school began, educational effectiveness suffered. In addition, the state funding formulas in some states ironically led to a decline in state support of SLC schools whose operating costs that were higher than normal due to the costs of serving the needs of needy students.

In the end, in many cases, community support for SLC began to wane due to student unhappiness, the difficulty of demonstrating increased student achievement and performance, the challenge of demonstrating to skeptics that additional money would improve achievement and performance, and the perception that the college-bound programs were being affected negatively by the diversion of scarce funds from traditional schools to a new or redesigned school. Communities were not convinced that the cost of all the changes would have the promised payoff, the same kind of response that eroded community support for the Model Schools and Coalition for Essential Schools projects.

Two statements from the Fouts' evaluation of the Gates project are relevant and instructive to any who undertake reform projects that include components similar to those of Gates.

> We cannot emphasize this enough: If the building leadership cannot present a clear case of why change is necessary, and if teachers or the public are not convinced that it is a moral question, conversion to SLCs or any other school reform effort for that matter, will face great difficulty (p. 11).

> When it comes to school reform, there is no conversion blueprint to ensure success (p. 10).

As you can see, educators do not have to reinvent the wheel of school improvement. They already have access to highly valuable literature for anyone embarking on a *planned* change endeavor, whether the classroom, school, or district is the target. This literature underscores the rationalistic or technological approach to change (discussed in the next chapter), and it contains useful lessons for change agents.

Michael Fullan's comprehensive work (2007) summarizes much of the historical and current highlights from the research to that date. The literature summarized earlier in this chapter also contains helpful summary chapters pointing out what was learned from these varied experiences.

A good example of a project that does not appear to have learned from the literature is the Sizer CES project. Although the Muncey and McQuillan book reveals many positive results, it also reveals, in my opinion, many more negative or at least disappointing ones (as do the studies by Cohen and Wagner).

For example, "lessons" from other projects have shown that a "school-within-a-school" strategy is not usually effective, whereas a more inclusive "whole-school" approach is; that time is critical when implementing a set of "principles" (or any less well-defined innovations) in any school context; that strong and consistent leadership from the principal (or a surrogate) is instrumental for success; and that traditional, suburban-type schools with a college preparatory emphasis are likely to be more resistant to significant change than are other schools.

Many of these outcomes emerged from the Trump Model Schools project, yet nowhere in Sizer's volumes (or ones written by associates such as Powell, Farrar, and Cohen, 1985) is Trump cited, nor do any of the books that form the foundation for the CES (particularly Sizer's three volumes) draw on the instructive literature described here or acknowledge work done by noted change researchers such as Michael Fullan or Matthew Miles who were producing insightful relevant works during the CES inception and during its later years. Such crucial literature is conspicuous by its absence.

Muncey and McQuillan asked, "Don't new reforms build on findings from those previously undertaken?" (1996, p. 288). They queried Sizer and his staff about this and were told that they did examine and use this literature to guide their work. But the formal evidence indicates a contrasting conclusion, that Sizer (a historian of education) and his associates skipped over the history of school reform as seen through the lens of the change literature, which is the focus of this book. Attending to it might have given them a greater chance of greater success than appears to be the case at present.

The external evaluators of the Gates project did not comment on this issue relative to that project's outcomes. But their findings signal that the creators of the project paid scant attention to the literature that could have informed project strategies. Had they learned lessons from that literature, they might have avoided repeating certain mistakes embedded in it.

LEVELS OF CHANGE

Three levels of change are common in organizations—system, subsystem, and individual—as illustrated by the literature reviewed.

Figure 2.2 shows that the system might be the district or the school; the subsystem might be the school, the department, or program; and the individual, the teacher. Most research has focused on change across districts and schools. This book focuses on departments, programs, and individuals.

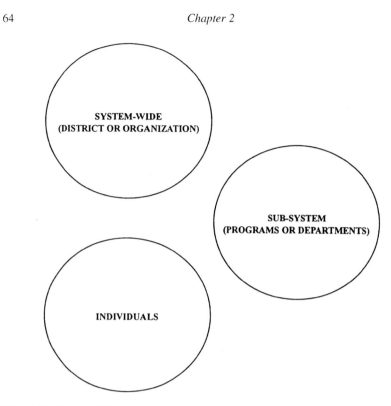

Figure 2.2. Levels of Change

At all levels, a number of variables exist, and they interact in numerous and often confounding ways. It is tempting to think that change is "simpler" at the level of the individual, but that is erroneous. As we will see in chapters 4 and 5, "micro" variables such as values, abilities, motivation, and relations with peers and supervisors, play a major role in one's reactions to change. Then, as one works up the system ladder, other organizational variables are added. These include power and authority, communications, decision-making, leadership, incentives and rewards, resources, and rules and regulations.

Ravitch concluded, after examining school reform efforts from the 1960s to 1980, that ". . . any planned reform is filtered through the experiences, intentions, and purposes of those who implement it" (1983, p. 265). This "layering" of variables contributes greatly to the confounding nature of change. One day in one setting, change seems relatively easy to accomplish, but on another day in the same situation, improvement is maddeningly hard. Conversely, with another change in that same situation but weeks later, walls of resistance are thrown up (Fullan, 1991, p. 350).

The impact of understanding or not understanding how these variables affect change was identified by Huberman and Miles (1984) in their "up close" field research. They found that administrators lived in different institutional worlds from teachers, tending at first to see the innovations as relatively simple and straightforward to use and having the potential to bring about considerable organizational improvement.

Teachers, on the other hand, saw the innovations as complex, inherently ambiguous, and difficult to use, and they were skeptical about eventual changes (p. 272). (As an aside, I would add that so, too, do most politicians and critics live in "different worlds" as we have seen via mandated change legislation.)

In general, eventual successful implementation hinged heavily on the administrator's ability to recognize and value the teacher's view of the innovation, the processes associated with its use, and the kind of administrative assistance they would need to overcome or dampen the impact of impediments.

Wolcott, in a study of one district's attempt to install a "top-down" programmed budgeting system, identified great differences in how teachers perceived and reacted to this "macro" level change contrasted to the way that the "technocrats"—the administrators—viewed it (1977 and republished in 2003).

The recent research on the Coalition of Essential Schools, the Gates project, and the studies by Supovitz and Weinbaum provides additional testimony to the power of these variables to enhance, to block, or to diminish the intended effects of innovations. As Fullan said again in the fourth edition of his analysis of the literature, ". . . planned change attempts rarely succeed as intended" (2007, p. 13). The exact statement is made in the first edition of the book (1982, p. 6).

"Will School Reform Fail?" is the headline of a 2010 issue of *U.S. News & World Report?* (January). The answer can be "no" if reformers pay attention to the evidence that presents itself so clearly in the literature cited. Rather than list them again, I encourage those engaged in a change project to read and think about the evaluation findings that emerged from the studies depicted in the previous pages. In general, they fall into the broad categories of *capacity and context* that will be examined in upcoming chapters.

Emerging from all these studies, as the evidence shows, is that reformers must understand the nature of small-scale change and the validity of the incremental approach discussed in the Introduction. It is this approach to change that is recognized in the private sector and historians of education have shown as a sensible and credible one for schools. As Tyack and Cuban, who examined a century of school reform concluded, "We favor attempts to bring about such improvements by working from the inside out, especially by enlisting the support and skills of teachers as key actors in reform" (1995, p. 10).

And after Ravitch analyzed reform efforts, she concluded, "In view of the number of actors involved, and the degree of their autonomy, lasting change in an institution as various as the school is invariably incremental and piecemeal" (1983, p. 265).

Clearly, organizational literature contains ample evidence that smaller-scale change *can be* a route to more substantial organizational improvement, provided that it can go deep in terms of large numbers of employees making such changes in purposeful directions (Fullan, 1993, p. 14). We cannot put schooling on hold or jump over existing situations while we debate and conduct more research on how to effect large-scale change and innovation. We now have much instructive literature available on that subject. We need to build on it and not repeat that research.

Instead, we need to embrace the fact that the inside-out, small-scale approach works when it comes to improvement in education and that it occurs already in numerous good schools. We need to find ways to make this level of change more potent for organizational renewal, so you will find that chapters 4 and 5 describe the dynamics of this process as it unfolds within a complex organization, the school, and the even more complex component of the school, the classroom. Failure to explore these complexities fully would ensure failure—or at least reduced results—for any change endeavor. Hence, the next chapter zeroes in on *Schools as Organizations.*

Chapter 3

Schools as Organizations

There are, in the school, complex rituals of personal relationships, a set of folkways, mores, and irrational sanctions, a moral code based upon them. There are games, which are sublimated wars, teams, and an elaborate set of ceremonies concerning them. There are traditions and traditionalists waging their world-old battle against innovations.

—Waller, 1965, p. 103

As a veteran practitioner turned professor wrestling with this puzzle, I have come to appreciate the fact that organizations have plans for dealing with reformers.

—Cuban, 1988, p. 343

While the society around them becomes increasingly complex, most schools appear to their external critics to be tidy bureaucracies, relatively simple to manage and to change. Perhaps this is because, as was discussed earlier, most citizens have spent several years in the organization, directly observing teaching and experiencing its rituals, folkways, mores, sanctions, and ceremonies. Thus there is little mystique to the education profession compared to other professions, and self-proclaimed experts in curriculum, instruction, and learning abound in every community.

Muddling the mystique of teaching is the fact that there are successful teachers who staff religious education programs and local community organizations and who, more likely than not, lack formal educational preparation. But easily overlooked is another fact, that these settings usually serve a selected clientele in contrast to the public schools that must serve all students. In sum, classroom teaching, according to popular misconception, is straightforward and relatively easy work: a teacher simply pours knowledge into the heads of students. To some observers, it is mainly an "art form" with little "science" involved.

To outsiders, schools will always be there, too. Until the increasing impact of the accountability squeeze, it was rare to have a school close for reasons other than declining enrollment. No matter what the budget reductions, the school always managed to deliver services. Small increases in class size, postponing buying those new textbooks or computers, cutting back on pencils and paper, reducing the times for room cleaning, not lining the athletic fields as frequently, and dropping some field trips, there can be a near endless list of "little cuts" that laypeople barely notice. Sapping quality is a subtle process.

Each of us wears a pair of sociopsychological glasses through which we see the education process and the organization within which it takes place. We identify patterns, and we make interpretations. We come to believe in our perspective. If the perspective is somewhat accurate regarding the realities of the setting and accompanying phenomena, then we conclude that it is helpful to rely on it. If the perspective proves to be inaccurate, however, we need to change our glasses, or we will continue to bump against reality and against those with a clearer vision of the workplace.

Bolman and Deal use the term "frames" to view organizational life and events. Frames are both windows on the world and lenses that bring the world into focus. Frames filter out some things while allowing others to pass through easily. Frames help us to order experience and decide what action to take (1991, p. 11). They identify the structural, human resource, political, and symbolic frames.

THREE PERSPECTIVES ON CHANGE

House describes three perspectives on educational change: the technical, political, and cultural (1981, pp. 17–41).

The *technical perspective* emphasizes rational behavior. To attain organizational goals, one must establish bureaucratic structures and processes to promote hierarchical control and suppress competing interests and values. Then the route to improvement can be a fairly clear means-ends route—one that emphasizes an effective technology leading to an identifiable product. This perspective is akin to Bolman and Deal's "structural frame" (pp. 37–97).

In terms of change, this perspective may focus on the innovation that often emerges from a research and development process and that "should" work in any setting where it is implemented (e.g., What Works Clearinghouse). Or it may focus on the process of planning, which can be treated in a highly technical fashion. Whatever the focus, it assumes that rational people ought to adopt a tested innovation on its merits or they should implement the outcomes from a well-outlined planning process.

The *political perspective* emphasizes that there is seldom one route to achieve goals. Issues of power and authority permeate every human setting, and, therefore, there is often conflict over what the goals should be and how to achieve them. Cooperation among groups is not automatic; one must often resort to negotiation and compromise to set a direction, and, even then, forces inside and outside of the organization may redirect energy and affect outcomes. A critical element in this mix is the impact of the external environment. This perspective is akin to Bolman and Deal's "political frame" (pp. 161–209).

With regard to change, this perspective focuses on processes working through issues of power, authority, and conflicting values. But because of the give-and-take, the final shape of the planning process itself or its outcomes—or the shape of an innovation—may not please all parties. However, once the affected groups have reached agreement, they should maintain fidelity to the adopted plan or innovation.

The third perspective, *the cultural*, is a more recent addition through which to understand organizational change in schools and in other organizations. In education, it is rooted in Waller's classic study, *The Sociology of Teaching*, written in 1932 (republished in 1965). Waller emphasizes the important role that the shared elements of norms, beliefs, and values held by groups of participants (e.g., administrators, teachers, and students) play in creating the context for change.

This perspective is akin to a combination of Bolman and Deal's "human" (pp. 101–158) and "symbolic" (pp. 215–262) frames; it assumes that few things in organizations are exact, precise, or predictable (p. xiii).

Each organizational group derives "meaning" about change through its culture of norms, beliefs, and values Lortie (1975) and Sarason (1996) published other classic works dealing with the culture of the school and dimensions of it not addressed by Waller. These dimensions will be identified in subsequent chapters. Wolcott's previously cited research—on a rational planning and budgeting process in an Oregon school district—portrays vividly the deep gaps of understanding and meaning between "technocrats" (administrators) and teachers that can subvert a technically well-designed innovation.

All individuals in a school work within such groups. (For teachers, other subgroups might be defined by grade level or by subject area, such as ninth-grade social studies or mathematics.) The respective norms, beliefs, and values of these groups may differ considerably from those of other groups or from those of the total organization (McLaughlin & Talbert, 2001, pp. 61–65).

Groups adopt these cultural features over time and thus they become guideposts for behavior and tend to preserve the status quo. They may become similar enough so that people can work together fairly effectively, but their differences may become so magnified that the organization is rife with conflict, controversy, and un-cooperation.

Hence change, from this perspective, unless imposed, tends to be evolutionary. Innovations are altered as they are implemented—as they sometimes are through the political process—so they fit better into the local context. Also, the culture of the group will likely inhibit organization-wide changes but nurture small-scale improvements. This is the "mutual adaptation" and "iterative refraction" described in the last chapter.

Each perspective is valuable for giving us greater understanding about organizational change. For example, we can explain successes or failures of the Model Schools project, the Coalition of Essential Schools, Outcomes-Based Education, the Rand Study of New American Schools, and the Gates Foundation project by analyzing them from the technical or political perspectives. But to my eye, what those perspectives lack is appreciation and understanding of the cultural, as was seen in chapter 2.

Therefore, we will focuses on school improvement from a cultural perspective with the goal of enlarging the knowledge base about its practical implications through the case studies of the Bromley and Mansfield secondary schools. The rest of this chapter sets the stage for the case studies by examining the *context* for change, demonstrating the power of organizational and professional characteristics to facilitate, block, and shape innovative practices. Such invisible complexity permeates educational organizations; we need to make it more visible.

SCHOOLS AS ORGANIZED ANARCHIES

Although schools possess characteristics common to all organizations—a division of labor, a hierarchy of authority, rules and procedures, and goals—they possess other characteristics that are not in keeping with the traditional notions of bureaucracy. March and Olsen (1979, pp. 24–93) apply the label "organized anarchy" to these features.

In broad terms, organized anarchies lack specific, well-defined, consistent goals; their processes for delivering their service cannot be easily explained, and the participants (in this case, educators and students) vary in their involvement in and commitment to the learning enterprise. Organized anarchies are thus rife with uncertainty and ambiguity, cultural features not usually associated with our operating image of a bureaucracy.

Let us examine this concept in more specific terms by drawing primarily on Elmore, 2004; Lieberman & Miller, 1984; March & Olsen, 1979; March, 1994; Miles, 1965; Waller, 1965; and Weick, 1995, to compile an illustrative but not exhaustive list of some characteristics of schools as organized anarchies.

- Problematic Goals and Goal Ambiguity
- Zero Client Rejection
- A Changing Clientele
- Fluid Participation
- Experience Valued Over Research and Education
- Transitioning toward Technology
- Loose Coupling
- High Teacher Autonomy and Low Peer Visibility
- Adult Interactions, Primarily with Children and Youth
- Low Professional Mystique
- Lay-Professional Control
- Internal and External Vulnerability

Problematic Goals and Goal Ambiguity

Organizational-level and even program-level goals are typically broad and indeterminate—"develop responsible citizens;" "appreciate and know how to use leisure time;" "and be adept at mathematical problem solving." Such goals are open to interpretation, so it is difficult to know how to achieve them or how to measure if they have been learned. One could make a similar argument about "standards," hence the increasing reliance on standardized tests.

On the other hand, because the school must meet a wide variety of student, parental, and community expectations, broad goals have traditionally been the best one can hope for, especially as communities become more and more diverse. Precise goals would likely generate conflict between school constituencies because such goals would leave little room to accommodate differing views. Since parent groups change with each entering first grade and exiting twelfth, school goals face continual parental scrutiny. And each new school board member carries around her perception of their meaning.

Let us return for a moment to the Outcomes-Based Education movement discussed earlier. As noted, by the mid-1990s, OBE became the center of considerable controversy and outright conflict. Not only was there a several-state upheaval, but the same unrest occurred in some communities (Chion-Kenney, 1994; Manno, 1995).

Administrators lost their jobs, boards of education were voted out of office, and children were pulled out of schools where deep disagreement arose over OBE—or what was perceived to be OBE—as illustrated at the Littleton (CO) high school where performance-based graduation requirements were dropped (Davis & Felknor, 1994). Overall, OBE largely faded from the educational landscape.

Despite such conflicts, the "standards/accountability" drive is here to stay, as we saw in chapter 1 (see also Elmore, 2004, pp. 133–147). All fifty states have boarded the bus with their destination defined by the specific expectations for learning expressed, at the moment, mainly by standards and standardized tests. "To pronounce against standards seems tantamount to being in favor of sin" (Hargreaves, Earl, Moore, & Manning, 2001, p. 3).

Zero Client Rejection

The school must serve all students, and the mix of students keeps increasing in its diversity as everyone reading this book can attest, no matter what part of the country you represent. Schools must deal with special education and at-risk youth in regular classrooms, an influx of immigrants from non-English speaking and non-Western cultures, and multi-languages spoken in a classroom. Polyglot students are the norm in most cities and towns from Hartford to Lincoln to Honolulu and from Anchorage to Wichita to Laredo.

How to teach these children? How does one capture the interest of this clientele and manage classrooms of captive audiences whose motivation covers the spectrum from cooperation to passivity to often vigorous resistance?

By accepting all comers, education in a democratic society holds great promise. On the other hand, that very act in a time of limited resources increases the risk that educators will not be able to serve all groups well, thus aggravating the inequalities between students and schools (Elmore, 2004, p. 207). In turn, the critics and politicians not sympathetic to public education will leap on any failures.

Newmann and his associates, who conducted extensive research about secondary school restructuring, state that, "The most immediate and persisting issue for students and teachers is not low achievement, but student disengagement" (1992, p. 2). Engagement, one's psychological investment in learning, is undermined today by many of the social forces affecting young people that were discussed in the first two chapters.

But the "take all comers" schools, which have always had some disengaged learners who might have sat at the back of the classroom, now cannot ignore the growth of this demographic without undermining public "report cards" on test results. Now educators must confront the issue as an organization-wide, moral challenge.

A Changing Clientele

Every year, a significant segment of the population changes as older students graduate and a new class enters kindergarten. Those entering include the tractable and eager to learn and the unstable and resistant. On any given school day, who enrolls is the "luck of the draw." The teacher on opening day always begins a new adventure aiming to build relationships with individuals and classroom groups. Just one unbending, reluctant learner or special needs child can require incredible teacher effort if that individual and other individual students in the class are to flourish during the year.

Without positive relationships between teacher and student, little of lasting value can be accomplished in the classroom. Clearly, any innovation that upsets or has the potential to upset these human dynamics is quite unwelcome. But to the contrary, innovations that facilitate positive dynamics are more likely to be embraced or at least given a trial run. They promote the "psychic rewards" that are so vital to teacher motivation (Lortie, 1975, pp. 101–106).

While teachers of selected students in charter and magnet schools do enjoy these rewards more readily, their colleagues in the regular system must soldier on, serving the remaining captive, changing, and challenging clientele.

Fluid Participation

Not only do student attitudes toward learning vary considerably, but even students who are generally motivated and interested in education differ in their degrees of participation in school affairs. Young people are tugged in many directions by their peers, their physical and psychological development, their parents, their personal heroes, their need to work to support their hobbies, cars, and college financing, the media, and social networking. Thus, the organization must expend considerable energy to capture and retain the attention of sporadically and often peripherally involved learners.

As McLaughlin and Talbert concluded from their study of sixteen high schools in California and Michigan, today's students differ in many ways from the often idealized images of the "good" students of days past who generally complied with teacher requests and projected some interest in the subject. By contrast, many students today seem "disengaged" from teacher expectations (pp. 13–17).

A few years ago, while conducting another research project, I interviewed teachers from our children's high school. When I asked how students now (1998) differed from those they taught who were our son and
daughter's classmates, I was struck by the consistency of their responses.
They said that, a decade earlier in this suburban school, reluctant or resistant learners were few. But now, even among the college-bound, there was
a more common attitude of "Here I am! Teach me!" Self-motivation was
noticeably less evident. And this was twelve years ago! The societal influences today—described in chapter 1—have an even more potent effect on
current students.

These influences test teachers with intensity each day, and the demanding pull and tug with students mentally and sometimes physically can be
exhausting.

As is true for any social institution, employees also vary in their commitment to organizational goals and involvement in organizational activities.
Although the hiring of capable and motivated people can go a long way
toward ensuring sustained involvement, a less-than-healthy organizational
environment can quickly undermine this attitude and behavior. There is anecdotal evidence that this is a serious side effect in schools under the gun of
NCLB and the testing movement.

Finally, the teaching profession is classed by several researchers as a
"semi-profession"—one that has (1) low-entry requirements; (2) relatively
low pay and societal status compared to other professions (certainly, pay
today in many systems is far from "low" with salaries at the top of the scale
often reaching $70,000-plus); (3) low organization level job autonomy (but
considerable autonomy within the classroom); (4) a considerable degree of
lay control over its affairs; and (5) little disciplinary control over peers.

In addition, there is (6) the lack of a body of professional knowledge and
skill that is perceived as "special" by the clients served or by other relevant
constituent groups; and (7) no differentiation in salary based on performance
(Lortie, 1975, pp. 1–24; Lortie, 1969, pp. 1–53). Therefore, schools must
expend some effort to gain and hold the attention of professional staff because
professional norms and role expectations may not do so.

If a school has a large number of such employees, it takes even more time
and energy to bring them into the fold, and that is time and energy taken
from school improvement endeavors. But beyond that, it must also *intervene*
to reshape norms and beliefs and actively promote the development of its
employees in order to remain a viable organization (Glickman, Gordon, &
Ross-Gordon, 1995, p. 27).

Now that NCLB failure can cause the closure of "underperforming"
schools and the firing of administrators and teachers, morale issues

have become more pronounced in many districts. Living with this new uncertainty cannot help but erode motivation and overall professional commitment.

Experience Valued over Research and Education

Unlike the time-honored professions of law, medicine, and theology that are rooted in traditional bodies of knowledge and research, public education is weak in this regard. Despite considerable educational research, it is rare to find enough agreement among researchers on any one finding so that practitioners feel they can, with a high degree of confidence, make decisions based on it.

Witness the seemingly endless battles between reading experts over the most effective means to instruct in that subject. And now there are questions raised about the small-school movement described in the last chapter. For example, Boston was involved with the Gates project for a decade and reorganized four large high schools into smaller units. Now the new superintendent is moving toward consolidation, citing high costs and little evidence of increased student performance. This is happening at the very time that New York City is citing success with small schools (Vaznis, J., 2010b).

Therefore, it is difficult to demonstrate to educators that one approach to instruction, a certain curriculum, or organizational configuration gets better results than another. Instead, educators more likely base decisions about programs and practices on their experiences and conventional tried-and-true wisdom. In other words, they need to see for themselves what works with their learners in the sociopsychological composition of their classrooms before adopting an innovation.

Given the nature of this professional ethos, it becomes clear that change in education will not come about readily if it is based on some distant research findings; education professionals place more credence in what their experience tells them has worked and will work, rather than in what research indicates might work.

Transitioning toward Technology

Schools are "labor-intensive" organizations. The basic work of the organization is done through people, and, despite the introduction of modern technology, social transactions are the major mode of instruction. They are the major mode because interactions with students provide primary rewards to teachers, the pupil-teacher ratio has historically been the main means to deliver cost-effective instruction, and typically technology has been too difficult to use on a mass basis or has been too unreliable.

So most teachers have been hesitant to adopt and adapt many technologies when they see that instruction could still be conducted at the secondary level via the traditional lecture/discussion format even though it may not be that effective.

Also, due to their labor intensiveness, some 70–80 percent of most school district budgets support personnel, leaving little room to increase effectiveness, efficiency, and productivity through technology. Nonetheless today, educators must become adept users of modern technology, a costly project when most budgets are stretched to the limit.

Gone are the days when the 16mm projector or the overhead projector would last for years except for an occasional bulb replacement. In contrast, computers and most other modern "high-tech" equipment require considerable maintenance, plus they enjoy only a limited life because they are on the road to obsolescence when purchased. Upgrade costs are significant. Witness how quickly one's home computer will not handle a new software package! For these reasons and others, educators often do not fully jump aboard the technology express.

But now, as we saw in the section, "Digital Overload," there is an explosion of technology that cannot be ignored. Most students are immersed in it, and, if schools do not take their lead to a reasonable degree, student achievement will suffer. Christensen, Horn, and Johnson (2008) make a compelling case for integrating computers and other technology into classrooms. We need to work away from "standardized learning toward customized learning," and technology is a key to that end (pp. 33–39).

In fact, American schools have embraced the purchase of computers and related equipment as evidenced by the fact that, during the last twenty years, schools have invested over $60 billion on technological growth (p. 81). But just as we have a great unevenness in school funding from state to state and community to community, so too is there unevenness in the upgrading of technology. Behind this backdrop, the larger question remains, "Can schools move to a student-centric classroom through the adoption of computer-based learning?" (p. 64). This issue and teacher innovation will be addressed further in chapter 7.

Loose Coupling

Schools are composed of classrooms, but the connections between them are "relaxed" so that each, even at the same grade level or in the same subject, has its identity and physical separateness. Weick refers to this structural feature as "loose coupling" (1976, pp. 1–19). Earlier, Bidwell labeled this feature "structural looseness" (1965, p. 976). Unless a teacher operates in a totally dysfunctional fashion, what happens in one classroom rarely has a noticeable impact on another.

This structure promotes quick responses by individuals or small groups to small changes in the environment and meets professional needs for autonomy. But the structure also impedes implementation and institutionalization of large-scale innovations according to educational historians such as Tyack and Cuban and Ravitch and studies reviewed in chapter 2. But test-based accountability has begun to alter loose coupling due to this new way that governments intrude into classrooms. Such intrusion challenges time-honored educational norms and values (Elmore, 2004, pp. 50–53).

In addition, features of the organization such as zero client rejection and a captive clientele can lead to professional behavior (e.g., relating to student discipline) that may be only loosely connected to school goals. Also, because loosely coupled decisions in one part of the school may not directly affect decisions made elsewhere in the organization, it is difficult to assess their impact on others, despite the fact that they often appear related. March points out that these phenomena guarantee some degree of "foolishness" within an organization that ought to behave rationally (1981, p. 274).

High Teacher Autonomy and Low Peer Visibility

Although longtime trends have promoted "teaming" or other collaborative arrangements among teachers, in most schools (and particularly high schools), teachers still work within classrooms largely independent of colleagues. They teach at the same time as their colleagues; they use break time for preparation rather than for conversations with peers. Teaming arrangements are the exception rather than the custom.

The autonomous classroom and logistics of the daily schedule make it almost impossible for teachers to observe each other's performance. "In most high schools, teachers consider individual autonomy and seniority prerogatives as sensible principles for organizing their work together" (McLaughlin & Talbert, 2001, p. 91).

Although people work across the corridor or in the next room—whether in a ten-teacher school or one with ten times more staff—they rarely see firsthand how colleagues teach, nor do they share materials or ideas. This pattern makes it difficult for educators to implement and institutionalize innovations that require staff to work together consistently.

Adult Interactions Primarily with Children and Youth

While isolated from their peers, teachers spend most of the day in close quarters with "kids." Despite real efforts on the part of many schools to find ways for teachers to work together more consistently, the structure of the schedule is difficult to alter for such purposes. An elementary teacher commented to me recently, "I spend most of my day in my classroom with my children. There are days when I don't talk to or see another adult." And a high school teacher said, "It can be emotionally draining to deal with adolescents all day."

An important side effect of these patterns is that, when some teachers are called upon to interact with adults as part of school business, they may not interact very effectively. Over my forty one years in the profession, I heard numerous comments made by parents and school board members that some teachers behave with them as if they were children, not adults. I have similar observations. Often, they come across in a patronizing way or as if they were still wielding authority in the classroom.

This behavior can also be an impediment to the increasing need for effective collaborative staff work and staff development in schools as the call goes out for more teacher leadership in site-managed organizations or in Professional Learning Communities (to be discussed in chapter 7). There is little room in undergraduate teacher preparation programs for instruction in this vital area.

Historically, success in the profession stems mainly from successful relationships with one's students, not one's peers. When it comes to considering changing one's practices, the opinions that matter most to teachers are likely those of their charges, not their colleagues.

Low Professional Mystique

Because everyone has been through school and observed the 13,000 hours of teaching, most laypeople feel quite familiar with how educators go about their work as discussed a few pages ago. This preordinate knowledge gives the general citizenry a sense of control that contrasts sharply with the sense of control it feels toward other professions. Therefore educators, to sustain relationships with the public, must listen to its complaints and often entertain seriously the proposed "solutions" to problems made by people outside of the system. Such activity takes time away from direct educational work.

Professional image is also eroded by mundane issues like obtaining supplies for one's classroom. A recent study in Washington of seventy five teachers from the Spokane schools reported that some spent $3,000 of their own money and others an average of $751 a year for basic supplies. Nationally, the figure runs around $1,700 (Lawrence-Turner, 2010). A San Diego mathematics teacher sells ad space on his test papers to raise money to print his tests (*The Week*, 2009, p. 6.) However, it is rare to read about these contributions in the local press.

Across the country, at all levels of public schooling, the budget crunch has led to administrators and teachers requesting of parents and businesses many basic supplies such as scissors, pencils, glue, copy paper, Kleenex, paper towels, and toilet paper (Clifford, 2010). These activities can be added to the plates of educators, as described in the last chapter, and siphon valuable professional time from the prime ongoing task of school improvement.

To bolster one's professional image is the opportunity for teachers to attain national certification through the National Board for Professional Teaching Standards. Board certification is an intensive three-year, ten-step process. (A similar program is available for principals.) The cost is $2,500 to apply. But only 82,000 teachers out of a pool of over three million have received this prestigious certification since the Board's inception in 1987 (www.NPTS. org, 2010).

And the recession is causing some states to reduce their commitment to support local districts in increasing pay for such certification. Between 2007 and 2009, states supporting local district incentives dropped from thirty eight to thirty one (Sawchuk, 2010b, p. 13). So moving toward this goal on a broad basis nationally is difficult.

Lay-Professional Control

School boards govern schools, and, because these policymakers often have not had any direct contact with schools for years, they carry in their minds an image of education as they experienced it. Even with their outdated perceptions, board members may see themselves as quite "expert" in a particular field; they feel they know quite well what the school should or should not do. This is particularly pronounced when individuals run for a board seat egged on and supported by political parties or interest groups with education agendas to fulfill.

Of course, the school must listen to them and, in some instances, respond to their change agendas because of dynamics in the political environment. Sometimes, the actions forced by board agendas may be beneficial and other times not.

In some communities, citizens and politicians have concluded that what they see as the dismal condition of education requires their intervention, whether or not their involvement is welcome. To legitimatize such involvement, school-level councils have been created in many districts. Such entities were created in Massachusetts by the Reform Law of 1993.

These councils, typically composed of educators, parents, citizens, and students, often have some degree of formal authority over organizational matters such as budgeting, curriculum development, selection of instructional materials, and hiring and evaluating personnel. But whether councils have authority over boards or are advisory to them varies considerably from community to community (Ogawa and White, 1994, pp. 57–64).

Internal and External Vulnerability

Because schools are built around children and youth, we have already seen that they are under the constant threat of disruption by the very clientele they serve. In addition, every citizen is a potentially vocal shareholder in the organization (as demonstrated by the school council movement) with a civic investment that fluctuates—depending on the issues and whether one has a child in school. Beneath it all flows the undercurrent of vulnerability caused by the turbulence of the social, cultural, economic, and political forces surrounding schools.

Glickman, who has worked on school improvement projects in Georgia that incorporated mechanisms like school councils, once observed that the overall context that supports such an endeavor conveys no assurance of permanency and stability, so ". . . there is always the feeling that the floor could fall through at any moment" (1990, p. 70).

CLASSROOMS AS BUSY KITCHENS

The classroom is where it finally all happens. It is here that the major formal efforts to teach children and youth occur. If there is no success at this level, there is, for most students, no other place to go to learn unless one can change enrollment to a charter, magnet, or some other alternative structure. And it is within the classroom that innovations succeed or fail.

Classrooms are, in the view of Huberman, "busy kitchens" (1983). They are a unique type of social system; no other profession is structured so that its service is delivered day after day, in a fairly set routine, to groups rather than to individuals, and groups that are often unwilling clients. Yet within the group, the needs of individuals must be met.

A letter to Ann Landers relative to a hypothetical competition between a group of businesspeople who were assigned to teach elementary school for six weeks captures the "busy kitchen" image nicely.

Each contestant will be provided with a class of 28 students and a copy of the district's curriculum. Each class will have five learning disabled children, three with Attention Deficit Disorder, one gifted child, two who speak limited English, and three labeled as having severe behavioral problems. (*Cape Cod Times*, 2002).

In many ways, teachers are like chefs, drawing on their recipes and preparing meals each day. They work, as we have seen in the previous section, in relative isolation from other adults. This isolation is not only from peers, but, in many instances, from supervisors. It is not unusual for teachers to work for fifteen or twenty years without observation by any adult.

With the busy kitchen as a context, then, the following characteristics of teaching have been gleaned from the work of Hargreaves, 1994; Hargreaves, et al., 2001; Jackson, 1968; Johnson, 1990; Lieberman & Miller, 1984; Lortie, 1975; Nieto, 2003 and 2005; Pellegrin, 1976; Sarason, 1996; Waller, 1965; and Wasley, 1994:

- Emphasis on Psychic Rewards
- Balancing Affect, Control, and Cognition
- Hectic Pace, Volume, and Variety of the Work
- Presentism, Immediacy, and Serendipity
- Importance of Instructional Style

Emphasis on Psychic Rewards

Although money, prestige, and power have some importance to teachers, as they have to any professional, most teachers teach for less tangible reasons. Lortie, the most cited researcher on the profession, states that, "The structure of teaching rewards, in short, favors emphasis on psychic rewards" (1975, p. 103). What happens for the learner in the classroom is of prime importance to teachers. A twenty-year update of the 1964 data upon which Lortie based his findings resulted in virtually identical conclusions (Kottkamp, Provenza, & Cohn, 1986). Nieto's more recent studies of high school teachers elicited similar outcomes (2003; 2005).

"The greatest satisfaction for a teacher is the feeling of being rewarded by one's students" (Lieberman & Miller, 1984).

BALANCING AFFECT, CONTROL, AND COGNITION

In my final thirty one years in education, I taught at a university. Then, if I wanted to, I could just lecture to my graduate students and give them examinations. If they learned the material, fine, but, if they did not, I was not subject to any organizational disapproval or state accountability expectations. I did not worry about classroom control.

Not so with the public school teacher. To be successful with a captive audience, one has to juggle the dimensions of attitudes, feelings, values, classroom control, what is to be taught, how it is to be taught, and, increasingly, how what is taught is to be measured. The quality of student-teacher relationships plays the critical role in establishing order and discipline; without order and discipline, not much learning will occur. Teachers must deal effectively with affect and control if they hope to create an environment that can produce learning and psychic rewards for themselves.

Lemov has developed a program to assist teachers in successfully integrating affect, control, and cognition. Central to his efforts ". . . is a belief that students can't learn unless the teacher succeeds in capturing their attention and getting them to follow instructions" (Green. 2010, p. 35). Educators, he says, often call this the art of classroom management. Whatever the label, the basic point is that teachers confront a myriad of fast-moving tasks every minute of the day.

This juggling act became personalized for me when I was on a sabbatical leave studying the Bromley and Mansfield high schools. Because I had not taught public school since 1964, I thought it would be good "reality therapy" for me to do so again. I was correct, and, while at that time I found little difference between the past and the present when it came to instructing the motivated, college-oriented social studies classes, such was not the case with other groups.

I was jarred by the differences in the attitude and deportment of students in these unmotivated groups compared to the difficult boys and girls I had taught almost thirty years before. I expended an immense amount of psychic and physical energy keeping control while trying to build and sustain relationships—and hoping to teach them something. Cuban, who also returned to a high school to teach after being in a university setting, came away with similar impressions (1990, pp. 479–482).

And by all indications, from my last research as mentioned earlier plus countless reports in the media, teachers today face more numerous and severe deportment and engagement problems as "deviancy is defined down" (as explained in chapter 1).

HECTIC PACE, VOLUME, AND VARIETY OF THE WORK

Classrooms are beehives of activity. Place one adult and twenty five young people within the close quarters of four walls, and one has a "busy kitchen." Teachers have to facilitate discussion. One study estimates that a teacher engages in at least 1,000 interpersonal interchanges each day (Jackson, 1968, p. 11); formulates a host of on-the-spot questions; assesses individual learning; decides what assignments to give; manages the overall use of time; chooses expectations to communicate and communicate them effectively; maintains a safe, orderly, and academically focused environment; deals with deviant behavior; and enhances a cooperative group climate.

This pace continues through the day, six to eight periods in a row for the school year at the high school level. For high school teachers, this all adds up to "900 shows a year" (Palonsky, 1986). Typically, there are three or four minutes between classes, a free period for planning, an extra duty (study hall monitor or cafeteria or hall supervisor), and a brief lunch break.

On top of these demands, teachers deal with a seemingly endless list of other tasks. Prior to setting foot in the classroom, teachers make decisions about content to be taught, the time to be allocated to it, methods to be employed, key questions to ask, how learning is to be assessed, and how to work with certain individuals or groups within the class. Once school ends, there are assignments to grade, tests results to interpret, grades to compute, parents to contact, parent/student conferences to arrange, meetings to attend such as multidisciplinary teams (special education), and then tomorrow's preparation, including media and Internet previewing.

How then, if teachers teach subjects governed by mandated tests, can they successfully address the required content so that all learners are learning—in essence, no child is left behind? Hargreaves, et al. (2001) studied twenty nine Ontario middle school teachers who were implementing what has become the new orthodoxy, standards-test-based reform. They portray the daunting challenge. "How is it possible to meet the ambitions of standards-based reform without getting bogged down in its frequent, practical problems of over-standardization, under-resourcing, de-professionalization, and curricular narrowness?" (p. 9).

Berliner examined teacher decision-making and sorted decisions into pre-instruction, during-instruction, climate, and post-instruction categories (1984, pp. 51–75). Gleibermann, a former humanities teacher in a San Francisco high school, calculated that, between these four categories, he spent (teaching five classes of 30 students each) an average of 140 hours a week at the tasks (2007, p. 455). Factored into the total was five hours a week keeping abreast of student popular culture (music, film, television, and sports) so that he did not become illiterate in that regard.

As a result of all these prescriptions, where could teachers like Gleibermann hope to address tasks related to innovation? The paperwork associated with regular classroom teaching is already formidable and enormously time-consuming. One study demonstrated that, over a seventeen-day period, fifty eight teachers handled 3,893 pieces of paper covering areas from tests to homework to discipline (Freed and Ketchem, 1987, p. 16). A department chair at Mansfield added other paper to the pile.

> At a recent retirement party, we presented the retiree with a kitchen cart full of the new initiatives, policies, rules, regulations and the like that are now on the plate of a new teacher from local, state, and national sources. Twenty years ago you literally gave the teacher the keys to the classroom and said 'go to it.'

The hectic pace, the volume, and the variety of the work forces teachers to create repetitive routines to help survive amidst the whirlwind of so many variables. Standardization, not diversity, becomes the norm; this survival strategy largely explains why classrooms look so similar everywhere and why the same patterns of instruction persist in the face of efforts to alter them (e.g., the non-graded school and open education). And innovations that add to this pace, volume, and variety, in most cases, are understandably resisted. Yet the news media continues to ignore factors such as this in their ongoing critiques of the schools (Ripley, 2010).

Presentism, Immediacy, and Serendipity

After my stint "in the trenches," I kept thinking that, for the high school teacher, the future is now—at 9:00 a.m. or 1:00 p.m., whenever the next class arrives; that is the overriding concern. In higher education, by contrast, the future is often next semester when we will be instructing that new course; next summer when that workshop will be offered; or next year when that book deadline arrives.

The need to respond immediately to learners forces teachers to focus their energy and interest on the present moment. Jackson's research led him to conclude that ". . . it is today's behavior, rather than tomorrow's test, that provides the real yardstick for measuring the teacher's progress" (1968, p. 123).

It is this emphasis on the present, however, that can lead to small-scale innovation, to serendipitous responses to what is happening in the classroom, the "tinkering" portrayed by Tyack and Cuban. Why? Effective teachers, in order to survive and progress, must constantly adapt to unanticipated demands (Huberman, 1983, p. 487). Chapters 4 and 5, describing findings from Bromley and Mansfield, will portray this process. To teachers, these "small wins" keep them moving forward.

Importance of Instructional Style

Teachers develop a very personal style for delivering curriculum and instruction as they aim each day to balance affect, control, and cognition. No one "formula" works for all teachers just as none does for lawyers in courtrooms. Personality is central to it. Rather, teachers undergo a process of trial and error that often involves considerable stress before they begin to find "what works." But what works with one group may not be as successful with another because of the particular mix of personalities and needs. And this mix is getting to be more complex than ever in our diversified classrooms. How they all mesh is the mysterious and marvelous accomplishment of an excellent teacher.

Style is never perfected because, each year, a new group of students arrives, and the process begins again. This always-evolving pedagogical demand diverts attention from delivering the content per se.

The issue of style plays a huge role in the success or failure of an innovation because teachers are reluctant to alter, except for very good reasons, something so personal that they have honed over many years. Style is the "bottom line," so to speak; upsetting it can threaten the pedagogical life of the teacher. Without classroom control, nothing is accomplished. Very likely, this reality explains why research in secondary schools consistently demonstrates that it is far easier to implement curricular as opposed to instructional innovations (Orlosky & Smith, 1972, p. 413; Rutherford & Austin, 1984, p. 54).

Christensen and colleagues have written about transforming schools with computer-based learning. After studying past attempts to make such changes, they concluded, "The sum of these assessments is that traditional instructional practices have changed little despite the introduction of computers and other modern technologies" (2008, p. 83). I contend that the "busy kitchen" workplace is a fundamental reason for the persistence of traditional pedagogy.

It is also a prime reason for teacher resistance to "disruptive innovations," those that can disrupt common ways of doing things and tilt the established plane of development (Christensen, et al., 2008, pp. 47–51). To veer in a new direction without adequate groundwork and support unsettles most teachers who are usually preoccupied with establishing and maintaining relationships with students and managing their classrooms.

Elmore, in his incisive analysis of the public school system at the policy level, observes that the work of school ". . . is fundamentally incompatible with the practice of improvement" (2004, p. 127). If improvement is conceived as the more ambitious type as described in chapter 1, then the organizational characteristics of schools and classrooms impedes that level of change severely.

SPECIAL FEATURES OF HIGH SCHOOLS

In addition to the characteristics discussed thus far, high schools possess other characteristics that have implications for effecting change.

They are usually fairly large—500, 1,000, 2,000-plus pupils—and size affects the way education is delivered. In rural areas where regional schools are not feasible, they are much smaller. High schools are usually organized into departments that further complicates organizational processes because departments reinforce separatism between teachers, and departments focus on their particular subject and on their often conflicting educational goals (e.g., social studies staff may emphasize affective-type goals, while mathematics teachers may emphasize cognitive-type goals).

Cooperation and communication between these subsystems can be difficult. Scheduling students into subject areas, along with trying to accommodate levels of ability and involvement in co-curricular activities, results in a complex daily schedule. Students usually only have contact with specific teachers one period a day, and they move through a six- or eight-period day. This pattern erodes the ability of the school to develop norms of affiliation with a significant segment of its prime clientele, norms that could help to motivate learners (although this is changing as many high schools implement block scheduling).

Because students are older, parents often have less interest in their children's school activities (or students do not want them involved), and thus it becomes more difficult and time-consuming to obtain parental cooperation and involvement. Adolescents also carry into the organization a greater variety of needs and attitudinal and value conflicts than do children.

These factors, combined with the reality that a higher percentage of them, compared to elementary and middle school youngsters, would rather not be in school, requires the allocation of professional attention, time, and energy to custodial functions, at the expense of matters relating to curriculum and instruction.

Injected into this complex secondary school environment are the dynamics of the "born digital" generation, as described in chapter 1. As Gleibermann puts it, "Besides mastering my own curriculum, I spend time mastering a second curriculum that my students expect me to know: popular culture" (2007, p. 457). When I began teaching in 1958, my "culture" in terms of the mainstream was the "culture" of my students, too. I had no need to invest extra hours in staying "up to speed" with them because we all listened to Tony Bennett, Rosemary Clooney, Doris Day, and Frank Sinatra.

Secondary schools also face numerous and more intense external pressures compared to elementary and middle schools. The media, jobs, and peer expectations all compete for student interest. In some communities, expectations surrounding varsity sports play an important role in the life of the organization. Social phenomena associated with drugs, alcohol, and sex have a real impact on a large portion of the student body, along with the resultant intervention of social agencies on behalf of many students, intervention that requires further time commitments from educators within the building. Add to that bullying and all its ramifications!

Figure 3.1 (see p. 88) depicts what is on the "plate" of a typical Massachusetts high school teacher in 2010.

THE ROLE OF THE PRINCIPAL

An axiom of school administration is that the principal is the instructional leader. Few principals would assert that this is not one of their key roles. However, as one study of the high school principalship revealed, there are many interpretations of the term. For some administrators, the role means that they get directly involved with teachers in curriculum development, management, change, and instructional improvement. For others, the role means that they primarily address the managerial dimensions of the work, all of which, in one way or another, has an impact on curriculum and instruction (Pellicer, et al., 1990, pp. 27–41).

Historically then, the principal's role has often been defined by the school in its local context. Sometimes, it is expected that whoever occupies the office will act in an instructional leadership capacity. Sometimes, it is expected that the principal will mainly be a manager and supervisor. Sometimes, it has been left to the principal to define, assuming that she has the ability and the luxury of time to do so. And sometimes, the size of the organization has permitted others to take on these functions such as department chairs or curriculum directors.

Trump, in conjunction with the previously described NASSP Model Schools Project, developed the most thoughtful, comprehensive definition of the high school principal's role that I have seen as well as an administrative structure within which the role would work effectively. In 1977, he said,

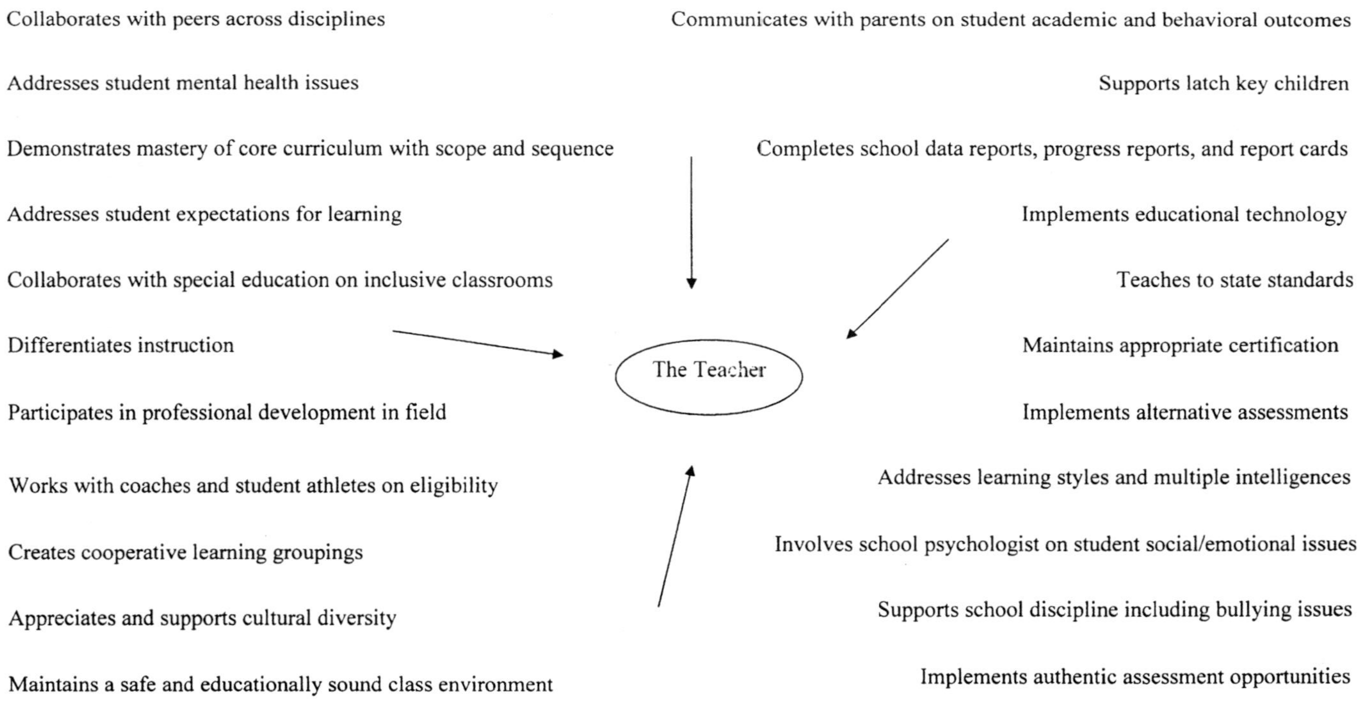

Collaborates with peers across disciplines

Addresses student mental health issues

Demonstrates mastery of core curriculum with scope and sequence

Addresses student expectations for learning

Collaborates with special education on inclusive classrooms

Differentiates instruction

Participates in professional development in field

Works with coaches and student athletes on eligibility

Creates cooperative learning groupings

Appreciates and supports cultural diversity

Maintains a safe and educationally sound class environment

Communicates with parents on student academic and behavioral outcomes

Supports latch key children

Completes school data reports, progress reports, and report cards

Implements educational technology

Teaches to state standards

Maintains appropriate certification

Implements alternative assessments

Addresses learning styles and multiple intelligences

Involves school psychologist on student social/emotional issues

Supports school discipline including bullying issues

Implements authentic assessment opportunities

The Teacher

Figure 3.1. The Teacher's Plate in a Small/Medium Size High School in Massachusetts

"Today's principals are bogged down even more than their predecessors as the job gets larger and larger, mostly with duties and assignments not directly related to the improvement of instruction" (p. 63).

John Dewey made a similar observation in 1946 (p. 68). Today, as we see from Figure 3.2 (see p. 91), principals have far more on their "plates" than sixty four years ago! It is truly a different administrative world!

To allow for principals to be more involved in instructional leadership, Trump proposed a "supervisory-management team" (pp. 65–77), using existing central office and existing (or new) building personnel to take on various tasks that would provide the principal more time for such leadership. The "team" would be structured in relation to the size of the school and district. Distressingly persistent budget problems since the 1970s, however, mean that today's principals actually get *less* rather than more of the help Trump advocated. As a result, principals today find themselves in a situation where instructional leadership happens around the edges of the job.

All around where I live, as schools confront a budget squeeze, it is common for boards to eliminate an assistant principal or reduce the role to part-time in order to accommodate budget shortfalls. The pages of every hometown newspaper across America report similar local actions. As one high school principal put it recently, "More and more I feel like I'm doing custodial duty."

This job reality clashes sharply with the image of principals as "superman or superwoman" that is still promoted by the media. A *Newsweek* story on principals included this line, "They set the tone for what happens from the moment the opening bell rings and can turn a troubled school around with a combination of vision, drive, and very hard work" (Kantrowitz & Mathews, 2007, p. 44). The article did admit that finding such a leader is harder than ever. Talk with any search committee in any community in this country, and a common theme is the "shallowness" of the current pool of administrative candidates. This trend has been increasing for the last two decades.

There is a vital need to "de-romanticize" the role of the principal at all levels of public schooling and to re-conceptualize it to be more realistic and functional in today's standards-based, accountability environment (Elmore, 2004, pp. 57–88).

The pace and the press of the work are key factors in the counter-trend to hire young principals with far fewer years of teaching experience than has been the norm. The job, regardless of its leadership level, requires the energy and stamina of a young heart! "Responsibility has increased, expectations are much greater, and accountability has grown exponentially. There is much more scrutiny with how your school is performing," said an NASSP employee recently (Moss, 2010, p. 32). Add to this list the demands of the "culture gap" between educators and their students, as has been discussed in earlier pages.

If the principal wishes to be an instructional leader, then research tells us that it is very difficult to act the part (e.g., Gottfredson & Hybl, 1987; Hallinger & Heck, 1996; Manasse, 1985; Martin & Willower, 1981; Pellicer, et al., 1988; 1990). The role is strikingly similar whether it is in an urban, suburban, or rural setting, whether it is in a large-, small-, or medium-sized organization, and whether it is in a high, middle, or elementary school. At the organization level, inhabited by administrators, the school building is also a "busy kitchen."

Principals' work is characterized by a high volume of activity, including a wide variety of tasks that are brief in duration, often interrupted, and often managerial rather than instructional. The tasks are so fragmented that rarely does a principal have an opportunity to give undivided and sustained attention to any one of them. The hectic pace of the principal's day leaves little room for reflection and planning. The result is that educational leadership happens ". . . within and around the edges of the job as defined and presently constituted" (Lieberman & Miller, 1984, p. 76).

Mintzberg conducted a broad empirical study of managers in all walks of life to answer the question, "What do managers do?" One main conclusion from his insightful book, based on work beginning in the 1970s, was that ". . . his activities are characterized by brevity, variety, and fragmentation" (1973, p. 31). Sounds like the work of principals today, as reflected in Figure 3.2.

Added to the routine within-house tasks are new tasks from the external environment over and above the ones from the accountability movement discussed in the previous chapters. Not long ago, a parent e-mailed a principal asking, "Is there any way that that you can keep my daughter off of Facebook?" The "born digital" generation is impacting schools in unusual ways.

And the new Massachusetts law on bullying places innumerable new tasks on the principal's plate with its broad definition of the act, detailed reporting steps and written report forms, and the requirement that principals investigate each case (Schworm, 2010, p. 1; A6). At this time, there are vast unknown ramifications just in terms of defining free speech and ensuring that the rights of the accused are protected within this murky new area of the law (Saltzman, 2010, p. 1; A9). By statute, the principal will have a central role in all this, and the odds are high that lawsuits by parents and students lurk in the wings.

Fullan reviewed the literature and his own studies of educational change relative to the principal's role and concluded, "I know of no improving school that doesn't have a principal who is good at leading school improvement" (2007, p. 160). At the same time, he said that the role has become "dramatically" more complex, overloaded, and intensified over the past

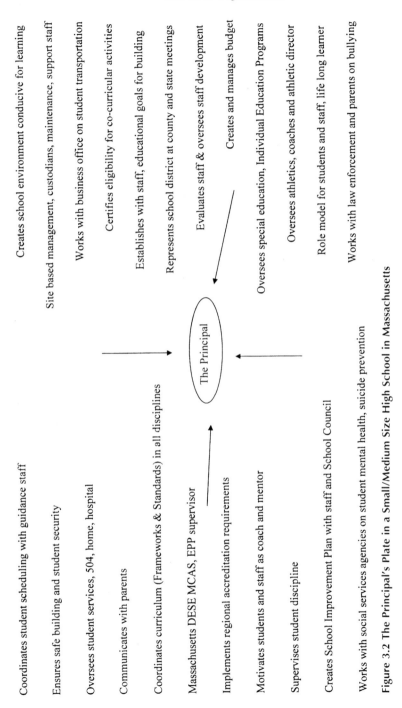

Creates school environment conducive for learning

Site based management, custodians, maintenance, support staff

Works with business office on student transportation

Certifies eligibility for co-curricular activities

Establishes with staff, educational goals for building

Represents school district at county and state meetings

Evaluates staff & oversees staff development

Creates and manages budget

Oversees special education, Individual Education Programs

Oversees athletics, coaches and athletic director

Role model for students and staff, life long learner

Works with law enforcement and parents on bullying

Coordinates student scheduling with guidance staff

Ensures safe building and student security

Oversees student services, 504, home, hospital

Communicates with parents

Coordinates curriculum (Frameworks & Standards) in all disciplines

Massachusetts DESE MCAS, EPP supervisor

Implements regional accreditation requirements

Motivates students and staff as coach and mentor

Supervises student discipline

Creates School Improvement Plan with staff and School Council

Works with social services agencies on student mental health, suicide prevention

The Principal

Figure 3.2 The Principal's Plate in a Small/Medium Size High School in Massachusetts

decade with the result that the principal has been placed in an impossible position (pp. 155–169). President Obama often says that a president spends 90 percent of his time reacting to unplanned-for events. The evidence is clear that this is, without question, the case for principals.

Yet the latest practice to "turn around" failing schools is to begin by replacing the principal and appointing someone else who will be in the same "impossible position." When that doesn't work, replace the teachers. When that doesn't work, close the school. Society continues to ignore the true conditions under which professional educators work and applies the cheapest "quick fix" to confounding problems. When will they, the policymakers, ever learn?

Do these "organized anarchy" and "busy kitchen" characteristics of schools and classrooms make it nearly impossible to effect school improvement? It often appears that way, and the changing conditions just discussed make it appear more so. The impediments and challenges can seem insurmountable, but, in chapters 4, 5, and 6, we will examine everyday processes within two "good schools" that demonstrate what is possible within such a challenging context.

Chapter 4

Bromley and Mansfield

Two Case Studies

Schools will improve slowly, if at all, if reforms are thrust upon them. Rather, the approach having most promise, in my judgment, is one that will seek to cultivate the capacity of schools to deal with their own problems, to become largely self-renewing.

—Goodlad, 1984, p. 31

Institutions are renewed by individuals who refuse to be satisfied with the other husks of things. And self-renewal requires somewhat the same impatience with empty forms.

—Gardner, 1965, p. 17

Given that all schools and classrooms possess the characteristics described in chapter 3, why is it that some high schools are judged to be "good" or "successful"?

WHAT IS A GOOD SCHOOL?

The notion of a "good" school has been around since schools were invented, but it was Lightfoot, in her noted book, who developed the best working definition. She states that "goodness" is a holistic concept, situationally determined, that includes people, their relationships, their motivation, their goals, and their will. It also includes measurable indicators such as attendance, vandalism, and truancy and aspiration rates (1983, p. 23).

Good schools are characterized by norms of cooperation, collaboration, and caring—norms that make the organization a generally pleasant place to work, whether that work is being done by the staff or the students. To understand what makes a good school good, it is instructive to examine its context through the cultural perspective outlined in chapter 3.

What Lightfoot does not include in her definition are two other factors integral to "goodness." The first is the autonomy to be "site-managed"—the practice that still gets much attention on convention agendas, in professional literature, in reports from foundations, and in speeches from politicians. Right now, it is a "hot topic," as it connects directly to "turnaround" schools that focus on the building as an organizational entity. But there will be degrees of autonomy depending on the role the central office assumes with local schools. The literature reviewed in chapter 2 also had a school focus, as has Fullan's review of the literature (2007).

The second factor in being "good" is the ability to change, to adapt, usually in small-scale, unobtrusive ways. One could liken this to "innovativeness," ". . . the capacities of an organization to engage in continuous improvement" (Fullan, 2007, p. 11).

In examining the question "Why Is It So Hard to Get Good Schools?" Cuban also addresses the issue of definition. He concludes, after analyzing the history of attempting to define what a "good" school is and after analyzing the characteristics of schools that he examined, that, "There is simply no scientific evidence that conclusively demonstrates that any of these schools are better forms of education for *all* (italics in original) than the others" (2003, p. 30). Instead, people make their judgments based on upbringing, life experiences, and values.

As society changes, there will be the continual struggle between the progressives and the traditionalists in most local contexts. It was noted in chapter 2, with the examples of community/demographic shifts in many school districts, that the "struggle" between those wanting more curricula and instructional changes to improve student learning and those who are satisfied with the status quo can be low-key and relatively amiable or it can be fierce and debilitating, such as the case with Outcomes-Based Education.

In chapter 1, the annual Phi Delta Kappa/Gallup poll showed that 77 percent of parents surveyed assigned either an A or a B to the school attended by their oldest child, the highest percent ever. It seems safe to conclude that they see that school as "good" in that situation, in that context. But there is often the nagging question of the criteria they use in making such a judgment. As societal changes rush onward, to what degree do parents "know" what kind of education their children need? To what extent do educators "know" better and therefore in a "good" school strive to educate parents and the community about new educational needs?

Taking such professional initiative is a central characteristic of Site-Based Managed (SBM) schools. SBM means that those who make decisions also implement them. Governance and management decisions, for the most part, are made by local stakeholders who are empowered to improve their school (Mohrman & Wohlstetter, 1994, p. xv). The schools studied by Lightfoot, by Goodlad (1984), by Lipsitz (1984), by Wilson and Corcoran (1988), and by Ogden and Germinario (1995) were administered in this way rather than being controlled by a remote, central office. (SBM will be discussed in more detail in chapter 7.)

In addition, evidence shows that these schools adopted or developed small-scale innovations steadily and incrementally, a characteristic, as we saw in chapter 2, that is essential to organizational health. Academic improvement came mainly through modifying courses or developing new ones as they are the prime change-bearing vehicle in high schools (e.g., Lightfoot, pp. 102–110; 196–207; 249–252; Cusick, 1983, pp. 72–103).

So the good news is that considerable innovation occurred in these schools. On the other hand, the authors of *The Shopping Mall High School* (Powell, Farrar, & Cohen, 1985) criticize this kind of change, along with many changes in co-curricula activities and social and psychological services, because they lack focus in relation to the overall mission of the organization. The authors contend that academic programs do not have enough rigor and that students have too much freedom of choice. Sizer shares these criticisms in his volumes relating to the Coalition of Essential Schools (1984, 1992, 1996).

Others, as seen in chapter 2, contend that these kinds of changes have little significance and will not lead to substantive educational improvement.

Thus we have a conundrum. Most high schools have the ability to innovate in "first-order," small-scale ways, and good schools have even more of that capability. Most students and parents seem quite satisfied with the education provided by these organizations. On the other hand, many critics conclude that these changes do not and will not make much of a difference in terms of the real impact the organization should have on its students. They will not be able to close the now-regularly cited "achievement gap." They assert that we need "second-order," larger-scale, more comprehensive change while, at the same time, promoting more standardized testing.

Yet given the turbulent external environment in which schools are imbedded and given limited resources and the accountability squeeze—combined with their organized anarchy and busy kitchen characteristics—that level of innovation is very difficult to implement and institutionalize, as seen in the literature reviewed in chapter 2.

While schools in today's rapidly changing environment often need to effect more ambitious change, we need to acknowledge the value of small-scale innovation. For many educational organizations, that is the more realistic route to improvement—perhaps the only route at a certain moment in their development. It appears to be the primary way in which the good schools got to be good.

We need to know more about how good schools become adaptable organizations. In 1981, Miles called for ". . . more contingent analyses, showing, for example, under what contextual conditions active teacher involvement in planning change will be productive" (p. 111). David, who synthesized the literature on SBM to 1989, concluded that there is a dearth of knowledge about the dynamics of local school decision-making and change (pp. 45–53). My recent Internet review of that literature affirmed her conclusion. Careful attention to such key details can increase the odds for success (Fullan, 2007, p. 8).

Clune and White, after a review of thirty SBM projects, contend that one important area for further research is to "unravel issues" relating to teacher participation in decision-making, educator roles, and patterns of communication and interaction (1988, p. 31). Johnson and Boles state that empirical literature on teachers' roles in SBM is still limited (1994, p. 113).

And today, disentangling these issues has become infinitely more complex due to the "new orthodoxy" of the accountability movement that has complicated teachers' lives immensely (Hargreaves, et al., 2001). With it comes the demands of combating the single measure mind-set, currently so dominant, of assessing student learning primarily with standardized tests instead of relying more on "multiple measures" for that purpose (Brookhart, 2009). And, in turn, learning how to use data from such measures in an intelligent, informed way (Hess, 2008–09), it is no easy task given that educators are literally drowning in it.

THE RESEARCH DESIGN

To contribute toward this unraveling, I conducted field studies of processes of curricular and instructional innovation in two Vermont high schools, Bromley and Mansfield (pseudonyms). The schools were selected from a pool of six medium-size high schools (by Vermont standards) judged by a selection panel to be "good" high schools, but not ones known for being innovative. (Readers interested in the qualitative methodology used may contact the author. See end of bibliography.)

Five years was the boundary for the analysis so that two major imposed organization-wide innovations, State Board of Education Basic Competency Regulations and the Individuals with Disabilities Education Act (IDEA) Multi-Disciplinary Team procedure, would be included (then called "staffings" under PL 94–142).

I spent five weeks, full-time, in each school interviewing, distributing questionnaires, reading documents, and observing informally. I lived in each community during that period. Initial interviews (an average of 100 minutes each) included every administrator, counselor, and teacher. Thus the findings are based on the *total* relevant professional population in each organization. No attempt was made to assess whether one organization was "better" than the other.

In Vermont, as is the case throughout New England (with the exception of larger cities), schools have traditionally had decision-making autonomy in budgeting, curriculum, and staffing, the three basic decision areas associated with decentralization or site-management (David, 1988, pp. 4–5; Ogawa & White, 1994, pp. 57–64).

Chapter 3 demonstrated that certain characteristics of schools are relatively enduring rather than ephemeral. So case studies can be immensely helpful in understanding change and gaining knowledge about effecting and managing it. But no generalizations can be made by the researcher to other organizations. Applicability to one's setting is made by the reader based on the credibility of the cases, in research terms, their "truth value" (Lincoln & Guba, 1985, pp. 301–305).

THE SCHOOLS

Bromley, a 9–12 school in central Vermont built in 1958, had 500 students, a dropout rate of 4.5 percent with 68 percent of its graduates going on to some form of higher education. The principal had been in his job for six years and had a full-time assistant. The average experience for the thirty six teachers was eleven years. Twelve staff had bachelor's degrees, and twenty four had master's degrees. Bromley was unionized.

Five elementary schools representing rural populations of 8,349 people were "feeder" schools for the high school. One-third of the population was employed in agricultural or forestry-related industries and about one quarter in manufacturing. Average per capita income was about half that of national per capita income. Close to half the population had a high school education, and close to 15 percent of families were classed as being below the poverty line. Despite these financial constraints, per pupil costs were slightly above the state average for schools the size of Bromley.

Mansfield, a 7–12 school in northern Vermont built in 1970, had 400 students, a dropout rate of 3 percent with 36 percent of its graduates going on to some form of higher education. The principal had been in his job for seven years and had a half-time assistant. The average experience for the thirty one teachers was ten years. Eighteen staff had bachelor's degrees, and thirteen had master's degrees. Mansfield was unionized. (Two years after my study, Mansfield became the first high school in Vermont to be selected as a "successful organization" under the U.S. Department of Education's Recognition Program.)

Three elementary schools, representing rural populations of 3,863 people, were "feeder" schools for the high school. About one quarter of the population was employed in agricultural or forestry-related industries and about one-fifth in manufacturing. Average per capita income was about half that of the average national per capita income. Close to half the population had a high school education, and close to 15 percent of families were classed as living below the poverty line. Despite these financial constraints, per pupil costs were just slightly below the state average for schools the size of Mansfield.

Each principal was delegated authority by the superintendent over building maintenance; budget construction and management; curriculum development and management; hiring (subject to board approval); supervision, staff evaluation and development; and construction of board agendas in cooperation with the board chair. These are all characteristics of a site-managed school. The buildings were clean and well-maintained. Graffiti was rare. Vandalism repair costs were less than $400 a year for each school.

The superintendents had business managers but no assistant superintendents and were responsible for the oversight of several elementary schools. Therefore, the site-managed high schools relieved those administrators of another direct major supervisory task.

A comment by the Mansfield principal captures the philosophy of the principals relative to their building role. "I'm the least important person here. I can be away all day, and this place will still run. I'm really trying to decentralize control. I can't control everything anyway."

Following this philosophy, the principals delegated considerable decision-making responsibility to teachers in matters relating to curriculum and instruction. Teachers still had considerable autonomy in the classroom as the "accountability squeeze" was in its infancy.

THE CONCEPTUAL FRAMEWORK

There are two major characteristics of this study that make it different from other studies about change. First, Bromley and Mansfield were selected on the basis of being "good"—not on the basis of being innovative. Other investigations typically begin by identifying schools that had adopted or developed an innovation or that were in a process of changing and then proceed to examine the dynamics of implementation. Such organizations were seen as innovative initially.

The second characteristic different about this research is its construction around the change model that emerged out of the Rand studies of "Federal

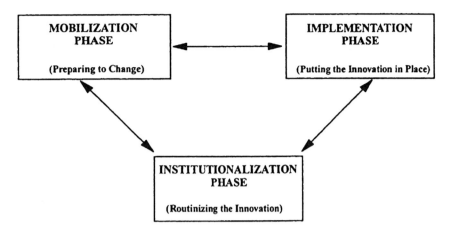

Figure 4.1. Three Phases of Change

Programs Supporting Educational Change" (Berman & McLaughlin, 1978, pp. 13–21; Berman in Lehming & Kane, 1981, pp. 264–274). That model (Figure 4.1) emphasized that change does not move in a linear fashion from one discrete stage to another; rather, it is a highly interactive, "snarled" process encompassing three phases—mobilization (sometimes referred to by other authors as "adoption" or "initiation"), implementation, and institutionalization or continuation (Fullan, 2007, pp. 64–106).

As discussed in chapter 2, to this model, Supovitz added the concept of "iterative refraction, . . . the process through which reforms are adjusted repeatedly as they are introduced and work their way through school environments" (2008, p. 153).

All three phases usually occur at different times and with different people. Even when something is institutionalized, conditions may lead to new thinking (mobilization), which, in turn, creates modifications in it. This was the case with the findings reported here. Change does not simply stop and start; in an adaptable school, change unfolds recursively.

ELEMENTS OF SMALL-SCALE CHANGE

Most change in organizations results neither from extraordinary organizational processes or skill, but from relatively stable, routine processes that relate organizations to their environments [March 1981, p. 564].

How does change begin? What stimulates it? What motivates people to change? The instrumental elements include: types of innovations; teacher roles; stimuli for and sources of innovation; motivation to change; and leadership. In describing them, the recursive, "iterative refraction" nature of the phases of the Rand model is very much in evidence.

TYPES OF INNOVATIONS

To begin the research, it was first necessary to identify the innovations that existed in the schools. Two forms emerged—policy and voluntary.

The policy changes were mandated ones—Basic Competency Regulations and the IDEA Multi-Disciplinary Teams, both of which were present in all high schools in the state. These will be discussed in chapter 6. The rest of this chapter focuses on the voluntary types listed in Table 4.1.

Table 4.1. A Typology of Voluntary Innovations

		Bromley	Mansfield
Course	A body of organized knowledge taught on a semester or year basis (e.g., Vermont Ecology, Data Processing)	$n = 14$	$n = 14$
Unit	A segment of a course (e.g., 4 weeks on mfg. in metals, 2 weeks on map skills in geography).	$n = 8$	$n = 9$
Theme	A topic of discourse or discussion (e.g., consumerism in home econ., sex equity in U.S. history)	$n = 7$	$n = 8$
Methods and Materials	Means of instruction and the implements for its delivery (e.g., games and simulations in French, new text in basic English)	$n = 5$	$n = 3$
Technology	A technological device for aiding the learning process (e.g., microcomputer in math, memory typewriter in business education)	$n = 2$	$n = 4$
Structure	Work patterns or working relationships of organization members (e.g., double period for transcription, open classroom area for math)	$n = 3$	$n = 3$
Total		39	41

OBSERVATIONS ABOUT THE INNOVATIONS

In a study of change in district high schools in Illinois, Daft and Becker point out that ". . . a good typology of innovations can enhance our understanding of the processes underlying innovation" (1978, p. 139). Although studies (e.g., of the National Diffusion Network by Huberman & Miles, 1984) identify types of innovations, they do not place them into a workable typology nor do they examine the factors that may affect their implementation.

For veteran educators, there are no surprises in Table 4.1. All schools implement innovations like these, and good schools are particularly adept at installing new courses. But what is interesting is the variety of ordinary, small-scale types. In most cases, individual teachers initiated them, taught them, and were thus most affected by them. However, other innovations affected entire departments such as several new courses, initiated in some cases by the principals, in social studies, English, and science that constituted an "innovation bundle" (Hall & Hord, 1987, p. 135) or could be classed as a "mosaic of innovations" (to be discussed in chapter 7).

Another project that had some twenty urban, suburban, and rural high schools as its database also found that the organizations had implemented, over two years, numerous small-scale innovations (Hall, et al., 1984, pp. 58–62).

Change in practice is usually multidimensional involving materials or technology, approaches or methods, and alteration of beliefs (Fullan, 2007, pp. 30–37). While these Bromley and Mansfield innovations appear commonplace against these criteria, for the innovating teachers—tackling the theme of sex equity in social studies, the origins of life in biology, or a death and dying unit in English—change was complex, multidimensional, and demanding work.

Usually, it required new materials, new methods, and changes in beliefs. The resulting combination altered teaching practices. It was the "deep" change that was explicated in earlier pages. The interviews with these teachers indicated strongly that the innovations had *meaning* for them, a central factor in real change. "Meaning fuels motivation, and knowledge feeds on itself to produce ongoing problem solving" (Fullan, 2007, p. 39).

Because they were site-managed, the only time Bromley and Mansfield required consistent principal, superintendent, and board involvement with voluntary innovations occurred when courses had to be approved. Then, budget implications, statutory responsibilities, and administrator philosophy brought the boards into the process because, in the words of the Bromley principal, "It's essential that the board knows what's going on around here in curriculum. The administration has a responsibility to educate the board so it can make intelligent decisions."

The board chair, in turn, expressed mutual respect and an endorsement of site-management, "The board is here to deal with policy and finances. We hire administrators to think and get for us the best school we can have. The staff is to teach, work with the administrators, and do the best job it can for the youngsters."

The principals had considerable latitude about when they needed to involve the superintendent and board in decision-making relative to innovations. While involvement always came when a change carried dollar signs (e.g., the purchase of computers or the acceptance of a new program), there was no hierarchical lid on innovations at Bromley and Mansfield as evidenced by the fact that each school had a family living course that dealt with sex education, often a red flag in many communities.

Note that the data in Table 4.1 are purely quantitative. This study did not include an "impact assessment" of the innovation on the organization. Just how does an instructional unit, for example, measure up against an open classroom area for mathematics in terms of its effect on student achievement? In isolation, the unit may not be that important, but, if it eventually leads to changes in virtually all units, the unit has produced a considerable change in curriculum.

I observed this phenomenon where teachers were developing "standards-based" units or "thematic" units. Writing such new units means difficult and time-consuming work that may or may not lead to real overall change in the complexion of the entire course. But success with the one unit and consequent increased motivation, staff development support, and time for development can make a real difference in spreading the impact of the small change.

Consider also the number of innovations. How many should high schools like these in similar settings have implemented over a five-year period? How does one establish an "innovation baseline" against which to examine innovativeness? Is it even possible to do so when local contexts differ and each organization is affected differently by osmotic phenomena?

Finally, how accurate is the tally? The principals contended that, if one included in the list changes in teaching styles, approaches to discipline, and alterations in professional attitudes and educational beliefs, there would be far more than eighty. I agree with them.

A reverse example of smaller changes spilling out of a larger change that would not often be recognized is when the principals talked about changing the schedule. At one time in each school, there were too many study halls and not enough elective courses. The teachers concurred, and the Mansfield principal concluded, "I can manage the curriculum by building the schedule. And the schedule gives the gestalt of the program." But to the observing eye, the "gestalt" was comprised of courses; most other changes were not visible.

On one level, the schedule change was a large-scale innovation that altered how the day was structured, but it also had an impact on student attitudes (more attention to studying); teacher attitudes (study halls were "no fun" to monitor, and teachers felt relieved of a real burden); and curriculum in that more courses could be offered to meet student needs (thus expanding options in "the shopping mall"). Educators recognize that schedule-making of this kind can lead to "innovation bundles."

But for the critic who wants radical change, the schedule will not pass muster; it appears to be merely a routine management task. Yet developing different schedules was a key goal of the NASSP Model Schools project discussed in chapter 2. Block scheduling emerged a few years ago as a key innovation in many secondary schools. From it, some educators see many other resulting changes that will effect classroom changes such as more ". . . engaging teaching methods, use of alternative assessments, more attention to individual student needs, fewer discipline problems, and overall improvement in school climate" (O'Neil, 1995, pp. 11–15).

INNOVATIONS AND ATTRIBUTES

The next step in the research was to place this topology of innovations in a grid against innovation attributes from the literature.

Rogers, one of the most noted students of innovation, states that change agents hoping to gauge potential reactions to certain innovations would find it helpful if they knew beforehand the critical attributes of innovations such as those listed in Table 4.2. He points out that the literature concentrates on the differences between people who might adopt an innovation and gives scant attention to differences between innovations (1983, pp. 210–211). Also, Daft and Becker conclude that it is much more useful to examine the attributes of innovations rather than thinking of them as a homogeneous category (pp. 120–127).

Hall and Hord use the term "configurations" as akin to the notion of attributes or characteristics of an innovation. Configuration is a central component of their Concerns-Based Adoption Model (explained further in chapter 6). It provides clearer ways to talk about and define an innovation (1987, pp. 107–140). In essence, what does an innovation look like in components that have to be in place for it to be successful? To give one specific example: What does real team teaching have to consist of in practice for it to be teaming and not "turn teaching"?

Table 4.2. Innovations and Attributes

	Relative Advantage (degree perceived as better than alternatives)	Compatibility (degree perceived as consistent with existing values and norms)	Complexity (degree perceived as difficult to understand and use)	Implementation Requirements (items and arrangements necessary to implement)	Trialability (degree of experimentation possible on limited basis)	Observability (degree to which innovation results are visible to others)
Course (e.g., Vt. Ecology)	hi	hi	medium	medium	medium	medium
Unit (e.g., Map Skills)	hi	hi	lo	lo	hi	medium
Theme (e.g., Consumerism)	hi	hi	lo	lo	hi	lo
Methods and Materials (e. g., Games and Texts)	hi	hi	lo	lo	medium	medium
Technology (e.g., Microcomputer)	hi	hi	hi	hi	medium	hi
Structure (e.g., Open area for Math)	medium	lo	hi	hi	lo	hi

Table 4.2 represents an analysis of specific innovations at Bromley and Mansfield against six attributes drawn from Rogers (pp. 21–232) and Zaltman, Duncan, and Holbek (1973, pp. 33–50).

The attributes include the four main characteristics of an innovation that Fullan (2007, pp. 87–92) found necessary for successful implementation—need, clarity, degree of complexity, and quality and practicality. The "high," "medium," and "low" assessments in Table 4.2 are qualitative, but represent an example of the kind of analysis called for by researchers. This is not to say that, in the hectic environments of Bromley and Mansfield, educators purposively passed all innovations through an innovation attribute screen before someone decided to mobilize for change. But it appears that the educators in these schools did that very thing intuitively.

Change agents, however, can purposefully use this attribute screen when considering certain innovations. For example, when schools introduce new technology, they may view it as relatively "simple" to implement. In reality, though, it creates numerous demands on the organization due to its inherent complexity and numerous implementation requirements, as was described in earlier pages. "Screening" the technology with the attributes could ensure a better planned change.

Doing so might help avoid the situation where the lack of such planning leads to adopted technology sitting relatively unused because of inadequate supervision and staff training. Proper screening should uncover such "hidden" requirements in order to ensure the successful implementation and institutionalization of innovations.

TEACHER ROLES

Historically, teachers have enjoyed considerable decision-making autonomy within the classroom. A theme common to all the reports and studies of the last two decades is that "Teachers should be provided with the discretion and autonomy that are the hallmarks of professional work" (Carnegie Forum on Education and the Economy, 1986, p. 56). Research tells us that effective employees in organizations like schools, which serve a reluctant, often unmotivated clientele, need considerable discretion to act (Katz & Kahn, 1978, p. 159).

To assess the presence of autonomy and job discretion at Bromley and Mansfield, each teacher completed a twenty four-item "Sense of Autonomy Questionnaire" scored on a one (low) to six (high) scale (Packard, et al., 1976, pp. 211–251). The mean score for the respective staffs was 4.5 and 4.6. These outcomes are congruent with a national survey of staff-reported involvement in school decision-making, where Vermont teachers ranked highest in choosing textbooks and instructional materials (93 percent) and in shaping the curriculum (85 percent) (Carnegie Foundation for the Advancement of Teaching, 1988, pp. 4–5).

If another such study were conducted today, very likely, the accountability squeeze would reduce considerably the sense of autonomy felt by similar teachers.

STIMULI FOR INNOVATION

Teachers were asked, "What was the stimulus for the innovation you've described?" Table 4.3 depicts the responses.

Table 4.3. Stimuli for Change

Student interest or dissatisfaction (e.g., students not electing elective courses, failing grades, or "acting up" out of boredom)	21
Teacher ego, interest, or experience (e.g., the poor image of a course, special affinity for a pet subject, new information from a graduate course)	13
Laws, regulations, and accreditation visits (e.g., Title IX, PL-94-142, accreditation team suggesting a new course)	10
Teacher observation (e.g., students needing first-aid instruction for farm work, students needing sex education information not available through a community agency)	7
Teacher dissatisfaction (e.g., "I had to do something with this material. It was driving me crazy")	6
Journals and newsletters (e.g., a death and dying unit from the *English Journal*)	5
Administrative direction (This category, although low in number, is not an accurate portrait of the principals' roles. It encompasses several changes through principal direction such as a "bundle" of course innovations in a department.)	4
School structure (e.g., a new study hall structure that affected "time on task," an open area that facilitated teaming in math)	4
Budget (addition or cuts) (e.g., a model office from state and federal vocational educational assistance, creating a new course out of two courses due to RIFing)*	3
Culture change (e.g., carry over activities in physical education to meet leisure time needs)	3
The local public (e.g., parental complaints about numbers of failures in a government course)	3
Peers (e.g., suggesting the local paper as an outlet for work of a journalism class)	1
Total	80

OBSERVATIONS ABOUT STIMULI FOR CHANGE

There was no pattern to the connection of certain stimuli with certain types of innovations. This conclusion—plus the fact that there was such a variety of stimuli—is similar to the findings of Huberman and Miles, who uncovered a host of what they called "reasons/motives" for adopting a National Diffusion Network or Title IV-C innovation (1984, pp. 44–52). Different, however, is the fact that administrative pressure on staff forced the adoption of most of those innovations. That factor contrasts with Table 4.3, which is dominated by teacher initiatives to effect small-scale innovations.

These stimuli have a distinct "inner directedness" (e.g., from teachers, students, and principals). The schools were not subject to much direct environmental pressure to change. Contrast this finding to the outcomes of the "Change Over Time?" study of high schools reported in chapter 2, where environmental factors over thirty years increasingly had a significant role in causing change. Such changes were connected to the press of accountability that is severely curbing autonomy for most high school teachers.

Many of the innovations at Bromley and Mansfield were aimed at the vocation-bound student. This outcome contrasts with Daft and Becker who found that teachers were inventive primarily concerning changes relative to the college-oriented curriculum, but needed to be prodded by administrators when it came to changes concerning the vocational-oriented program (pp. 51–96). In that case, local values focused on higher education.

At Bromley and Mansfield, local values did not favor the college-bound over the vocation-bound student (less than 40 percent of the graduating classes went on to higher education). Hence, teachers felt the press of needs from a significant number of non-college-bound youngsters and responded to them with various innovations. In numerous instances, the principals made innovation interventions on behalf of all groups of students. Clearly, educators must attend to the range of local values as stimuli for change and not neglect some students in the process.

Although Bromley and Mansfield had a written philosophy and goals, they were not mentioned as a stimulus. This is not an uncommon research finding. For example, Boyer, in his analysis of high schools, found, "When we asked teachers, principals, and students about school goals, their response frequently was one of uncertainty, amusement, or surprise. 'What do you mean? Goals for what?' Some teachers just smiled. Others apologized for not knowing" (1983, p. 61).

And other studies of school improvement, such as those conducted by Muncey and McQuillan and Joyce and Calhoun (in chapter 2), showed that up-front philosophy and goals did not stimulate change.

However, no one (at Bromley and Mansfield) perceived the innovations as a bad fit with what the school was all about. There was an implicit "philosophical glue" bonding them. Innovation decision-makers saw a positive relationship between changes and organization purposes and made rational choices, a finding similar to one in Daft and Becker's study (p. 129). In an organized anarchy, the connection between individual and organizational goals may be quite loose (March & Olsen, 1979, p. 16). Therefore, schools need to make more than a routine effort to connect them.

According to much of the literature, change should follow the classic pattern of problem-search-solution. However, at Bromley and at Mansfield, the usual initial stimulus for small-scale change did not grow formally out of a rationally defined problem, but emerged instead from educators' intuition, hypothesizing, and experience—modalities that some authors advocate as important ways to stimulate organizational improvement (March & Olsen 1979, pp. 78–79; Kouzes & Posner, 2007, pp. 103–129).

Other literature demonstrates that such mobilizing phenomena are not unique to these schools (Huberman & Miles, 1984, pp. 44–52; Daft & Becker, 1978, pp. 127–136; Louis & Miles, 1990; Joyce & Calhoun, 1996; Muncey & McQuillan, 1996).

SOURCES OF IDEAS

At Bromley and Mansfield, teachers were asked, "Where did you get the idea to respond to the stimulus?" Twenty-one teachers named professional journals and newsletters, thirteen named discussions with peers, and twelve named college courses. Other responses were scattered among areas such as conferences, television, the school librarian, the principal, and textbooks.

Reading, talking, and listening, these are the pivotal behaviors for acquiring ideas to respond to a change stimulus. The schools subscribed to journals, as did many staff, and the schools supported teachers financially when they enrolled in college courses. These information sources had considerable payoff and demonstrate the vital connection between knowledge and change. This is a similar conclusion to one of Joyce and Calhoun in their study of "school renewal" (1996, p. 187).

As is true for most schools, however, there was little money budgeted at Bromley and Mansfield for staff to attend conferences, places where professionals routinely obtain considerable information. Today, professionals have easy access to the Internet so they have no problem obtaining information; rather, the challenge is to make sense of what is found and to decide what is valid and potentially useful. Is that gold or not at the bottom of this landfill of information?

In keeping with the nonlinear nature of change discussed thus far, it should be pointed out that, in several instances, the source of the idea for the innovation (the possible solution) "arrived" in someone's mind before a stimulus or need was apparent. As March contends, in a "garbage can model" of decision-making (to be discussed further in the next chapter), "Solutions are answers to problems that may or may not have been recognized" (1995, p. 200).

For example, a Mansfield teacher attended a university course on writing and subsequently searched the curriculum for a place where the teaching of writing needed improvement. The result was an elective writing course. At Bromley, a teacher attended a course in vocational-technical education that led to the development of a new unit on metals for an industrial arts course.

The professional desire to be "enlightened" was a major factor in this process. As one teacher put it, "Most schools don't identify the problem. They come up with solutions first."

Sieber, in an extensive analysis of key incentives that encourage teacher innovation, points out that enlightenment has been undervalued, noting that, "There are reasons to believe that more up-to-date, informed, 'tuned-in' individuals take more initiative in educational change" (1981, p. 148). Such individuals search for solutions before there is an identified problem so that, when one arises, they are well armed to respond.

Despite the importance of information in this process of improvement, it is interesting to note that no one in either school mentioned the ERIC system, the National Diffusion Network, or the State Department of Education as a source of ideas.

MOTIVATION TO CHANGE

At Bromley and Mansfield, autonomous teachers were stimulated to change by a variety of factors in the work environment. Consider their responses to interview questions (drawn from Lortie's classic study of the teaching profession (1975, pp. 248–254) related to motivation.

When asked, "What are the most important tasks you have to do as a teacher?," 47 out of 59 responses dealt with role modeling, meeting the needs of students, and planning and organizing the day. Only four respondents mentioned "developing and updating curriculum. When asked, "What are the greatest satisfactions you get from teaching?," 81 of 111 responses had to do with seeing students do well in school, working with them, and having control over the logistics of the day and the way work was done.

Finally, the survey asked, "If you were given a gift of ten extra hours a week for work (and you were paid for it), how would you spend the time?" Answers ranged (Bromley to Mansfield) from 25 percent to 18 percent on class preparation; 22 percent to 10 percent on curriculum development; 12 percent to 28 percent on counseling students; 16 percent to 13 percent on advising school activities; and 10 percent to 20 percent on more teaching. These responses are highly similar to what teachers told Lortie in 1963 (p. 163) and what they told follow-up researchers twenty five years later (Kottcamp, Provenza, & Cohn, 1986).

For these teachers, the prime motivators to innovate were rooted in a variety of psychological factors. While there are other types of rewards that teachers can earn—extrinsic (money, prestige, and power) and ancillary (work schedules, job security, and school vacation breaks) (Lortie, pp. 101–106)—both types do not fluctuate very much and cannot be manipulated directly by teachers. Psychic rewards, on the other hand, are within easy reach of teachers, if the workplace climate permits them to be obtained by the staff.

The schools overall provided a strong professional community so essential to motivation. While this research did not examine the department climates within Bromley and Mansfield, as did McLaughlin and Talbert in their study of high schools (2001), these schools had developed the work contexts essential for effective professional practice.

As the answers to the Bromley and Mansfield questionnaire demonstrate, teachers do not get "kicks" from dealing with discipline problems or building management. In schools where teachers have to spend inordinate time on issues such as these, creative energy is diffused, rather than focused, on tasks relating to instruction and learning that can affect psychological rewards. Getting these rewards is an incentive; it may be more important to stimulating innovation than first responding to a need. One teacher summed it nicely, "I love to work with kids when I see them learn."

But the changing demographics in most communities across the nation, some more radical and impactful than in others, often alter the student mix (as described in chapter 2) and make it more difficult to "see them learn." Often, these students require a different approach to teaching. Much of the time these students " . . . do not conform in appearance, comportment, or academic preparation to earlier generations of students" (McLaughlin & Talbert, 2001, p. 17). Teachers have to work much harder to benefit from the typical rewards described in prior pages.

In good schools, teachers feel focused on curriculum and instruction, and their sense of efficacy is enhanced. Efficacy shows up frequently as a key variable in the school improvement process because feeling that one can have a positive impact on one's immediate situation boosts energy and persistence in the face of challenges (Ashton & Webb, 1986, p. 3; Darling-Hammond, 1997, pp. 170–172).

In turn, one gains power in the workplace, and teacher empowerment is a frequent theme in reports on teaching (e.g., Carnegie Forum on Education and the Economy, 1986; Maeroff, 1988). As Rogers stresses, "Individual innovativeness is affected both by the individual's characteristics, and by the nature of the social system in which the individual is a member" (1983, p. 260).

Empowerment, and thus innovativeness, increases when employees achieve success at what Weick calls "small wins"—concrete, completed outcomes on a moderate scale. Small wins motivate people to respond to problem stimuli by doing something rather than becoming frustrated by inaction. Acting with success brings rewards. Continued frustration leads to a feeling of powerlessness rather than empowerment (Weick, 1984, 40–48). Continued frustration creates morale problems. Today's shifting and often mercurial school and community environments can lead to increased frustration and thus a sapping of staff energy.

Teachers at Bromley and Mansfield, as the data show, drew on small wins to respond to the various needs they encountered. "Small wins produce results for a simple reason: it's hard to argue against success (Kouzes & Posner, 2007, p. 197).

Schools have often undervalued the impact that organizational climate and its accompanying forces can have on staff motivation. As was the case with Bromley and Mansfield, a vast reservoir of teacher talent, creativity, and drive is present in most schools, and it costs little to release it. But policymakers and some education leaders tend to skirt this reality in favor of a continued reliance on extrinsic approaches to motivation.

This tendency to skip over these "soft" organizational factors is illustrated by a publication on teacher incentives—developed under the auspices of the three national administrator organizations—that includes no discussion about psychic rewards, but rather an extensive treatment of topics like compensation plans, career options, and enhanced professional responsibilities (Cresap, McCormick, & Paget, 1984).

Hence, we see again the resurrection of merit pay, this time under the guise of "pay for performance" as the carrot that can "turn around" the school, despite abundant research demonstrating that it does not work in nonprofits, as supposedly it does in the private sector.

Figure 4.2 depicts the variety of stimuli for decision-making and innovation uncovered from the Bromley and Mansfield staffs.

Figure 4.2. Stimuli for Decision Making and Innovation

LEADERSHIP

At the time of the study, the Bromley principal had been in his job for six years and the Mansfield principal for seven. Both men were active and assertive individuals who practiced "management by walking around"; were highly involved with staff, students, the board, and the community; and were concerned about and engaged in matters of curriculum and instruction. However, they had to make an extra effort to engage in the latter because the demanding pace of their work was similar to the national research findings about the position discussed at the conclusion of the last chapter.

The Bromley principal saw his role through this frame, "I plant the seed, leave it there, and water it from time to time. When it takes root, you give away the ownership of it. The only people who may be aware of the change may be those involved in the transaction." The Mansfield principal noted, "The focus here is on change as a process and not an event. People have to come to feel that an idea is theirs before they'll move. Things happen subtly in low-key ways."

How did the staff at Bromley and Mansfield view the principal's leadership?

• Bromley: "He's very responsive and accommodating. He understands curriculum and knows the details of what's going on around here. I'm very dependent on him being willing to support an idea and advocate for it. Without that backing, after a while, you just give up."

• Mansfield: "He's on top of the latest trends. He seems to read all the magazines. He challenges us to think about what we're doing. If we as a department don't buy it, though, he doesn't force it on us. He's continually trying to upgrade curriculum. I have the feeling that he's never quite satisfied with what's going on. He wants excellence."

These principals were a mix of the initiator, manager, and responder styles of change facilitation identified by Hall and Hord (1987, pp. 215–257). Change facilitators who are administrators see themselves more as colleagues rather than as bosses, and, hence, they support and assist teachers in their work. Each principal was far more an initiator and manager than a reactor to events. Both engaged in countless interventions with their staffs, and these interventions influenced the use of an innovation (p. 143). They were not the "controlling" leaders who research shows have low credibility (Kouzes & Posner, 2007, p. 291).

Intervention incidents (the smallest level) included casual, isolated conversations in the hallways or over the lunchroom table; leaving an article in a mailbox; or repeated assistance to a teacher who was implementing an innovation. These patterns of behavior for the Bromley and Mansfield principals are in line with the Hall and Hord, finding that responder/reactive administrators make far fewer interventions (p. 244).

By themselves, most interventions of this sort are rarely noticed. But through them, the principals were able to nudge many small-scale changes so that bringing them about had become part of the normative climate of the organization. As a result, these successes with innovations provided incentives that boosted efficacy and empowered staff. This is strikingly similar to the dynamics of small wins found in the private and government sectors through the international surveys conducted by Kouzes and Posner (2007, pp. 27–31).

Corbett (1982), in a study of effective principal behavior relative to classroom change, and McAvoy (1987), in a study of effective principal behavior relative to staff development, found that administrators who provided commonplace intrinsic incentives—such as talking to teachers about their needs or inquiring how an innovation was progressing—had great impact on teacher attitudes and motivation. Such "everyday acts" play an important role in helping new practices become part of the curriculum.

In addition to their change facilitator styles, the principals also exhibited other leadership qualities described in the literature (e.g., Hersey, Blanchard, & Johnson, 2001). Each had the ability to respond to people with behaviors appropriate to the situation. Each was able to be directive or task-oriented as well as relationship-focused. For example, the Mansfield principal said, "Most faculty are basically on their own. They are in charge. However, there are a few that I've got on a shorter rein—they have less freedom now."

This is not to say that the two principals were perfect models of administrative behavior. At times, the Bromley principal was seen as not directive enough regarding needed curricular and instructional improvements; as not intervening with a teacher when he should have; and as placing too much emphasis on relationships. At times, the Mansfield principal was seen as too task-focused, directive, and somewhat overbearing. But, in sum, these men received positive marks by their staffs, the students, the board, and the community.

They chose to be the instructional leaders of their schools despite the intense demands on their schedules and thus demonstrated what research points to as the critical element of leadership accomplishment: positive leader-member relationships. "The *most important* (emphasis in the original) single element in situational control is the amount of loyalty, dependability, and support you, as the leader, get from those with whom you work" (Fiedler & Chemers, 1984, p. 47).

> For better or worse, principals set conditions for teacher community by the ways in which they manage school resources, relate to teachers and students, support or inhibit social interaction and leadership in the faculty, respond to the broader policy context, and bring resources to the school (McLaughlin & Talbert, 2001, p. 98).

But, as Figure 3.2 in chapter 3 demonstrated, the "principal's plate" in 2010 in most high schools is heaped with more tasks than can be handled effectively. Fullan's synthesis of the literature substantiates that conclusion. Principals today find themselves in an impossible position (2007, p. 168). We have a serious public policy issue on our hands that is beyond the pages of this book to address.

In one of the early classic books about management theory, March and Simon concluded that most people in leadership/managerial roles must adopt behaviors of "satisficing" (a step up from "satisfactory") rather than optimizing solutions because there are "cognitive limits on rationality" due to the complexity of the workplace (March & Simon, 1958, p. 149). The "rational man" of classical decision theory " . . . makes optimal choices in a highly specified and defined environment" (p. 137).

Clearly such environments, as we have seen in chapters 1–3, no longer (if they ever did) exist for schools. Satisficing choices, of course, belie the image of leadership to which we are accustomed. Indeed, they instead require new adaptations by principals in how they work with their staffs. Chapter 5 will illustrate how such adaptations can be made drawing on a "marketplace model of change."

Chapter 5

Good Schools
and Small-Scale Change

An organization is a collection of choices looking for problems, issues and feelings looking for decision situations in which they might be aired, solutions looking for issues to which they might be the answer, and decision makers looking for work.

—Cohen, March, and Olsen, 1972, p. 2

The picture (garbage can decision-making) is one of seeming chaos, of disorder. And yet there are patterns under the confusion and these can be modeled once the parameters are known. The process is not truly random and can be predicted to some extent, although it can feel like chaos to participants. Decisions do get made, although the process is about as far removed from rational choice prescriptions as it is possible to get.

—Miller, Hickson, and Wilson, 1996, p. 303

If decision-makers were to follow conventional wisdom, they would take actions largely connected to the goals of the organization. After all, should not thinking precede action and action relate to the societal mission of the organization? This conception of decision-making is fused in our culture. Underlying it is the Deweyian model of felt difficulty, problem analysis, search for solutions, consideration of alternatives, and choosing. The model is in line with the technological perspective on change discussed in chapter 3.

Within this framework, impulse, intuition, faith, and tradition are not given much conscious credence; they are outside of the mainstream of what is most trusted as the basis for choosing and changing. (The above ideas and many that are integrated into this chapter are drawn primarily from March, 1981; March, 1983; March & Olsen, 1979 & 1986; and March, 1994).

115

This model stresses planning and orderly change. Many good books on the subject stock library shelves. Because we "ought" to do things according to this model, we try to act that way in schools because it is widely accepted, logical, and sensible. Politically, it becomes difficult to espouse publicly a radically contrasting approach. "The appearance of rational action legitimates the organization in the environment it faces, deflects criticism, and ensures a steady flow of resources into the organization" (Weick in Lincoln, 1985, p. 110).

Sometimes, we are successful in following convention, but, as the literature review demonstrated in chapter 2, the "sensible" approach does not have a starry history within the organized anarchy and busy kitchen features of educational organizations. In addition, the usual approach, given the hectic and fragmented pace of work, demands too much time and information from decision-makers and assumes that most of them share the same goals.

Often, the "round" theory (new views of the earth) does not fit with the reality of the "flat" experiences (the conventional maps of Columbus' time), thus creating frustration and sometimes disenchantment with academic precepts (March, 1983, pp. 32–35). Employees begin to doubt their abilities and become frustrated when they are unsuccessful at influencing organizational events.

Fortunately, the expanding cultural perspective discussed in chapter 3 liberates us from the narrow focus of how organizations "should" behave according to classical theory. "Rational decision-making processes can be observed in schools; so can accidents" (Clark and McKibbin, 1982, p. 671). Our broader vision allows us to view the "accidents" as more than anomalies.

For while the traditional perspective is deeply imbedded in our collective psyches and in our political and social institutions, the new perspective allows us to see another path through the thicket of emerging concepts. It recognizes our "limited (bounded) rationality" within situations that are increasing ambiguous, uncertain, and unpredictable, as was seen in chapters 1 and 2.

> The core of limited rationality is that individuals are intendedly rational. Although decision makers try to be rational, they are constrained by limited cognitive capabilities and incomplete information, and thus their actions may be less than completely rational in spite of their best intentions and efforts (March, 1994, p. 9).

It is these conditions that often result in the "satisficing" behavior discussed in the last chapter relative to principals.

In what has become a classic new perspective on how the natural world works, Gleick presents "chaos theory" wherein he describes how the combination of relativity, quantum mechanics, and chaos will be the third great revolution in the physical sciences (1987, pp. 1–48). He analyzes how quantitative measurement and deterministic thinking have tried to make scientific outcomes "predictable."

One of the most cited dimensions of the book is his discussion of how small changes or "perturbations" (he calls it the "butterfly effect") can have an enormous impact in the natural world (e.g., weather and climate changes). Although it is certainly a stretch to apply his theory to organizations, some writers are beginning such explorations. Garmston and Wellman (1995) and Marshall (1995), for example, see some connections to schools. Wheatley has written about "chaos" ideas relative to organizations in general (1993).

The overall perspective fits with some newer views of organizational dynamics, views that are central to the overall thesis of *Changing Schools from the Inside Out: Small Wins in Hard Times*.

In this chapter, we shall fit together the findings from chapter 4 into a "marketplace model of change" that can be an effective approach to improvement in all schools. The term "model" should not be seen as another standard rationalistic conception of organizational change and innovation. It is not. Rather, it incorporates the affective and cognitive elements identified at Bromley and Mansfield with new concepts from the literature. The intent is to evoke and not to predict. The goal: a new route through the maze, a working map of new understandings about educational change for educational leaders.

THE MARKETPLACE AND INNOVATION

Some general outcomes from this part of the research are strikingly similar to findings from Daft and Becker's study of high schools.

For example, they concluded that there was a disorganized nature to the processes, that innovation takes place in different areas within the organization, and that different innovations follow different routes to adoption. They also found high compatibility between their findings and the ideas of the organized anarchy, garbage can decision processes, and loose coupling (pp. 164–181). However, their survey project did not obtain qualitative data to explain the dynamics behind their observations; this book does.

The marketplace is an appropriate metaphor through which to explain the mobilization phenomena that emerged from this more detailed study of Bromley and Mansfield. These phenomena connect strongly to those uncovered by research into other good schools (described in the last chapter), and they are also similar to the innovation processes found in excellent businesses (e.g., Kanter, 1983, pp. 129–205).

In those situations, supportive work climates provided rewards to relatively autonomous individuals or groups who invented new products or practices that led to improved organizational performance. "Innovating companies provide the freedom to act, which arouses the desire to act" (Kanter, p. 142). Many creative activities were undertaken without planned precision.

Picture a marketplace. The incentives connected with buying and selling govern behavior. Individuals exchange incentives; organizational level incentives are less powerful as has been demonstrated by the literature reviewed. The market structure provides loose boundaries within which individuals buy and sell. People come to the market because they believe in its mission which is to facilitate the exchange of desired wares between participants.

However, what is most important to them is their satisfaction and perhaps even rewards. Intentionality certainly undergirds action, but it is primarily the intentionality of individuals and not that of the market. There is rationality in the marketplace, but feelings, intuition, and values are powerful determinants of behavior (Clark & McKibbin, 1982, p. 671).

GARBAGE CAN DECISION PROCESSES

Within the marketplace, organizational decisions are made commonly through "choice opportunities" (CO), the occasions when the organization is expected to produce a decision. These situations are a "meeting place" for issues and feelings, solutions, and participants (March & Olsen, 1979, pp. 25–27). At the administrative level in schools, some typical routine CO include analyzing test results; budgeting; scheduling; assigning staff; classroom evaluation visits; staff development sessions; and meetings of various kinds.

At the teacher level, some routine CO are lesson planning; course development and revision; and test construction, giving, and interpretation. The CO can be thought of as a garbage can, a collection device for the streams of problems/concerns, participant interests, competencies, attitudes, values, and potential solutions to problems/concerns. The streams mix—in ways not clearly observable—and the can (situation) gets full. Eventually, it has to be emptied through a decision. That decision may be to change or not to change.

Measured against the conventional rational view of how organizations *should* function, this process may seem to be a clear indicator of organizational ill health. However, given that schools are not tight and tidy bureaucracies, but instead operate as loosely coupled structures—particularly in curriculum and instruction—the process is "normal" (Cohen, March, & Olsen, 1979, p. 37). Fullan points out that one key faulty assumption in thinking about change is that of overrationalizing a situation; that is a serious misreading of the culture of schools (2007, pp. 108–111).

The garbage can process . . . is one in which problems, solutions, and participants move from one choice opportunity to another in such a way that the nature
of the choice, the time it takes, and the problems it solves all depend on a relatively complicated intermeshing of the mix of choices available at any one time,
the mix of problems that have access to the organization, the mix of solutions
looking for problems, and the outside demands on the decision makers (March &
Olsen, 1979, p. 36).

Figure 5.1 depicts the concept. The arrows should not be interpreted to
indicate that all streams enter the can at the same time; they usually do not.
"Intervening variables" refers to organizational and environmental forces that
affect when and how the streams enter the can and cause decision-making to
sometimes be predictable and sometimes unpredictable.

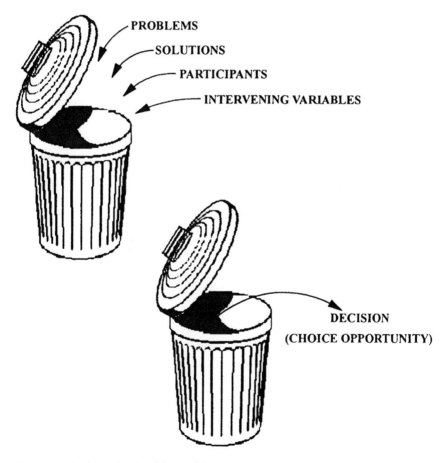

Figure 5.1. Garbage Can Decision Making

THE MARKETPLACE MODEL

Figure 5.2, drawing on the garbage can motif, depicts how the contributing elements might look in more specific terms, using the findings from Bromley and Mansfield. Nowhere in the garbage can literature have I found a schematic to illustrate the central ideas. The stream of problems/concerns (from Table 4.3) represents stimuli that prodded teachers and administrators that meshed with the motivators to change (from Table 4.4), leading to the generation of the stream of solutions (the types of innovations represented by Table 4.1).

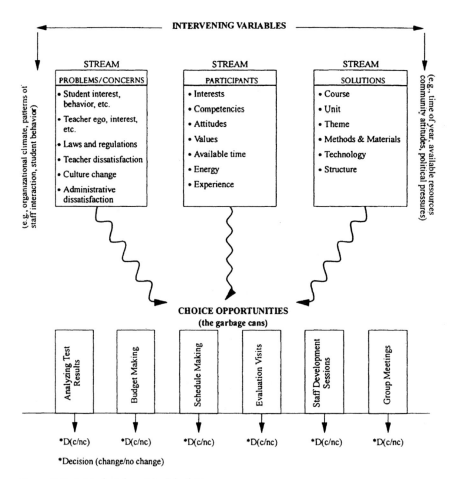

Figure 5.2. A Marketplace Model of Change

These streams flow into the choice opportunities that exist within Sarason's programmatic and behavioral "regularities," which are present in all human situations. In schools, regularities include the schedule, the size and composition of classes, the organization of curriculum, patterns of instruction, and student-teacher interaction (1996, pp. 95–117). These commonplace events, processes, and practices are powerful impediments to large-scale change or any type of restructuring; packed together, they serve to reinforce the image that "the more things change, the more they stay the same." Meanwhile, small-scale changes occur, often unnoticed by most observers.

Innovations at Bromley and Mansfield were effected largely through existing CO. There is much formal evidence (and common sense) to support the value of CO and "everyday acts" (as described in chapter 4 relative to the principal's role) as key factors in school improvement.

For example, a review of the literature on the instructional management role of the principal revealed a host of ordinary activities that can be associated with change and innovation. Some such activities are budgeting, scheduling, appointment of people to committees, public recognition of teachers for their achievements, strategic control of information flow about a new program, and lobbying for program support with senior administrators (Bossert, et al., 1982, p. 51). All principals engage in these activities if they are to administer a well-run organization. As another study put it:

> They require no new program, no innovation, no extensive change. The success of these activities for instructional management hinges, instead, on the principal's capacity to connect them to the instructional system (Dwyer, et al., 1983, p. 54).

Making this connection is very dependent on conscious use of the CO for improvement rather than just routine purposes. Being more aware of when they occur, who is or could be involved, how often they occur, and their value/ utility is a first step in this direction.

For instance, rather than observing a teacher and then filling out an evaluation form and placing it in a mailbox without discussion, the effective principal uses the opportunity to also discuss curriculum and possible needs for change. Rather than merely placing the standardized test results on his office shelf and not informing the staff of the outcomes, the effective principal develops a "game plan" of incidents (Hall & Hord, 1987, pp. 177–213) whereby the tests fit into the larger scheme of school improvement plans. The Bromley and Mansfield principals and teachers were adept at using the available CO to make their organizations better.

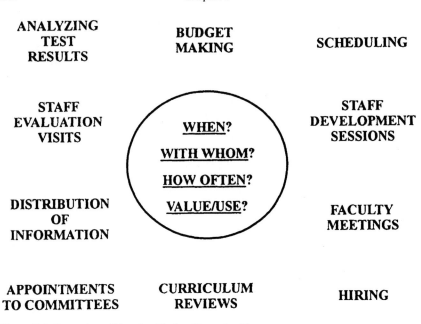

Figure 5.3. Examples of Regular Choice Opportunities

HOW THE PROCESS WORKS

Here are some examples that show how the marketplace process of change worked in the schools. Cusick, in his study of three high schools, found a similar pattern to individual teacher innovation. "More important to curriculum than collective agreement or mutual cooperation, were the personal predilections of each teacher" (1983, p. 3; see also pp. 72–100).

BROMLEY

- A social studies teacher with a strong psychology background was "getting bored" with his history courses, wanted to use his psychology training, and wanted to provide students with a course in adolescent psychology. As he put it, "It was largely self-serving on my part." His department chair, department members, and the principal agreed that such a course was needed and that he should make a proposal to the board before late fall to make sure there were not any budget implications (the budget was usually finalized by the board before Christmas).

- Also, the course would need to be approved before late winter when the program of studies would be printed in anticipation of student scheduling in the spring. The board turned down the initial proposal because of concerns about a unit on sexuality. However, the principal encouraged him to address the concerns and resubmit the proposal. He did, and it was approved.
- Basic competency regulations of the State Board of Education (in reading, writing, speaking, listening, reasoning, and mathematics) presented Bromley with an opportunity to help students who had low literacy skills (a concern of teachers and the administration). At first, after the regulations were in effect and students had been tested, those needing additional help were aided by teachers in study halls. This arrangement was not satisfactory because staff had monitoring duties to perform and could not give the necessary attention to tutoring.
- The chair of the English department proposed to the principal the idea of a "Competency Class" that would be part of a teacher's load and that, during every study hall, a teacher would be available to work with students on a "pull-out" basis. To make that teacher available, an aide would be hired for study hall supervision. The principal thought that it was a "super idea" and took it to the board because it had budget implications. It was approved for the next year. The principal also had to manipulate the schedule to accommodate the innovation.
- Part of the assignment for a new Home Economics teacher was a course in "Child Development." Within a year, she found the content unexciting. "I couldn't stand the material any longer." Students did not find it interesting either, as enrollments had been declining. As she put it, "Image was a big problem. Kids think of Home Ec as all cooking and sewing." She talked with the principal about her concerns. They agreed that the course was important, particularly because there were so few opportunities in the immediate area for students to gain this formal knowledge out of school.
- He found money to support her taking a summer graduate course that would strengthen her background and perhaps lead to ideas to change the situation. The next year, she began to modify course content and methodology and gradually converted it into a laboratory.
- Students observed and worked with preschool children who came to the school for the class. Parent relationships and birth control were added as units (since this was an existing course, the board was not asked to approve this additional content). The course became one of the most popular ones in the department.

MANSFIELD

- A science teacher was assigned some mathematics courses as part of his schedule. Mathematics was not his first love, and he did not feel that he was doing his best work in that subject. So he began to think about other possibilities in science that would address student needs. He talked with his chairman and the principal about his concerns, and they decided to do a student survey regarding current and future science offerings.
- The result was an experiment with a new forestry course for students who wanted to learn about managing a woodlot for home maintenance purposes (the school was in a rural area where knowledge about forest management for lay or career purposes was important) or for students in the vocation-oriented curriculum who might seek employment in a forestry-related field. A considerable amount of mathematics and engineering material was included in the content.
- The course became one of the most popular courses in the school curriculum. In addition, a very successful outcome was the construction by students of a sugar house in the woods near the school. Students produced and sold maple syrup, with profits going to the school for other projects.
- An industrial arts teacher observed the unmet needs of a small number of high-achieving students, too few—for budget reasons—at each grade level for the school to offer them a course. He could see that failure to respond to these students might adversely affect future enrollments in his elective program.
- He proposed to the principal an independent study option as the solution, one that would also compliment the school's goal of doing more for gifted and talented youngsters. To implement it, he would not supervise study halls, and his extra assignments would be minimized. The proposal was accepted by the principal, and the innovation has been an important part of the industrial arts program.
- The principal, who met regularly with the business education department, reminded the staff that there were state and federal vocational education grants available for the purchase of equipment and materials. In his words, "Budgets are a planning tool. They force people to think about what they're doing. They should have a maintenance and a change function."
- After one of these discussions, a teacher, influenced by some articles and her work on a state curriculum guide committee, realized that this might be a time to modernize the department's office equipment and also provide more simulation experiences for students. These ideas coincided with a grant proposal deadline. The application was approved and resulted in the acquisition of a word processing unit and a model office occupations' room.

OBSERVATIONS ABOUT SMALL-SCALE INNOVATION

As you can see, the garbage can decision process was guided primarily by small-scale innovation, not the traditional rational problem solving decision approach. However, the teachers and administrators at Bromley and Mansfield were not irrational in their behavior. Their actions were intentional, but intentionality was not attached to explicit organizational goals, as we saw in the previous chapter.

Egan, who studied change agent behavior in the helping professions, calls this "arational" behavior—behavior affected by emotions, intuition, and ambiguous and unpredictable workplace phenomena (1985, pp. 260–276). These phenomena make it very difficult to decide always on the basis of pure reason (an explanation for why people operating mainly from a "theory of change" rather than "theory of changing" often are less than successful).

The phenomena also verified Guskey's observations, based on an analysis of change and staff development literature, that often significant change in teacher beliefs and attitudes takes place *after* (emphasis in the original) testing out a new practice. The conventional view is that change in behavior typically occurs after changes in beliefs and attitudes (1985). Fullan observes, "Nothing is more gratifying psychologically than attempting a change that works and benefits students. Success can beget more success" (2007, p. 93). This is the sense of efficacy and empowerment discussed in chapter 4.

Schools, as we saw in chapter 3, are laden with special characteristics that cause marketplace-driven behavior to be a potent spur for small-scale change. According to March and Olsen:

> Measured against a conventional normative model of rational choice, the garbage can process does seem pathological, but such standards are not really appropriate since the process occurs precisely when the preconditions of more 'rational' models are not met (1979, p. 38).

At the same time, these characteristics are additional reasons why it is so difficult to "restructure" schools, while, at the same time, so relatively easy under the right conditions to effect important improvements through small-scale innovations. Weick, who has extensively studied the processes of change in loosely coupled systems, concludes that change in such systems is continuous, small-scale, improvisational, accommodative, and local (in Goodman, et al., 1982, p. 390). These dynamics were evident at Bromley and Mansfield.

As we saw in chapter 3, a major force maintaining the basic regularities of schooling is the inherent instability of the classroom that centers on a clientele that would rather be somewhere else. However, this fact can also be the cause of innovation because good teachers continually modify what they do to keep attention and control and promote learning. Realizing that such adaptive behavior is vital to success, teachers work to add to their stock of "recipes" for their "busy kitchens" so they will be armed to meet a variety of unpredictable situations. At Bromley and Mansfield, the adopted or developed innovations were teacher-driven vehicles for school improvement.

"Since schools have to take and provide something for everyone, they are constantly casting about for ways to interest their students" (Cusick, 1983, p. 75). Information was the key factor in the success of teachers stockpiling tentative solutions to the problems they faced or anticipated facing. Information is instrumental to solution generation.

As we have seen, long-recognized acts of reading professional literature, having discussions with peers, and attending college courses topped the list of ways in which the Bromley and Mansfield staffs garnered ideas for change. Joyce and Calhoun concluded—from their five case studies of districts undergoing system-wide change—that connecting educators to the professional knowledge base " . . . can expand the possibilities for effective action" (1996, p. 187).

The teachers in these schools were similar to the "idea-champions" studied by Daft and Becker: those individuals who effect real change. In such cases, their willingness to believe in an idea, to expend effort on implementation, to persist in carrying it over the inevitable rough spots, and to enlist support and help of someone else were critical dimensions of successful innovation (1978, pp. 210–211).

However, why do innovations sometimes fail to "stick around"? Fullan contends that those trying to get others to change too often ignore what a particular innovation means to those who actually would do the changing. How people experience change is their phenomenology, their subjective reality (2007, p. 8). The teachers at Bromley and Mansfield had worked out their phenomenology for change through the steps they used in initiating small-scale innovations.

They paid attention to their environments and responded with innovations that fit their organizational territory. The principals, because they were knowledgeable about that territory and their teachers as individuals, did not force innovations on them that were alien to that phenomenology.

As has been pointed out, the organizational climates of Bromley and Mansfield played a key role in the generation of the innovations discussed. The principals were pivotal to the creation and sustaining of that climate. They initiated and managed events, rather than merely reacting to them.

However, because so many innovations were initiated by teachers, at first glance, these administrators appeared to be more managers and reactors. Here it is appropriate to mention again that the most evident initiating behavior was connected to the "bundles" of innovations within a department. Often, the principals "got the ball rolling," but then left the main responsibility to the staffs to mobilize for and implement a change. Also, the initiating actions were often of the "incident" type, invisible to most observers.

Both men realized that ". . . much of the job of an administrator involves making the bureaucracy work" (March 1983, p. 22). By making the schools work, they provided teachers an additional slice of time to initiate change and created and sustained a climate conducive to such action. The staffs did not have to be involved in the student control and building maintenance activities that they did not see as part of their role.

All organizations compete for the attention and time of their employees, and schools—being organized anarchies as well as bureaucracies—have a particularly difficult task in this regard. Many internal and external forces want a nibble or a chunk of an already lean helping of attention and time. Good schools find ways to husband these resources more for improvement rather than for maintenance of the status quo.

Before concluding, a word about what "ideally" the principals could have done to take more advantage of the marketplace dynamics. For example, they could have initiated or "created" (Christensen, 1979, pp. 373–377) more CO to deliberately try to alter teacher thinking about "what is and what could be" (e.g., using an in-service day to examine societal trends and their possible impact on programs).

And they could have given leadership to implementing innovations that would have had more organizational-level impact (the only larger-scale innovations that had been adopted or developed in each school within the five-year period of the study were imposed from outside). But their "principal plates" were jam-packed with demands so they chose to focus on other needs.

We now see more clearly the dynamics of small-scale innovation within the organized anarchy and busy kitchen features of good schools, particularly as the dynamics relate to the mobilization phase of change. In chapter 6, we will examine additional findings from Bromley and Mansfield that emerge when we look closely at the implementation and institutionalization phases. There we will discover that interaction and recursiveness permeate all phases.

Chapter 6

Magnifying the Innovation Map

Sustainability of educational improvement, in its fullest sense, is unlikely to occur without a theory and a strategy that is more historically and politically informed.

—Hargreaves and Goodson, 2006, p. 35

Change will be most successful when its support is geared to the diagnosed needs of the individual users. If change is highly personal, then clearly different responses and interventions will be required for different individuals. Paying attention to each individual's progress can enhance the improvement process.

—Hord et al., 1987, p. 6

In this chapter, we will look "up close" at two policy innovations and some voluntary ones, placing them under a symbolic magnifying glass. We want to gain additional understanding about the details of change, particularly the way individuals experience the process during the phases of implementation and institutionalization. Chapters 4 and 5 provided insights into factors involved in mobilization or initiation.

We will magnify the details by using the "Levels of Use" and "Stages of Concern" components of the Concerns-Based Adoption Model. After completing this chapter, we will be better equipped to develop our "theory of changing" because the chapter contains additional concepts, technical information, knowledge of human relations, and knowledge of the social psychology of the workplace that, as described in the Introduction, are the components of such a theory. They all can be joined with material contained in the Marketplace Model.

IMPLEMENTATION

The literature we reviewed in chapter 2 revealed that, since the 1970s, implementation has been studied more extensively than either mobilization or institutionalization. Adoption and development were the focus of research in the 1960s and were discussed in chapter 2, as were the concepts of adoption, fidelity, development, mutual adaptation, and iterative refraction. More current studies, as seen in that chapter, have attempted to extract the factors involved in change. And others have focused on the process itself.

A quick review of concepts is in order here. Adoption is a sensible avenue to improvement because it shortcuts development time, utilizing an innovation that has been "debugged" to some degree elsewhere, hence reducing time and financial costs. Fidelity is the degree to which the use of an adopted innovation stays "true" or "faithful" to the original design. Local development of a curricular or instructional innovation usually takes time and money to ensure its effectiveness.

But if adoption is the choice, then because situations or contexts differ in terms of the organizational characteristics outlined in chapter 3 and numerous "intervening variables" depicted in chapter 4, many of these innovations have to be adapted, before or after implementation, to fit the local setting. And then, as time goes on, iterative refraction occurs, the ongoing adjustments necessary to maintain effectiveness.

However, excessive adaptation or neglect of a vital component of an innovation may lessen its intended impact. Excessive adaptation may lead implementers to believe that they are really using a new practice and have changed how they do things when, in fact, they have not changed in the way intended by the innovation. This is the "false clarity" described by Fullan (2007, p. 89).

For example, some schools have adopted mastery learning but have not supported the creation of correctives or enrichment activities that are integral to its integrity. Others have adopted cooperative learning without the staff development to train teachers in the essentials of its "technology"—creating positive interdependence, individual accountability/personal responsibility, interpersonal and small-group skills, and group processing. Others have adopted alternative assessments without training teachers in identifying new learning outcomes, selecting and developing tasks, developing assessment criteria and rubrics, and scoring for reliability and validity.

What then happens to an innovation after it moves from the mobilization phase into implementation? Will it be used as intended by the adopters or developers? How do "users" react to the innovation, and how do those reactions affect its implementation? What factors help make an innovation a "permanent" part of organizational routines? What causes such dramatic modification of an innovation that it is difficult to recognize it in its original form? What causes it to disappear?

To answer these questions, let us examine two policy innovations and several voluntary ones, placing them under that symbolic magnifying glass so that we can gain additional understanding about the details of change, particularly the way individuals experience the process during the phases of implementation and institutionalization.

THE CONCERNS-BASED ADOPTION MODEL

I chose to examine change relating to larger-scale processes at Bromley and Mansfield through the Concerns-Based Adoption Model (CBAM) instrumentation. This model (Figure 6.1) emerged from extensive research conducted on innovation in public schools and colleges (Hall & Hord, 1987; Hord, et al., 1987). The CBAM instrumentation allows the researcher to probe into change phenomena through questionnaires and interviews rather than relying on observation.

In the model, the *Resource System* represents the people, materials, money, and other resources available to the change activity. The *Change Facilitator* is the person(s) responsible for giving leadership to the change effort. In schools, this person may be the principal, a teacher, or department head. *Stages of Concern* represent the affective side of change—the feelings, atti-

Figure 6.1. IMPLEMENTATION

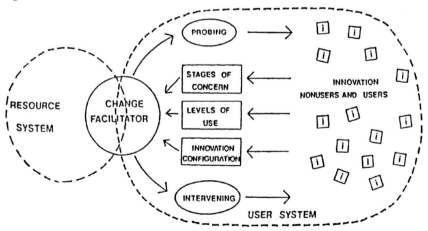

Source: The Concerns-Based Adoption Model. (Hord, et al. 1987, p. 10. Copyright, Southeast Educational Laboratory, 1987. Reprinted by permission.)

tudes, and perceptions of the implementer and sometimes others involved with the innovation.

Levels of Use represent the actual behaviors of the implementer. *Configurations* represent the forms that an innovation takes as it is used. *Interventions* represent the actions of the facilitator that influence the individual's use of the innovation.

Underlying the model are several assumptions:

1. Change is a process, not an event.
2. Change is accomplished by individuals.
3. Change is a highly personal experience.
4. Change involves developmental growth.
5. Change is best understood in operational terms (what it will mean to the user; how practice will be affected).
6. Change facilitators should focus on individuals, the innovation, and the context (Hord, et al., 1987, pp. 5–7).

Drawing on this model, we will examine the Levels of Use and Stages of Concern at Bromley and Mansfield as they apply to two policy innovations that were the only large-scale innovations found in the schools. We will also examine some voluntary innovations.

The first policy innovation was the Vermont Basic Competency Regulations, mandated in 1977 by the State Board of Education. (This policy was phased out as a regulation in 1991; the state determined that the competencies had now been infused into the regular curriculum.) These competency regulations, the first ever at the state level, initiated the accountability squeeze that is still evolving, required schools to test all students in the areas of reading, writing, speaking, listening, mathematics, and reasoning.

Beginning with the class of 1981, the successful mastery of competencies in these areas became a prerequisite for graduation. *How* to develop a plan to locally address this regulation and then implement it was left to the local district and/or school. Today, a similar task for schools relates to testing programs relative to NCLB and to those of individual states such as the Massachusetts Comprehensive Assessment System.

The second policy innovation was the staffings (now TEAM) procedure required by the then Public Law 94–142, the Education for All Handicapped Children Act (now the IDEA) that became federal law in 1975. Under this procedure, each school had to hold periodic meetings of teams (composed, at minimum, of the special education teacher in the school or district, the teacher of the child with a handicap, often a parent, and one other staff member, usually a counselor or administrator) to assess the needs of children who appear eligible for special education services, and to recommend appropriate assistance.

Eligibility resulted in the writing of an Individualized Educational Program (IEP). As with the Competencies, it was the school's responsibility to design its method of implementation. Today, schools still have autonomy to establish their processes for responding to IDEA requirements.

Both the competencies and the staffings were broadly defined rather than specifically delineated. Neither of them met the four criteria that are associated with successful implementation: (1) the degree to which users see it as needed; (2) the clarity of the goals of the innovation and the means to implement it; (3) its complexity or the degree to which it is difficult to implement; and (4) the degree to which it is perceived to be of quality and practicality (Fullan, 2007, pp. 87–92). In other words, practitioners were given no "template" for either innovation that would help them with implementation, so there was considerable need to develop a workable *process* for each.

As seen from the literature reviewed in chapter 2, it is the norm rather than the exception for mandated innovations to be lacking in all or some of these criteria when schools then have to implement them.

The principals assumed an active role in assisting their staffs to implement these policies, but, as we shall see, each approached the task differently.

LEVELS OF USE

Levels of Use (LoU) is explored through an interview—a validated, focused methodology that enables a researcher to assess the behavior of individuals implementing an innovation (Loucks, Newlove, & Hall, 1975). Table 6.1 outlines these behaviors.

In the two schools, twenty nine interviews were conducted at Bromley and twenty four at Mansfield, each for an average of fifty minutes. The purpose was to examine how teachers used the voluntary innovations (i.e., courses, units, themes, etc.) and the Competencies. No teacher declined to be in the LoU population. (Staffings for special needs students were not included in this research because they are not a classroom-type innovation but rather a school-wide process and practice.)

OBSERVATIONS FROM THE LOU INTERVIEWS

The voluntary innovations had been in use for an average of two years, and the process to test for the competencies had been worked on for three years. So it is interesting to note:

Table 6.1. Levels of Use of the Innovation: Typical Behaviors

Levels of Use	Behavioral Indices of Level
0 NONUSE	No action is being taken with respect to the innovation.
I ORIENTATION	The user is seeking out information about the innovation.
II PREPARATION	The user is preparing to use the innovation.
III MECHANICAL USE	The user is using the innovation in a poorly coordinated manner and is making user-oriented changes.
IVA ROUTINE	The user is making few or no changes and has an established pattern of use.
IVB REFINEMENT	The user is making changes to increase outcomes.
V INTEGRATION	The user is making deliberate efforts to coordinate with others in using the innovation.
VI RENEWAL	The user is seeking more effective alternatives to the established use of the innovation.

Source: Hord, et al., p. 55. Copyright, Southwest Educational Development Laboratory, 1987. Used by permission.

- With one exception, all teachers involved with the mandated innovation were at the IVA routine level. The one exception was at the LoU III mechanical level.
- On the other hand, eighteen users of voluntary innovations were at Level IVB, refinement, six at Bromley and twelve at Mansfield.

At the IVB level, the users try to increase the impact of the change on the client. They are not satisfied, and they aim for improvement.

Teachers at the refinement level revealed that their innovation was having a considerable positive effect on student learning and attitudes and that it had potential to have even more of an effect. Therefore, it was well worth their time and effort to refine it. Those staff members felt the sense of efficacy (discussed in chapter 4) that research tells us is an important factor in successful implementation. The mandated innovations did not foster a similar reaction.

Being able to refine an innovation can be an important source of satisfaction and even revitalization to a teacher operating in a "busy kitchen" where psychic rewards are so important to motivation. Empowerment is being generated. Staff at the refinement LoU are also at a readiness level in terms of ability and willingness to change (Hersey, Blanchard, & Johnson 2001, pp. 175–197). Hence, a supervisor would have considerable opportunity to affect teacher behavior even further in the direction of school improvement tasks.

THE PRINCIPAL'S ROLE

One factor seems to explain the difference between the number of staff at the refinement level in one school compared to the other: the greater initiating and interventionist behavior of the Mansfield principal in matters relating directly to curriculum and instruction. During the research, I observed each principal in numerous situations over a five-week period. A scan of the frequency of incident interventions by them with their staffs (e.g., hallway conversations, leaving articles in mailboxes for teachers to read, and following up on requests for assistance) gave a decided edge to the Mansfield principal.

However, the difference was not only in the sheer number of small-scale interventions. The Mansfield principal operated with *policy*, *game plan*, and even *strategy*-type interventions in his repertoire (Hall & Hord, pp. 177–213).

Policies, formal and informal, set parameters within which change can occur. For example, the process of budget-building involved teachers systematically throughout the school year.

A *game plan* is where a facilitator orchestrates incident interventions into a larger scheme to achieve a goal. At Mansfield, the principal's game plan involved distributing readings about new curricula trends, staff evaluation sessions, parent and student feedback about the quality of a department's curriculum, and meetings with individual teachers and department members—all of which led to a decision to drop several elective courses and to replace them with several new courses (a "bundle of innovations").

Strategy interventions move beyond game plans into major actions that shift organizational direction. At Mansfield, calculated changes in departmental offerings over a period of years altered the complexion of that component of the school's program.

The Mansfield principal's favorite analogy for his role was that of an orchestra leader, describing it this way:

> The principal is the key to where the school is going. He is an orchestra leader, keeping the sections of the orchestra in balance. But he doesn't have to play

every instrument. And it's crucial for him to remember that a fifth grade orchestra is very different from a high school one.

This behavior is similar to the directive, task-focused behavior that Hersey, Blanchard, and Johnson (2001) and Glickman, Gordon, and Ross-Gordon (1995) emphasize as important for administrators to exhibit, along with a range of other behaviors. This kind of behavior tells staff that what they are doing is important, that the administrator is interested in the activity and is willing to put energy into supporting and helping staff so it will succeed, and that small wins are vital to organizational improvement.

As Hall and Hord assert (1987, p. 102), individuals at the LoU IVB refinement level make adaptations aimed at increasing the chances that the innovation will have positive outcomes. Sometimes, the assistance of a facilitator can help someone move further along the LoU continuum. At Bromley and Mansfield, the principals assumed this role most of the time because department chairs had heavy teaching loads along with the administrative part of their roles.

By all indications, the Mansfield principal, on matters relating to daily curriculum and instruction, had developed an effective "theory of changing." The Bromley principal had not.

STAGES OF CONCERN (FROM INTERVIEWS)

At the conclusion of the LoU interviews, teachers were asked an open-ended question about the concerns they had about the use of the innovation. "When you think about _____, what are you concerned about?" Stages of Concern (SoC) are depicted in Table 6.2.

OBSERVATIONS FROM THE SOC INTERVIEWS

The relatively veteran faculties (average experience at Bromley, eleven years; average at Mansfield, ten) did not have concerns about the innovations per se, but some had intense feelings about the management of the change—handling time, securing materials, and the like.

Some Stage 3 concerns were:

• A teacher responsible for implementing Basic Competencies said, "All I seem to do is file stuff."

Table 6.2. Stages of Concern: Typical Expressions of Concern about the Innovation

	Stages of Concern	Expressions of Concern
I M P A C T	6 REFOCUSING	I have some ideas about something that would work even better.
	5 COLLABORATION	I am concerned about relating what I am doing with what other instructors are doing.
	4 CONSEQUENCE	How is my use affecting kids?
T A S K	3 MANAGEMENT	I seem to be spending all my time getting material ready.
S E L F	2 PERSONAL	How will using it affect me?
	1 INFORMATIONAL	I would like to know more about it.
	0 AWARENESS	I am not concerned about it (the innovation).

Source: Hord, et al., p. 31. Copyright, Southwest Educational Development Laboratory, 1987. Used by permission.

- A social studies teacher was trying to find ways to bring more guest speakers to class, to get students out on field trips to apply course content, and to manage those activities with "less hassle."

Others on the staff were concerned about the impact (Stage 4) of their work on the student. Twenty years of research on the Concerns concept suggests that, as people gain experience, knowledge, and skill in relation to an innovation, consequence concerns become more intense (Hall & Rutherford, 1990, p. 23). Such an evolution of feelings would be consistent with maturing staffs like the ones at Bromley and Mansfield.

Some Stage 4 concerns:

- A science teacher, integrating contemporary material into her course (e.g., genetic counseling, euthanasia, and holistic health) said, "Kids today need to be made aware of controversial issues."
- An industrial arts teacher, wondering how to stimulate and sustain student interest in new material, observed that, "Their interest controls the whole thing. The more they're into it, the better it works for me."

Given the individualistic, single-classroom pattern of instruction in schools, it is not surprising to see only one teacher at Stage 5, collaboration, and none at the refocusing level. This pattern was reinforced by the fact that neither Bromley nor Mansfield had staff development programs aimed at bringing teachers together in any consistent way to work on matters of curriculum and instruction or to create innovations that would require staff interaction for implementation.

THE PRINCIPAL'S ROLE

Just as it appears that principal behavior had an impact on teachers' LoU of the innovation, the same appears to be the case for the concerns expressed by many teachers. Because the Bromley principal was not as much of an interventionist as the Mansfield principal, Bromley staff had to deal with more management concerns about voluntary innovations, while Mansfield teachers did not. Bromley staff did not feel that they received the help they needed. On a day-to-day basis, the Mansfield principal was more skilled at using the "one-legged conference"—any opportunity that presents itself—to check on teacher concerns.

Hall and Hord allege, "Principals do not take advantage of these one- to two-minute conferences to monitor or facilitate change. All too often they become forgotten moments of informal exchanges of pleasantries" (1987, p. 63). Again, CBAM research demonstrates that, when those who intervene target specific individual concerns, there is a greater likelihood that the person being helped will move to the next SoC (Hall & Rutherford. 1990, p. 24).

The feelings, attitudes, and perceptions that surfaced through the open-ended "concerns" question show again how important it is that change facilitators understand and appreciate the subjective dimension of teaching—its phenomenology—before trying to get users to alter their current practices. In any organization, due to individual job assignments, distance grows between employees so that, over time, a lack of appreciation and understanding develops among them.

Miles, after a detailed and instructive study of twelve National Diffusion Network innovations, concluded, "It was clear in our sites that administrators and teachers lived in separate worlds" (1983, p. 19; see also Huberman & Miles, 1984).

In good schools, this separateness (among teachers, teachers and administrators, and others) is minimized. It can be decreased in various ways, such as through ongoing supervisory processes that take administrators into classrooms on a regular basis or through the "simple" practice of a principal serving periodically as a substitute teacher or even teaching a course as part of her assignment.

Of course, these actions, although helpful in this respect, in themselves, will not break down the separatist norms or lead to considerable staff collaboration. Such a change requires a long-term, concerted effort such as through the creation of a Professional Learning Community (to be discussed in chapter 7).

STAGES OF CONCERN
(FROM QUESTIONNAIRES)

As was mentioned earlier, two mandated, organization-wide policy innovations were identified at Bromley and Mansfield, the Competency Regulations and the then-IDEA staffings (now Multi-Disciplinary Teams).

In each school, the mandates were met with less than an enthusiastic response, but each principal was clear and firm that the organization had a responsibility to implement these innovations, that compliance would be in good spirit, and that implementation would be done well. As Loucks and Zacchei put it, a key factor in school improvement efforts is an administrator who says, "We're going to do this together, and we're going to get all the help we need" (1983, p. 30).

To examine concerns associated with the competencies and staffings, I drew on the SoC questionnaire, a thirty five-item, validated instrument.

In both schools, the English, mathematics, social studies, and science departments were responsible for implementing the regulations, for teaching and testing the competencies, and for keeping records. While the staffings could, in theory, affect every teacher, some teachers, due to their assignment (e.g., basic math or English versus calculus or French), had considerably more contact with lower-achieving youngsters who had difficulty passing the competencies.

Such differentiated assignments are similar to what is happening in all schools today under mandated state testing programs. The SoC instrument was administered only to those staff involved in implementation. All staff who were asked to complete the questionnaire did so.

Processing the questionnaire responses, we can view the results in a profile plotted on a grid that displays relatively "higher" and "lower" concerns. It is important to stress that higher or lower concerns are not synonymous with "good" or "bad" feelings. Instead, the scores indicate an individual's intensity of concern about an innovation at a moment in time. The higher the score, the stronger the feelings, attitudes, and perceptions. The most important aspect of the profiles is not how high or low they are on the grid, but the relative difference in the peaks and valleys.

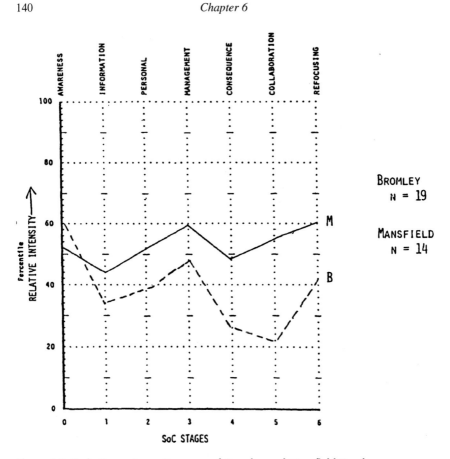

Figure 6.2. Basic Competency Concerns of Bromley and Mansfield Teachers

Also, according to Concerns theory, a difference in intensity of a least ten percentile points is an "important" difference in concerns—important in that the concerns could interfere with one's work and therefore need attention. Outcomes from the questionnaires are displayed in Figures 6.2 and 6.3.

OBSERVATIONS ABOUT THE PROFILES

The factors shown in Chart 6.1, drawn from interviews, documents, and limited observation, are offered as reasons for the differences in the SoC profiles.

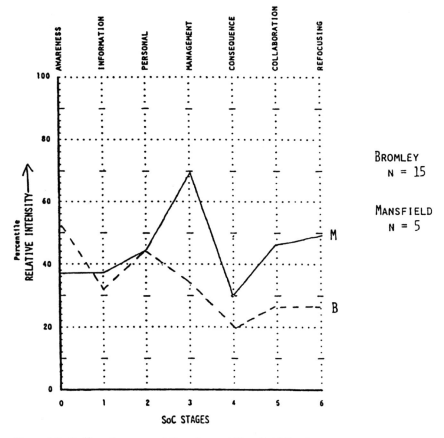

Figure 6.3. Staffing Concerns of Bromley and Mansfield Teachers

Clearly, the management of these policy innovations had an important impact on teachers. In contrast to his reactive behavior toward the voluntary innovations in his school, the Bromley principal had a "game plan" for implementing these organizational-level changes. The Mansfield principal, in contrast to his initiating behavior toward his school's voluntary innovations, did not have as strong a "game plan" to guide his management of the competencies and staffings. For dealing with these mandated innovations, the Bromley principal had developed an effective "theory of changing" whereas he had not relative to the regular pattern of small-scale change.

These outcomes are very aligned with the Huberman and Miles findings relative to National Diffusion Network and Title IV-C innovations. They found that the presence of a sound support system, plus active assistance to

---

Chart 6.1.

Basic Competencies (BCs)

Bromley (N = 19)

- A three-page, detailed set of instructions on managing the competencies was available to staff, including how to record pupil progress.
- Each department responsible for competency implementation had at least one teacher (some had two) assigned to a Competency Class in place of a regular class assignment. By using this period in combination with a regular unassigned period, a teacher was able to take youngsters out of study hall who were in need of more help with BCs. Teachers felt that they were able to contact "90 percent" of students in need of assistance.
- Competency tests were in place in all departments responsible for BCs and were being used with results recorded. The principal used these results to follow up on problem students and to identify weak spots in the BC system.

Mansfield (N = 14)

- A one-page less detailed set of instructions was available, which did not address items such as recordkeeping.
- The English and math departments had a teacher assigned to a "lab" in place of a regular class assignment. This period was used similarly to that at Bromley. Teachers felt that there were still many students who they were not able to assist.
- Tests were in place in English, math, and social studies and were being used with results recorded. The principal used these results similarly to the Bromley principal.

Bromley (N = 19)

- Each department was required to keep a BC file on each student for whom it had responsibility; the file was used in combination with a once-a-year computer printout. A typical teacher comment was, "I trust them more than the printout as I *know* they are my entries." These were kept up-to-date and monitored periodically by the principal, who also monitored the system through printout data.

Staffings*

Bromley (N = 15)

- Four pages of detailed instructions on placement procedures, staffing procedures, and staffing protocol were available to staff.
- The written material made it clear that any staff member identified as "regularly in contact" with the student was required to attend. Anyone not attending " . . . will be so noted for the record."
- Staffings were held before school, were limited strictly to thirty minutes, and were taped. People attending arrived on time and did not leave early.

Mansfield (N = 14)

- Files were kept on a voluntary basis by the English, math, and social studies departments. Computer printouts were provided quarterly. The principal monitored the system through the printouts.

Mansfield (N = 5)

- No written instructions were available to staff.
- "Required attendance" was stated verbally and in writing by the principal and the resource room teacher.
- Staffings were held after school, often started late, and often ran over the set time frame. People attending sometimes arrived late and left early.

Bromley (N = 15)

- The principal regularly chaired staffings. Of 106 staffings between January and October, he chaired 103. He once stated, "I take a trip every time we have a staffing. It is the one place where professionalism really comes through day after day."
- At least five days before a staffing, the resource room teacher notified, on paper, those people who were to attend. This notice instructed them to come prepared to discuss the strengths and weaknesses of the student and to make tentative recommendations.
- The resource room teacher was beginning to observe eligible students in regular classrooms on a systematic basis.
- The resource room teacher was starting her third year full-time on the job.

Mansfield (N = 5)

- The principal only attended when requested by the resource room teacher.
- At least five days before a staffing, the resource room teacher notified, on paper, those people who were to attend.
- There was no systematic observation of eligible students in regular classrooms.
- The resource room teacher was starting her first year full-time on the job.

---

*The difference in the Ns of teachers highly involved in staffings was due to these reasons:

1. Although PL 94–142 at that time required only one staffing every three years on an eligible student, at Bromley, they were held every year, and any teacher who had that individual in class was *required* to be present. Therefore, many teachers in grades 9–12 were involved. There were also numerous requests for staffings from teachers.
2. At Mansfield, because students were coming right from the three elementary schools into the 7th grade, the focus of early staffings was on junior high youngsters. Therefore, only those teachers were highly involved.

---

teachers by change facilitators (building and central office administrators), were prime factors in the successful implementation of the innovations.

Support (in this instance, from principals) took the form of ongoing contact between the facilitator and staffs, offers of help from the facilitator, and concrete assistance by him in the form of actions such as schedule modifications, assigning aides, obtaining resources, and offering solutions to problems (1984, pp. 88–114). This kind of leadership helped immensely in stabilizing the new programs and practices and led to their institutionalization.

Although the competencies and staffings were mandated for Bromley and Mansfield and thus would not "disappear," the differences in how they were being managed affected their organizational impact. If they had been voluntary changes, it seems very possible that those at Mansfield would have had less of a chance to survive than those at Bromley.

These conclusions about the importance of managerial acts to successful change are consistent with other conclusions, addressed in chapters 4 and 5, about the role of leadership. There are some things that only administrators can do, and, while each individual administrative act may appear insignificant in the total scheme of things, to the change agent, each is critical to success—even if it is a relatively isolated incident intervention rather than part of the game plan.

In addition to the impact of these management factors on the competencies and staffings, there were other reasons for the differences in their implementation.

First were human factors, such as the personnel available at that moment in organizational history who could assume added responsibilities. At Mansfield, a new resource room teacher was not too confident when it came to running the staffings. Therefore, the less active involvement of the principal had a real impact on teacher concerns about them. She was at a lower level of "readiness" for the assignment than was perceived by the principal. Application of the Hersey, Blanchard, and Johnson theory would have helped the principal greatly.

Second were managerial philosophies about the degree to which principals should be engaged in regular activities related to the implementation of mandated innovations. Given that these innovations did not meet the four criteria (described earlier) that Fullan identified as critical to successful implementation, it seems that the choice of philosophies should have been on the side of more active intervention.

If administrators should be involved, then in what ways? The Bromley principal chose to intervene in several specific ways on a sustained basis, which contributed to "program settledness" or stabilization (Huberman & Miles, 1984, p. 126). Considering the special organizational features of schools, in which teachers already expend considerable energy maintaining classroom control and dealing with myriad job details, creating a situation where they have to confront even more details and have their frustration levels raised—particularly regarding changes imposed on them—will have a negative impact on their attitude and motivation.

By becoming "settled," the innovations increased the sense of efficacy felt by teachers. There was a decided difference between Bromley and Mansfield teachers, with those at Bromley feeling more comfortable, confident, in control, and gratified in relation to their use of the competencies and staffings. Interestingly, these four indicators of efficacy were present in the NDN and Title IV-C sites (Huberman & Miles, 1984, p. 115).

A cogent point at this juncture is that where the change facilitator chooses to focus his or her attention and energy can have a decided impact on implementation. In turn, it may well be that such choice-making has more of an impact on the success of certain innovations than the importance of the innovation itself (in this instance, two mandates) (Hord, 1991).

Data from the LoU and SoC support Berman's contention that two activities have been found to be frequently identified with successful implementation. The first is thoughtful adaptation, which means the tailoring of an innovation (that is not highly defined) to fit the local situation.

At Bromley, according to CBAM data, adaptation was a more effective process. The second is clarification, which is how users become more clear about the nature of the innovation, its objectives, what is needed to make it work, and their role in the process (1981, pp. 271–273).

With fairly broad policy innovations like the competencies and staffings, clarification emerged as the policies were gradually implemented. Again, this seemed to happen more effectively at Bromley than at Mansfield. As mentioned at the beginning of this chapter, there are lessons here for readers involved in mobilizing for, implementing, and attempting to institutionalize current approaches to responding to state and federal testing mandates and the use of IDEA Multi-Disciplinary Teams.

INSTITUTIONALIZATION

Institutionalization, the third phase of the Rand framework, occurs when the innovation continues (i.e., when it has become a "permanent" part of the organization). The innovation becomes "routinized," and, despite the fact that the novelty has worn off, there is no flagging of enthusiasm. Lack of enthusiasm can shove a good, new change aside in favor of old practices.

Huberman and Miles state that the ultimate measure of institutionalization is when members of the organization indicate that the innovation will eventually be revised just like other programs or practices in the normal cycle of organizational events (1984, p. 209). Loucks-Horsley and Hergert, drawing on the same database of NDN studies, point out in their handbook for school improvement that, "Institutionalization does not just happen naturally. It takes planning and effort, often with the people who, up to this point, have not been part of the effort" (1985, p. 65).

We know from research that the press of everyday activities tends to cause behavior to regress to former routines and thus often undermines continuation. But it is also difficult to determine when an innovation meets the conditions of continuation because this phase is the least studied of the three and is complicated by the reality that often one phase of change seems to blend into the other (Fullan, 1991, pp. 88–90; Larson, 1988, pp. 53–54). As was discussed in chapter 4, the three change phases are interactive and recursive, not linear.

Muddying things, too, is the fact that, even if an innovation seems to have become institutionalized, it may get "shelved" permanently or temporarily, often due to the difficulty of using it or because it no longer seems to do the job it was intended to do. Voluntary innovations often gradually disappear if adopted or developed in a situation where there is little supervisory oversight, interest, or support shown to innovators who may want and need it.

Critical here is staff development assistance because change agents often require more help at this phase than they do during mobilization and implementation. Research findings are firm in this conclusion (e.g., Evans, 1996, pp. 63–66; Fullan, 2007, pp. 291–293; Huberman & Miles, 1994, pp. 255–258).

Finally, even when the organization decides formally to discontinue an innovation, some employees may still use elements of it. Books, films, software, videotapes, CDs and DVDs, methods, and print materials of various kinds may find a new home in the regular program within a teacher's workspace.

While the mandated innovations required planning and effort, as we have seen, voluntary innovations at Bromley and Mansfield—which we will look at next—demonstrated that institutionalization and discontinuation often "happen" in less than visible ways. At times, these phases of change appear to be a naturally occurring process.

Other than the ten-year self-evaluation conducted in each school in preparation for a visit by a regional accreditation team, neither organization had developed a systematic means for deciding what programs and practices it should retain.

As was discussed in chapter 4, school philosophy and goals were not conscious reference points for mobilization and implementation decisions, and neither were they for those related to institutionalization.

Rather, these kinds of decisions presented themselves at various times, imbedded in choice opportunities. Because these opportunities occurred on a "rolling basis," they are illustrative of the

> . . . complicated intermeshing of the mix of choices available at any one time, the mix of problems that have access to the organization, the mix of solutions, and the outside demands on the decision makers (March & Olsen, 1979, p. 36).

Considering the work demands on the principals and teachers, it was next to impossible for them to find the time to engage in calculated, collaborative decisions about continuing or not continuing the many small-scale innovations existing in each school. The policy innovations were mandated to continue, but, as we saw earlier, there were real differences between the schools in how continuation was managed.

DISCONTINUATION

Over the five-year period covered by this study, through the initial seventy eight exploratory interviews with administrators, counselors, special education personnel, and teachers, twenty six courses were identified as having been eliminated at Bromley and twenty three at Mansfield. Two curricular units had been dropped at Bromley. Teachers had a difficult time identifying anything else that had been dropped.

The reasons given by interviewees for eliminating a program or practice were:

- material too difficult for students
- community discontent with electives
- enrollment decline
- loss of staff
- lack of student interest
- boring material, inability to get speakers, and cost of film rentals
- students' procrastination in doing work
- community reaction to kids out in town during the day
- no time to do justice to material
- material covered in another class

OBSERVATIONS ABOUT DISCONTINUATION

Dropping an innovation may be an innovative act and another indicator of a positive organizational climate. Sometimes, it is far more difficult to jettison a program or practice than it is to adopt or develop it because, if it has been used successfully for some time and is seen as a beneficial addition, users often come to have an investment in it (a finding from the Gates project described in chapter 2).

For example, a teacher who has developed an elective course may want to retain it, but the school board may decide that new required courses demand a reduction in electives. In good schools, there is a willingness to look beyond vested interests if it appears that programs and practices no longer serve the purposes of the organization.

In a high school, dropped courses can be tracked by examining programs of study from year to year. Structural innovations usually have to be scheduled, and technological innovations can be observed. However, it is virtually impossible to track dropped units, themes, or methods and materials and software. Hence memory, which is not very reliable, becomes a key retrieval device. Considering the number of voluntary innovations identified at Bromley and Mansfield, it seems reasonable to conclude that, over five years, more things were discontinued than could be remembered in order to make room for the "add-ons."

More courses were dropped than were added. The main reason for this was the elimination of numerous English and social studies electives in each school in favor of more required courses and fewer choices. The injection of the "back-to-basics" movement that began in the mid-1970s caused a gradual phasing out of electives (Ravich, 1983, p. 255). English and social studies courses were prime targets of criticism for offering less than rigorous experiences for students. Regardless of how well received such courses were, the schools found it impossible to resist the external pressures to drop them.

Because courses are important change-bearing vehicles in secondary schools and have to be brought before the school board for approval or discontinuation, the principals played an active decision-making role in relationship to them. Some of the "drop" situations even involved "bundles" of several courses, and the board acted on them during a relatively short period of time. This dynamic is an illustration of Weick's contention that a major positive feature of loosely coupled organizations like schools is their adaptability.

> Loosely coupled systems can also adapt to small changes in an environment, especially when that environment is diverse and segmented. Departmental units that are free to vary independently may provide a more sensitive mechanism for detecting changes in the environment, and they allow the school to adapt quickly to conflicting demands (1982, p. 674).

Course "drops and adds" did not occur on a one-to-one match. In some cases, content was simply eliminated from a curriculum. In other cases, it was integrated into other courses. For example, content from an introduction to physical science course was integrated into basic chemistry, physics, and biology, and American government was absorbed partially into U.S. History. Such processes enabled many such decisions to be made with minimal disruption to the rest of the school. They show that adaptability works in many subtle ways.

The myriad of reasons for discontinuing something that once was an innovation illustrate that a rational planning process was not the prevalent path to that decision. Many of the factors involved in discontinuation were similar to those causing weak implementation, as seen in the chapter 2 literature review. This outcome is in line with Fullan's review of other studies (2007, p. 101).

The findings about phenomena of implementation and institutionalization and findings relative to mobilization demonstrate that change is very much a process and not an event; that there is not *one* change process; that they are accomplished primarily by individuals; that they are highly personal experiences; that they entail developmental growth; that they are best understood in operational terms; that the focus of change facilitation should be on individuals, innovations, and the context; and that leadership plays a central role throughout all phases and processes of change.

The findings also demonstrate that factors associated with most innovative activities, especially those of a larger scale, are numerous and sometimes nearly overwhelming. Without doubt, the dynamics illustrate the "detailed and snarled" nature of the processes (Fullan, 2007, p. 67). Therefore, an effective "theory of changing" and not "change" will have enough breadth to apply to a variety of change situations despite their contextual differences. In the next chapter, we will see how other approaches to school improvement require such a perspective to ensure success.

Chapter 7

The Potential of Small Wins and Related Strategies

A small win is a concrete, complete, implemented outcome of moderate importance. By itself, one small win may seem unimportant. A series of small wins at small but significant tasks, however, reveals a pattern that may attract allies, deter opponents, and lower resistance to subsequent proposals. Small wins are controllable opportunities that produce visible results.

—Weick, 1984, p. 43

In *reinforcing processes*, such as the Pygmalion effect, a small change builds on itself. Whatever movement occurs is amplified, producing more movement in the same direction. A small action snowballs, with more and more and still more of the same, resembling compounding interest.

—Senge, 2006, p. 80

We have seen the cultural factors that help to nurture small-scale innovation. We have also considered the factors at the heart of larger-scale innovation, based on a review of relevant literature and application of the Concerns-Based Adoption Model to real-world change situations. Building on this foundation we have developed or refined a working theory of changing from an "inside out" perspective, fused with organized anarchy and busy kitchen features. This theory of changing contrasts considerably with the more familiar rationalistic perspective.

Most of what we have learned has grown out of our focus on the high school. But this learning also has very strong application to elementary and middle schools in urban, suburban, or rural settings, a fact that became clear to me over two decades of experience using the ideas with graduate students in a variety of work settings plus similar settings as a consultant.

SMALL WINS

What we have discussed lines up well with Cuban's first-order type of change, which was discussed in chapter 1. As Weick points out, isolated small wins in themselves will not lead to fundamental, second-order alterations in goals, structures, roles, curriculum, or instruction. Fullan also says that "simple changes" may not make much of a difference, but that, while larger, more complex ones can accomplish a great deal, failure has greater impact (2007. p. 91).

But as we have seen in chapters 1 and 2, large, complex, top-down reforms have failed or fallen far short of their goals despite the political muscle often behind them. This conclusion is supported by the cited research of educational historians such as Ravitch and Tyack and Cuban. Marzano's analysis of thirty five years of school improvement literature led him to conclude that, in this new era of reform, change will need to be on an incremental basis (2003, p. 159); he came to this conclusion before the onset of the current Great Recession.

However, the historic tug-of-war between advocates of sweeping, radical, total-system reform, or something more moderate such as the Model Schools Project and those supporting the incremental, evolutionary approach continues.

Nonetheless, the thousands of schools (like Bromley and Mansfield) that possess the capability to be adaptable and to renew themselves can become far more effective and perhaps lay a foundation for second-order change by using a strategy of small wins, a strategy consistent with Senge's contentions. He makes clear in his best-selling book, based on research in corporations, that small changes can provide the "leverage" to push the system in the right direction, but such changes are often the "least obvious" (p. 64).

But, at Bromley and Mansfield, many small wins, as important as they were to the innovators, were less obvious to most staff. But the "wins" have to be engaged in by more than a handful of employees to achieve the "deep" change described by Fullan, "When personal purpose is present in numbers, it provides the power for deeper change" (1993, p. 14).

At the risk of overdrawing comparisons between the private sector and education, these observations fit well with the notion of "continuous improvement" that is central to W. Edwards Deming's writings about how to create more effective organizations (popularly labeled TQM or Total Quality Management). In one of Walton's books about Deming, his theory of management, and his methods, she states, "Great gains can be made through a continuous process of improvement in the design and performance of already-existing products, even ones that seem to be in trouble (1986, p. 57).

Peters and Waterman call this dynamic a "bias for action," the willingness of the excellent companies they studied to try things out, to experiment (1982, pp. 119–155). Hersey, Blanchard, and Johnson, in the eighth edition of their influential text on leadership, also contend that continuous or incremental change is of a first-order nature and central to the organizational life cycle. However, it may or may not provide a foundation or stimulus for second-order change (2001, pp. 387–389).

Kouzes and Posner, based on their extensive research in private, public sector, and nonprofit organizations, find that real progress comes about through an incremental approach. Small wins allow people to act with relative immediacy, to be invested in the process, to feel success, and to gain confidence in their ability to effect change. Hence, employees are likely to become more committed to long-term improvement goals and concomitant learning (2007, pp. 188–203).

Rauch conducted an in-depth study of federal government reforms from the Truman through the Clinton years. He found that more and more is being expected of Washington, but that less and less gets accomplished due to the power of outside special interests (he does not use the term pejoratively), the power of internal programs that resist change and become "entitlements" in themselves, the growth of more programs developed to "go around" the bureaucracy, and the consequent insidious increase in bureaucracy resulting in more anger and disenchantment with the federal government (witness the current "Tea Party" movement).

He concluded that large-scale, comprehensive change is increasingly difficult to accomplish (witness the recent struggle to enact a national health care program). Instead, Rauch sees "radical incrementalism," or evolutionary change, as the realistic route to improvement. "But incremental change on a steady course can be surprisingly powerful" (1999, p. 267). Clearly, we need to readjust our vision in order to see what is actually feasible (p. 277). That is a major contention of this book.

Systemic impediments of a different kind, as have been described in chapters 1, 2, and 3, also inhibit larger-scale change in public schools, particularly at the high school level. Educators wrestle with what can be attained in terms of improvements that will bring about a boost in student achievement within a context of societal and educational uncertainty and turbulence.

In a persuasive small volume with a psychological bent on "the power of small," Thaler and Koval say:

> Small, seemingly insignificant acts are powerful agents of change—if we pay attention to them. Unfortunately, we live in a world where we are constantly told to concentrate on the big things, to not sweat the small stuff. Because of that, we often feel that incremental change doesn't count for much or doesn't pay off (2009, p. 3).

Adaptability, as has been stressed throughout these pages, is the ability to take on newer and more appropriate educational practices. It is an environment for improvement, when needed, within essential stable parameters. Small wins are central to the process where effecting larger-scale change is most difficult. Small wins can have real payoff.

These conclusions from the private and government sectors parallel Conley's conception of "incremental restructuring," derived from an exhaustive analysis of some 600 sources relating to school restructuring (1997, p. 113). It parallels the conclusion of historians of public education such as Ravitch who, after an extensive analysis of school improvement efforts, 1945–1980, concluded that "piecemeal," incremental change may be the more sensible route to changing schools because of the decentralized nature and particular organizational features of schools (1983, p. 261). And, as we saw in the Introduction, Tyack and Cuban concurred after their analysis of a century of school reform.

But will that approach satisfy the reformers and business and political critics who are calling for dramatic reform and restructured organizations? Most likely, it will not, given their history. Sarason (1990) is an outright pessimist about the probability for success of externally driven reforms that the reformers and critics endorse and/or demand. He contends that, until we confront the deep-rooted social, institutional, and organizational obstacles prevalent in schools, most reforms will fail. That is the contention of this book. Many of these obstacles are connected to the nature of the school as an organization depicted in chapter 3.

For him, power relationships between teachers and students, teachers and administrators, and schools and parents are a key to reform. Yet altering them in fundamental ways is extremely difficult, making schools "intractable" to startling innovations. In his 1996 revision of *The Culture of the School and the Problem of Change* (1970), Sarason admits to underestimating how issues of power permeate all relationships within that culture and that "the problem of change is the problem of power" (1996, p. 335). Today, the press of accountability, represented by NCLB and other state statutes, has injected power more sharply than ever into the school's power field.

> Schools are political institutions in that their organization reflects conceptions of power, how it can be obtained, who should have it, what can be done with it, and what one should do when the possession of power is challenged (1996, p. 292).

Sarason additionally points out that power issues are rarely discussed in the change/innovation/school improvement literature. I agree based on my review of that literature for chapter 2. Yet they lurk in the wings as a formidable obstacle to change.

I also agree with him, to some extent, about externally driven reforms and "failure." In the current case of standards and assessment, factors are at work from the "top" via mandates and from the "bottom"—via media, parent, and community pressure—that will probably ensure that these practices (in most instances) will not "fail." Their effectiveness for students is another matter.

And the current economic situation and increased polarization and heated rhetoric between wings of the political parties exacerbate and complicate the power field, making it more difficult to have considered discussions about keeping or dropping hierarchically imposed innovations. Witness the difficulty of current attempts to revise the Elementary and Secondary Education Act.

SITE-MANAGED SCHOOLS

The potential of small wins needs to be joined to the potential of the site-managed school because the local school has historically been the focus of improvement efforts, even as it is today with the expectations placed on it by NCLB and various state statutes.

Unlike past broad, diffuse goals of "back to the basics," "humanize education," "equity," or "excellence," the strategy of site-managed schools is very specific: change local organizational structure and governance. Hence, the strategy is quite compatible with "inside out" change through small wins. The Coalition of Essential Schools approach depends upon site management, as do the projects described in chapter 2.

In the mid-1980s, site-managed schools emerged more formally as a key means to stimulate local educational improvement. The building principal would manage the school building, not the relatively remote central office that would be less in touch with what was needed to facilitate change in local education. A major boost to the strategy came from President George H.W. Bush who, in *America 2000: An Education Strategy,* advocated that there should be a decentralization of authority and decision-making to the local site, with schools being held accountable for attaining their goals—"The school as the site of reform" (U.S. Department of Education, 1991, p. 15).

He also said that there should be ". . . real consequences for persistent failure" (p. 42), but these were not named. "Hard" measures of accountability through the coercive and legitimate power of the federal government (e.g., the standards and testing associated with NCLB) were skirted in favor of the "soft" touch.

Some schools adopted formal programs called "School-Based Management" (SBM), but most developed their own because they needed to invest considerable work in order to sort out issues relative to power, authority, decision-making, goals, objectives, and accountability (Ogawa and White, 1994, p. 53). There was no *fidelity* to implementing most site-managed approaches. Indeed, *adaptation* was critical to ensure success.

But, as we have seen, many schools around the country, such as Bromley and Mansfield, have operated for decades under considerable local autonomy delegated by central offices. Not all schools have been puppets on the strings of a central office (as is implied by many critics) and thus have not needed the pressure of large-scale system redesign to improve. While these districts have not labeled their approach SBM, they have acted just that way, particularly in the essential areas of budgeting, curriculum, and staffing.

Absent from SBM processes until the 1990s, formal parental involvement now has a role in school governance through mechanisms like school-site councils, and those councils are often mandated by states (such as in Massachusetts). Parent involvement in schools is on the rise, but it is a challenging process to bring it about effectively. At the core of it is again the issue of *power.* Inviting busy parents to participate in school governance can present them with a formidable challenge, and their participation leads straight to power-sharing questions, a topic beyond the scope of this chapter.

Research is slim as to how formal SBM programs have led to change in curriculum and instruction. It has been assumed that improvements in these areas would be primary outcomes of such programs, but actual impact has been inconclusive. In preparing this section of the chapter, I conducted an Internet search on the topic. It, too, was inconclusive with the best, most recent summary, published by the North Central Regional Educational Laboratory (2000).

In the fourth edition of his foundational work on change, Fullan (2007), although focusing on the school, does not mention the term "site-based management." He devotes a chapter to parents and the community that largely supports the value to children of parent involvement in their education (pp. 188–205).

More site-management responsibilities will add to the already hectic work pace that exists in the organized anarchy and busy kitchen environments of schools. With such responsibility comes increased demand on the time of school personnel. Time becomes an issue because today's norms call for participatory decision-making through committees and councils of all kinds, involving varying configurations of school personnel, parents, and other relevant groups. That process demands many extra hours from personal schedules, more than most educators can hope to find in the press of day-to-day operations.

Union contracts present a significant impediment to finding more time because contracts specify what extra hours teachers can be assigned to spend beyond the classroom without extra pay. A recent outcome of union resistance to extra time for school reform work without additional compensation was the firing of the administrators, teachers, and staff at Central Falls (R.I.) high school in March 2010. Central Falls is a highly impacted city in terms of poverty, unemployment, literacy levels, and a high dropout rate.

The State of Rhode Island concluded that the school, one of six "worst-performing schools," needed to be radically reorganized (the state had assumed responsibility for the school in 1991). The event got national news coverage.

Teachers had rejected proposals to work ninety extra minutes a week and two extra weeks in the summer (some of it for pay) for specific training and twenty five minutes more instructional time per day (MacQuarrie, 2010a, pp. A1; A10). In mid-May, a new union contract was approved by the teachers with them accepting most all of the state's demands in exchange for retracting the firings. Hardball was the name of the game. Now the staff begins the work to "turn around" the school (MacQuarrie, 2010b, pp. B1; B6).

Dufour, et al., developers of the increasingly popular strategy of Professional Learning Communities (PLC), describe the challenges of working with and around the union contract at Adlai Stevenson High School in order to implement new approaches to student intervention, reduce remediation efforts, reduce the dropout rate, and increase student learning and achievement. Essential to those goals were the creation of a student advisory system, tutoring centers, guided study, and a mentor program, the roots of which can be traced to the Model Schools Project.

The long-tenured principal expended considerable effort to collaborate with teachers so that they could solve logistical problems. The solutions helped the school to meet with success through a series of "small wins" (2004, pp. 67–91). The entire effort illustrates that making this kind of headway to improve a high school demands real commitment from administrators and staff—accompanied by energy, persistence, and a focus on educational goals.

This lack of regular, significant collaborative time for focusing activities or programs that might eventually boost student learning exerts an enormous drag when it comes to effecting change beyond the classroom level. Most schools face formidable obstacles when they try to either extend the school year to include more in-service days (in this case, contractual), to gain more instructional time, or to take more time from the regular schedule for such purposes (working parents complain about child-sitting problems and that teachers have less time with students).

Since 2006, Massachusetts has had a program of grants to support extending the school day or the school year or both. By the spring of 2010, twenty two schools (with 11,000 students) were experimenting with extra time within the "new" normal day for instructional time along with staff planning hours. No schools chose to extend the year. Most are in urban districts. The typical day has been extended from six to eight hours with $1,300 per student allocated by the state to pay for staff time and other expenses.

An evaluation conducted for the three years indicated that, overall, learning in the Extended Learning Time schools was not "substantially different" from those of control group schools (MA DESE, March 2010). But funding limitations prevented the program from being offered for 2010. So once again, budget limitations place a restraint on finding whether or not a promising policy might make a difference, over time, to student learning outcomes. Central to those outcomes would be more staff time for planning the design and delivery of curriculum and instruction and the assessment of learning results.

But not everyone agrees that just adding more time to the day or year provides the most desirable option to improving student learning. Cuban, in an incisive analysis of the history of the use of time in schools, says that it is often the "recipe trotted out" by policymakers and business elites to supposedly boost student achievement, although the research is thin at best in making that connection. It is much more difficult to grapple with the real variables affecting learning such as adequate classroom resources, teacher quality, leadership, and the socioeconomic and cultural backgrounds of students (2008, p. 244).

Additionally, *how* time is spent is far more critical than " . . . counting the minutes, hours, and days students spend each year getting schooled" (p. 249). Nevertheless, time for staff planning purposes as just discussed is central to improving the effectiveness of the local school—that is if one assumes that local educators are motivated to take on that task and are capable of advancing the core educational agenda.

David, in her 1988 synthesis of the then-school-based management literature, concluded that time was a core factor in meeting with success (1989, p. 52), and later research in forty-four schools engaged in the process came to the same conclusion (Wohlstetter, 1995, p. 23). This is time not paid for beyond the standard teacher contractual day.

Involvement in organizational governance also requires time to train participants in communications and decision-making skills if educators and laypeople are to work together effectively (Wohlstetter and Mohrman, 1994a, p. 7). Such collaboration is not easy to achieve in any situation, but it is compounded in the case of schools because administrators and teachers have been educated on a psychological "independent agent" model (see the Introduction), and teachers, once employed, are accustomed to working in that mode in their busy kitchens.

In her oft-cited study of "teachers' workplace" involving twenty three elementary schools, Rosenholtz honed in on what conditions are necessary to promote staff collaboration. She concluded, "Norms of collaboration don't simply just happen. They do not spring spontaneously out of teachers' mutual respect and concern for each other" (p. 44). Schools have to work very hard to bring it off.

In addition, many board members and parents have little or no background for work in group situations that require participative processes. Moreover, they are often not motivated to receive training in group leadership and processes of power sharing. In order to take serious steps toward reform, unions and management in some communities have begun to recognize the need to alter these norms and working conditions, rooted as they are in the adversarial model of bargaining.

Both the American Federation of Teachers and the National Education Association have been engaged in innovative contract experiments in several districts that represented important new thrusts in regard to decision-making and participatory management, thrusts that address long-standing issues relating to roles, authority, responsibility, accountability, and time for teachers to engage in substantive tasks (Watts and Mcclure, 1990; Tuthill, 1990; Raugh, 1990).

For two decades, there has been some movement in these directions. Recent statements by the president of the AFT stressed the importance of labor-management collaboration in efforts to reform public schools (Sawchuk, 2010b).

But the new pressure to factor student performance into processes of teacher evaluation, conveyed forcefully by the federal Department of Education in the *Race to the Top* competition, is diverting union attention and energy toward job security and ensuring due process. This dimension of the accountability squeeze is, at the moment, seemingly counterproductive to the goals of increased staff participation in site-managed schools.

The new Colorado law abolishing tenure and mandating that at least half of a teacher's evaluation be based on student performance is a vivid example of this new dynamic (Slevin, 2010). So, too, is the new Washington, D.C. teacher contract that creates two compensation tracks that teachers can opt into, one the traditional step salary scale and the other a performance-based system (New York Times, 2010).

At the national level, reflected in debates at their 2010 conventions, the NEA resists negotiating contracts that factor student achievement into evaluating teacher performance with any implications for merit pay. However, the AFT is more open to experimenting with new contracts tying test scores to some dimensions of staff evaluations and compensation (Sawchuk, 2010d). Clearly, the ground is now moving more than glacially on this subject at the local, state, and national levels.

If site management is to further the goal of moving toward second-order change, then it will likely require additional staff to reduce current instructional workloads and the need for staff to cope with increased demands to implement more individualized programs, to analyze and utilize test data, and to evaluate, learn how to use, and integrate technology into the classroom. The principal, already stretched by tasks, as we have seen in previous chapters, will need assistance, too. But in these hard times, it will be a while before monies are restored to budgets to allow for such administrative planning and creative problem-solving.

If more time is not provided or some kind of staff redesign achieved, it is likely that burnout will prevent educators from meeting the expectations for what should happen in a site-managed organization. It might also cause them to regress to past practices or to disengage from change activities, behaviors we have observed (in chapter 2) in schools involved in change projects.

Failure to site-manage effectively and to have that site management result in noticeably improved learning may also result in more public disenchantment and redoubled demands for voucher, charter schools, and choice plans or even a spike in the homeschooling movement that has grown significantly in recent years. Although the move toward vouchers has lessened, charter schools and choice have gained decided momentum, with charters used as a bargaining chip by the federal government if states want to win grants through Race to the Top funds.

Proponents of site-based management face other challenges. How will schools in the same district coordinate and articulate their programs while maintaining building autonomy? How will autonomous schools deal with district and sometimes building-level union contracts; with changed roles among administrators, teachers, boards, parents, and even students; and with increased demands for more financial resources and ways to reallocate existing resources? In the words of one researcher, "SBM is not for the faint of heart or for those who are ambivalent about getting involved in making major decisions about kids and programs" (Carlson, 1996, p. 280).

Evans' experience in the Cambridge, MA, school system is an example of the sometimes struggle involved in implementing site-based policies in an urban district. Hired as the high school principal to reorganize the school into several small schools (like the SLCs of the Gates project), Evans initiated shared decision-making as a central practice, along with delegation of core decision-making autonomy from the principal to the staff. Yet as time went on, she and other school administrators increasingly ran afoul of the superintendent and school committee over matters of attendance, organizational redesign, and hiring. Power was at the root of the situation (Evans, 2003).

Finally, Evans resigned, leaving behind the likelihood that the central office and board "resolved" these contentious areas of decision-making by simply taking them over.

As did Bromley and Mansfield, thousands of schools can implement elements of SBM in the basic areas of budgeting, curriculum, staffing, and decision-making. Schools can move ahead in such areas without adding the time-consuming structural features of formal SBM that, absent time and other resources, will undercut success. They can achieve deep and fairly rapid incremental change, provided they proceed with a healthy dose of common sense.

Effective building management of schools is vital for schools that want to avoid being tagged as a "turnaround school" with all that that label entails. To attain effectiveness, all parties within the power field will need to operate on a foundation of trust, respect, and cooperation.

RESTRUCTURING

Emerging from a site-managed organization, as numerous critics and policymakers see it, is "restructured" education. "Restructuring" in the 1990s replaced "reform" and "renewal" as the popular term for describing a variety of expectations for school improvement. It was on the covers of professional journals, was on convention agendas, and was a high-profile topic among national, state, and local policymakers. David Tyack, the noted educational historian, said then that, "As U.S. education enters the 1990s, *restructuring* has become a magic incantation" (1990, p. 170).

The term conveys an expectation of second-order change, and, no doubt, that was the general expectation in the minds of most of those who promoted it. For example, a report on education released at the 1990 annual meeting of the National Governor's Association asserted, "We need dramatic and fundamental changes in the way we design and structure education if we are to compete globally and achieve economic success" (Branstad quoted in Olson, 1990, p. 7).

In Vermont, where I worked for thirty-one years, the State Board of Education and the Department of Education promoted restructuring. It was rare to find an administrator in the 1990s who did not assert that her school was "restructuring." Sample conversations with teachers confirmed that the concept had entered the ethos of many classrooms. But it was equally rare to find someone who could offer a definite definition of the term. I never saw a definition by the Department of Education. "Block scheduling," for example, was often equated with restructuring.

A concept like restructuring is so broad that it can mean virtually anything the user wants it to mean. It has been used in the name of minor reforms or changes in schools, what a person might call tinkering with the system. On the other hand, it can signal a revolutionary set of changes for the entire educational system (Ellis & Fouts, 1994, p. 25).

Ellis and Fouts constructed two sets of restructuring perspectives. One was "Goal-Driven/Participatory" with its focus on collaboration, deliberation, an internal needs focus and planned actions leading to more fundamental, second-order change. The other perspective, "Arbitrary/Mandated," stresses a top-down, external needs focus (i.e., responding to public pressure) and random actions that can create the impression that real change is occurring. The change that does occur, however, usually leads to differences of a first-order nature (1994, pp. 25–38). Today, the accountability movement fits into the latter perspective.

In *America 2000: An Education Strategy,* President George H.W. Bush discussed restructuring in the context of the six ambitious (and many said unrealistic) national goals set out in the 1991 document (e.g., "By 2000, U.S. students will be first in the world in science and mathematics achievement.") America 2000 typifies the "Goal-Driven/Participatory" approach. Nowhere in the document is there even an allusion to "turnaround schools" or government takeover of organizations. It is an ironic twist to history that just twelve years later, the younger Bush succeeded in getting Congress to pass the NCLB legislation with all its coercive accountability components.

Conley (1997) analyzed thoroughly the restructuring literature and, from it, derived an integrating model of twelve central variables integral to the concept (pp. 112–121). In addition, he identified three levels of change—renewal, reform, and restructuring (pp. 8–9).

Renewal activities are those that help the organization to do better and/or more efficiently that which it is already doing.

Reform driven activities are those that alter existing procedures, rules, and requirements to enable the organization to adapt the way it functions to new circumstances or requirements.

Restructuring activities change fundamental assumptions, practices, and relationships, both with the organization and between the organization and the outside world, in ways that lead to improved and varied student learning outcomes for essentially all students

Reflecting on the findings from Bromley and Mansfield, we can see that considerable teacher-driven renewal—adaptation—took place within each school. Reform occurred through the implementation of IDEA staffings and Vermont Basic Competencies. If restructuring had been part of the educational lexicon and ethos at the time, both principals might have used these small wins as the foundation for more ambitious changes in their schools.

By the end of the 1990s, it appeared that a consensus was emerging that the basic goal of restructuring was in line with Conley's concept, that of long-term, comprehensive change that would lead to higher expectations and higher levels of student learning (a goal similar to those in the literature discussed in chapter 1 relative to "future learning").

Lewis' book, *Restructuring America's Schools*, focused on what was happening in schools in the 1980s, and her ideas provided a foundation for the decade ahead—changing the nature of schools from the inside; creating new relationships for children, youth, and teachers; examining our basic beliefs about teaching, learning, the nature of human beings, and the kinds of environments that maximize growth for teachers and students alike; and opening up the process of learning and teaching, of human interaction and decision-making (Lewis, 1989, pp. 3–6).

Newmann and his colleagues also made a major contribution to the restructuring literature with their longitudinal and focused research on instruction and "authentic" student achievement in secondary schools (1992; 1996). Their convincing studies served as a key element in their model of restructuring that drew on a data base of some 1,500 elementary and secondary schools (1995). The model includes four areas of support for restructuring—student learning, authentic pedagogy, school organizational capacity, and external support. Each area includes several "standards" for gauging where a school is in implementing the circle of support.

The authors point out that, while "restructuring offered no panacea," it advanced student achievement when it honed in on student learning, built organizational capacity to deliver authentic pedagogy, and received external support (p. 4).

Joyce and Calhoun (1996) give descriptions of five well-designed, researched, and implemented projects on restructuring (although the authors use the term "renewal" and nowhere mention restructuring). They detail clearly the positives and the negatives of the project outcomes in five districts, projects that drew on the school improvement knowledge base.

This period, the decade from the mid-1980s to the mid-1990s, was one of great ferment and inventiveness (as we saw in chapter 2) that rode high until the upheaval around OBE in 1993. The ambitious goals of restructuring contrasted considerably with those of policymakers who each election cycle focus more on legislation and regulations relating to higher academic standards, on new ways of assessing learning, on manipulating time, and on raising the standards for those entering the teaching profession.

The birth and growth of the term itself, "restructuring," is an interesting example of osmotic change—a word that simply began to creep into the literature and the public agenda, gradually replacing "reform" in the organizational jargon. Tyack and Cuban say that "a *vague* word became a *vogue* word" (their emphases) (1995, pp. 80–84). Ironically, Russia gave the word a major push into world dictionaries in the mid-1980s when Mikhail Gorbachev came to power and initiated restructuring that radically altered internal economic and political policies, resulting in the eventual fall of the Soviet Union in 1989.

At the same time the concept began to enter business vocabulary in the United States where many businesses were "downsizing" and "right-sizing." Today, newspapers and magazines routinely carry stories about restructuring in the private sector and in local and state government, moves driven largely by our current "Great Recession." Restructuring is usually driven by economic crises and is the response to questions of organizational or institutional survival.

But restructuring in the late 1990s went off in a radically different direction from its original conception, forced there by social forces and the passage of *No Child Left Behind* in 2002 It included reference to "restructuring" in terms of what eventually occurred at Central Falls High School, dismissal of the entire staff and starting over with a new one. Standardized testing and Annual Yearly Progress reports are the mechanisms that power this kind of restructuring.

Accountability and restructuring have become synonymous in most circles. "Restructuring" has morphed into a different definition, perhaps more aptly called "re-stricturing" with its mandated "turnaround schools," "turnaround strategies," and castigating tone.

This morphing also spread to the now inactive Center for Comprehensive School Reform and Improvement that was part of the U.S. Department of Education. The CCSR in 2004 did not highlight educational restructuring initiatives as they were envisioned in *America 2000: An Education Strategy*. Instead, it was given an accountability responsibility: focus on "chronically struggling schools failing to meet AYP" (The Center had a five-year contract with the department that expired in September 2009) (CCSRI, 2010).

Restructuring, as eventually understood in the late 1990s, was an admirable goal that has considerable potential to shift our thinking about change and to move us to actions that can improve schools in important ways to meet the demands of the future. The knowledge base it generated is invaluable to our understanding of school improvement. But at this time, the term has been hi- jacked by policymakers and the media and given a different meaning, one pejorative to the mission of education. Yet again, something promising to the art and craft of education has been distorted by the political establishment and the media.

So today, educators have a responsibility to understand these definitional differences, to have a solid understanding of the knowledge base, to educate other groups about restructuring, and to get agreement at the local level—among professionals, the school board, and the community—about the meaning of the term if it is used operationally.

Otherwise, we could again get mired in a morass of clashing expectations that divert attention and energy from the real issues, possible solutions, and the kind of support needed to implement them. Worse, we could again dash the hopes of various school constituents, thus contributing to the already considerable disillusionment about public education that we have seen in prior pages.

Carlson says that, "School restructuring cannot be accomplished over a summer break but requires thoughtful and committed effort over a long haul, at a minimum three to five years" (Carlson, 1996, p. 256). That is the challenge that must be conveyed to our various "publics," what prior-to-2002 restructuring really means to the future of public education.

PROFESSIONAL LEARNING COMMUNITIES

The concept of a PLC emerged in the late 1990s, developed by Dufour, Dufour, and Eaker. For more than a decade it has been a highly popular topic at the national, state, and local levels as it offers a commonsense, practical, and somewhat adaptable approach to participatory change. They define a PLC as:

> . . . educators committed to working collaboratively in ongoing processes of collective inquiry and action research to achieve better results for the students they serve. Professional learning communities operate under the assumption that the key to improved learning for students is continuous, job-embedded learning for educators (2008, p. 14).

The PLC is an appropriate change strategy with which to conclude this chapter because it is a *process* for involving all organizational staff in grappling with the challenging, complex, and often confounding issues facing all schools today. Forming a PLC is a site- or building-level enterprise. That environment requires collaboration because the challenges are too formidable to be "solved" (to the degree that ever is the case) by solitary teachers operating in isolation from colleagues. And certainly the same is the case for principals. The old hierarchical, all-knowing model of leadership is archaic in this 21st-century world.

As with site-managed schools, there are thousands of schools that have created collaborative working environments. For those organizations, the PLC literature provides additional instructive material as to how to make those environments more effective. The PLC concept and accompanying practices contain much potential for adaptation in the local context.

Rosenholtz makes the case ". . . that when collaborative norms undergird achievement-oriented groups, they bring new ideas, fresh ways of looking at things, and a stock of collective knowledge that is more fruitful than any one person's working alone" (1991, p. 41). Such norms are an essential factor (but certainly not the only) in moving from a "learning-impoverished" school (today's "turnarounds") to a "learning-enriched" school (1991, pp. 79–96).

Moving in that direction requires an adaptable organization. Adaptability, as has been stressed throughout these pages, is the ability to take on newer and more appropriate educational practices. It is an environment for improvement within essential stable parameters. Small wins, I have argued, are central to the process where effecting larger-scale change successfully is most difficult. The goal is to grow and develop as professionals and as an organization rather than being rooted in routine processes and standardized approaches.

The school that eventually builds a true PLC would find that it should have at least nine important "common threads" that would make it similar to other such organizations. These are: (1) clarity of purpose; (2) collaborative culture; (3) collective inquiry into best practices; (4) action orientation; (5) commitment to continuous improvement; (6) focus on results; (7) teachers empowered by principals; (8) commitment to handle adversity and conflict; and (9) a common investment to make "every kid a winner" (DuFout, Defour, Eaker, & Karhanek, 2004, pp. 133–148). (Developing a PLC is ready-made for a chapter 6 "innovation attribute checklist.")

Attaining the collaborative working ethos that is the heart of a PLC requires an organizational culture that supports it, that enables the positive relationships to be anchored in the assumptions, beliefs, values, expectations, and habits that define culture (DuFour et al., 2008, p. 90). Individuals shape culture, and the culture shapes people. "Cultural norms are typically invisible, implicit, and unexamined, made up of scores of subtleties in the day-to-day workings of the school" (p. 109).

Although the positive "anchors" of any organization's culture are quite enduring, they can also change fairly quickly in a negative direction. An example today is the injection of evaluating teachers based, at least partially, on student performance. Traditionally, such a practice has been anathema to schools because of the formidable challenge of accurately determining the degree to which a teacher is responsible for student achievement (made extremely difficult by the already overloaded managerial roles of principals and other supervisors) and the degree to which student characteristics, family background, and cultural influences are responsible.

The norm of cooperation can shift to competition, and it can undermine the goal of establishing a PLC. Of course, to many external critics, competition is the salvation of the schools as seen in the promotion of choice plans and charter schools. Other external changes such as axing tenure in Colorado can have a similar effect. The ultimate goal of a PLC—that of high levels of learning for all students—means more stress on learning and less on teaching. That worthy goal can be seriously deemphasized by top-down decisions and sudden reliance on business practices, foreign to school culture, that challenge job security and erode collegiality.

The key books about establishing PLCs stress the challenges of the task whether it be in an elementary, middle, or high school. The commitment to generate classroom interventions for students falling behind and to alter schedules to find time to deliver them is most impressive, but simultaneously devising and implementing such vital logistics is "damn hard work" (Fullan, 2007, p. 151), as described a few pages ago regarding such efforts at Adlai Stevenson High School.

Jacobson sees two approaches typical of "the work." One is "inquiry-oriented," where teachers take ownership of the process and basically make the decisions for how the respective team or teams are to collaborate within the parameters of available time. A team may be grade level, across the same courses, or vertical content area. The other is "results-oriented," where administrators are more involved in goal and agenda setting, in planning, and in overall decision-making. More structure and direction comes "downward" rather than "upward" with the second approach.

Rather than an "either or" choice to building a PLC, he advocates a "Common Priorities" approach that integrates elements of both approaches in addressing issues relative to curriculum, instruction, and learning. The article illustrates how complex a PLC can become and the challenges to make its operation "simple" enough to be functional and effective (Jacobson, 2010).

PLCs do intrude on teacher autonomy. They also intrude on the "traditional" work of principals and on people in other roles. Hence permeating a PLC are issues of power, similar to those discussed relative to site management. Hersey, Blanchard, and Johnson define power as "influence potential—the resource that enables a leader to gain compliance or commitment from others" (2001, p. 204). In a PLC, the word "leader" can mean not only the principal or superintendent, but also a teacher, a department chair, a school board member, a student, or a parent. As we can see then, a PLC usually demands considerable role change.

Because we are human, we want some degree of control (or at least influence) over our lives and minimally over our immediate (in this case) work setting. Goals cannot be attained, and work cannot get done in a condition of disorder and instability. To get that work done, Hersey, Blanchard, and Johnson portray seven forms of power—coercive, connection, reward, legitimate, referent, information, and expert (pp. 210–212) that, in one form or another, are instrumental to stability and progress within a certain context.

Some or all forms are available to those in the roles just mentioned. How we use that power depends greatly on organizational culture and history. If one school has always valued and welcomed staff contributions, for example, it would very likely rely on power that is referent, information, and expert power. Another school with administrators operating from a "top-down" approach with staff—"telling" them what to do and not welcoming their input to decision-making—would find more reliance on coercive, connection, reward, and legitimate power. More dysfunctional behavior is likely in the second school than the first. Therefore, the odds for success in establishing a PLC are much greater in the first rather than the second organization.

Today, as the accountability squeeze increases, schools everywhere feel the effects of coercive and legitimate power from outside of the system as we have seen throughout these chapters. Already scarce time shrinks even more, desiccated by demands relative to testing and assessment.

Administrators and teachers experience more pressure with their already overloaded full plates (as seen in chapter 3), so finding time for a PLC will be difficult. Because these effects will not go away in the near and distant futures, a PLC must acknowledge and discuss them if it is to play a significant role in maintaining organizational morale and sustaining a climate for continuous improvement.

DuFour, DuFour, and Eaker stress that creating a PLC in ordinary times is a "complex and challenging task" (2008, p. 92), and we are not in ordinary times as we enter the second decade of this new century. In these extraordinary times, nevertheless, the PLC strategy will require "fundamental shifts" in purpose, the use of assessments in responding to the needs of students who are not learning, in the work of teachers, in school focus, and in professional development (pp. 93–95).

The task can be daunting in the best of times and certainly difficult most of the time, but the ultimate goal, a PLC as described at the outset of this section, can be central to real reform at the local level. There is real power in a professional community that is truly one entity.

In this chapter, we have examined the topics of small wins, site-based management, restructuring, PLCs, and the interrelationships between them. The first three are less defined "innovations," whereas the latter is characterized by specific examples of implementation, steps to take, and recommendations for success. Each contains concepts intertwined with process. There is no issue with "fidelity," that is being "true" to the original design, with these four as compared to innovations discussed earlier.

Adaptation is very much a key guideline, dependent on the local context and its capacity to accept and embrace change. With that in mind, we will next look at "levers and footings" for change that can aid and abet efforts to "change schools from the inside out" as they may or may not link with small wins, site management, restructuring, and a PLC.

Chapter 8

Levers and Footings for Change

Although policy talk about reform has had a utopian ring, actual reforms have typically been gradual and incremental—tinkering with the system. It may be fashionable to decry such change as piecemeal and inadequate, but over long periods of time such revisions of practice, adapted to local contexts, can substantially improve schools.

—Tyack and Cuban, 1995, p. 5

The best course may be a middle course. One approach would be to encourage incremental reforms by using schools such as those described in this book as natural laboratories while also supporting limited and carefully designed experiments with new organizational forms.

—Wilson and Corcoran, 1988, p. 147

In the pages preceding this chapter, research reveals the difficult, but not impossible, challenge of effecting large-scale change in any system. But in schools, as we have seen, large-scale change is often more problematic because of limited financial resources, contradictory and conflicting political forces, and the complex nature of schools as organizations.

Given these facts, along with the evidence that it is possible to bring about smaller-scale change fairly readily in most systems, I will conclude this book with some practices that have grown out of my foundation of four decades as an educator either working in or with public schools, plus my research-based observations of the educational workplace over the past decade. Some "levers for improvement" you can use fairly quickly with a modicum of reading, thought, and preparation, but you will need to use a considerable dash of common sense. "Footings for change" are more long term in nature but still quite achievable.

Use of the levers and footings could encourage the more rapid, authentic, inside out, incremental change Wilson and Corcoran observed in the schools they studied, schools recognized as excellent schools under the U.S. Department of Education's Blue Ribbon Schools Program (Mansfield was one of those first 571 schools).

The "levers" are in no order of import or potential impact. Their use is highly contextual depending on conditions in the local site. All can be used separately for some purposes, and many can be combined with others into a set of strategies. No doubt you, from your experiences, can add to the list. Here we can apply Senge's notion of "leverage" ". . . where small, well-focused actions can sometimes produce significant, enduring improvements if they are in the right place" (2006, p. 114).

Not all of the "levers" that follow are equally "small and well focused," but they are in line with the spirit of Senge's contention that, most of the time, such actions, or the possibilities for such actions, are not obvious to organizational inhabitants even though they contain considerable potential for organizational improvement.

LEVERS FOR IMPROVEMENT

Mosaics of Small-Scale Innovations

If an innovation is pure "hardware," yes, it can stand alone. But even hardware requires software, so an interrelationship begins. But most innovations, as we have seen, are composed of parts of a whole that developers see as a logical, coherent pattern. They are an example of how a mosaic of innovations can have far more impact on the organization than each would have had on its own. Thus calculated, "small change" could lead to a very different school if innovators see the gestalt of a design revealed by the components. A mosaic is similar to the notion of a "bundle of innovations," but "mosaic" conveys a more intentional arrangement.

In the previous chapter, PLCs were described. They are comprised of several potential components that could well fit under the umbrella of a mosaic of innovations. Also, the NASSP Model Schools Project is a prime example of challenging components—such as team teaching, differentiated staffing, flexible scheduling, learning activity packages, and new roles for educators. While the components were intended to be a coherent whole, each could be used individually but not nearly as effectively.

Consider, for example, the way a physical education program might be transformed over a few years from a traditional program into an innovative combination of exercise and academics that challenges and involves students. The combination of small-scale strategies might include changing the gym dress requirements; improving the appearance and functioning of locker rooms; cutting back of team sports; adding aerobic activities and group games; stressing wellness and lifelong activities; and linking many outcomes to the regular academic program.

Home economics has changed considerably over several years at the high school level. From a focus on traditional domestic skills, appealing largely to girls, many co-ed programs now emphasize relationships and communication skills; managing time; budgeting; diet and nutrition; and dealing with contemporary issues facing teenagers (such as bullying, drugs, pregnancy, sexual harassment, and child rearing). Each of these mosaic components can be implemented individually, but make much more impact as a whole program.

Some high school mathematics programs have been altered considerably through a mosaic approach. Over four years, the adoption of an integrated mathematics approach could change significantly the content as well as pedagogy of a traditional mathematics program. Courses such as pre-algebra, geometry, Algebra I and II, and pre-calculus are replaced by a sequence of mathematics courses that integrate most traditional content with newer content such as logical reasoning, probability, and statistics. Along with new content, teachers use methodologies that emphasize real-life applications, problem solving, technological applications, and group work.

Technology today presents numerous opportunities for joining several elements so that the individual parts make a larger innovation. In terms of "hardware," one high school language teacher in my local school uses, at one time or another, a radio, a television, a Bluetooth wireless tablet, an LCD projector, a DVD and video player, a computer, a digital camera, an old-fashioned tape player, and a blackboard. And the Spanish textbook has a Web site that includes updates of book chapters and supplementary materials like games and videos.

Within this classroom, next door to a similarly innovative one and next door to a traditional one, this teacher has "done a 180" over a couple of years in terms of moving away from a primarily didactic to a heuristic approach to instruction. Students engage much more readily. As she said in an interview, "They are beyond a paper environment. They are very quick with the technology so now I can keep their attention. Their capacity and knowledge make it easy to go beyond traditional methods. Technology is such a part of their lives that they rarely realize it." These students are the "digital natives" discussed in chapter 1.

This teacher is just one example of several others who are (as one put it) "embracing the technology in order to be comfortable with it." They are configuring the technology to suit their competencies at this time and opening themselves to the gradual integration of new hardware and software into their classrooms. "Small steps" are the strategy for these teachers as, for most, who are veteran staff. Technology in all its forms is a challenging new pedagogical world.

My school district (1,300 students, K-12) added a full-time instructional technology specialist to the staff two years ago. He said that our superintendent realized that the major way to encourage teachers to adopt new technology and adapt it for their classrooms was through staff development. He is available to assist teachers in a coaching mode and offers periodic workshops for them on hardware and software. This past year, these sessions covered topics such as Web site design, use of SMART Boards and SMART Notebooks, use of software—such as Google Earth and Google Applications—and all McIntosh and Windows software.

Hardware and software have virtually unlimited potential for adaptation to meet teacher and student needs. In chapter 2 (section on Voluntary Innovations), I described the "blizzard" of just online resources (many free) available from sources like Google and Microsoft that open doors to new creativity opportunities. Other sources include textbook companies that give teachers an "entrance key" for entry to that publisher's site if a school purchases a text. In addition, Web 2.0 social bookmarking sites enable participants to share "freeware" as well as ideas and methodologies. These sites have enormous potential for stimulating innovation.

A science teacher said, "Now I can create stuff that really looks authentic, and I can change it immediately. Kids now see how course material that they use can be altered, too. Chalk and talk teachers are going to be pressured by students to change." Gone are the days when I created purple spirit masters and had to correct them with a razor blade and a piece of the backing! That "technology" called for permanence rather than change in preparing one's lesson plans.

But teachers need significant time if they hope to simply learn what is "out there" in just software alone and how it meshes with available or needed other software and hardware. Then, they require time for previewing what is found, time to learn how to create and manipulate images, time to maneuver in sites, time to upload and download material, and time to become technologically facile. And they would really like time to plan strategy to (if one is a beginner) decide where in the curriculum to begin taking their first steps. As a teacher put it, "Today technology is becoming the new foreign language." Learning a language requires times and immersion.

A "mosaic strategy" works for these examples of technology because only certain combinations and configurations of hardware and software will "fit" a particular classroom (I use the term literally and figuratively as many schools are organized around instructional settings quite different from a standard, self-contained classroom). For a busy teacher committed to taking the leap into this relatively new universe for delivering curriculum and instruction, a unit of study (as was seen at the Bromley and Mansfield schools) could be a way to begin with a "small win."

Reflecting on the typology of innovations uncovered at Bromley and Mansfield (Table 4.1), we can see that there was considerable potential in both cases to create more of a mosaic of innovations out of the innovations that stood relatively alone.

Mosaics correspond to what Weick refers to as "small stable segments" within the larger organization. Because they are parts of the whole, they are not necessarily disorderly and unconnected to each other any more than are sentences within paragraphs. "Instead, what seems to be true within organizations is that coherence occurs in smaller-sized entities than may be true in other settings" (1985, p. 117).

Such appears to be the case in the "excellent" businesses described by authors like Kanter (1983) and Peters and Waterman (1982), in which small-scale change was a key to their effectiveness and competiveness. Waterman, in *The Renewal Factor*, devotes several pages to the value of "tiny steps" as one way to keep "change as the norm" (1985, p. 245).

The most detailed picture of this process of change emerged from Kouzes' and Posner's study of managers in private and public sector organizations. They state:

> A series of small wins therefore provides a foundation of stable building blocks. Each win preserves gains and makes it harder to return to pre-existing conditions. Like miniature experiments or pilot studies, small wins also provide information that facilitates learning and adaptation (2007, p. 198).

Their book describes several ideas about management and leadership such as continuous experimentation, dividing tasks into manageable chunks, reducing the essence of the "win" to its essentials, and building, obtaining, and sustaining commitment to a course of action. "The most effective change processes are incremental, not one giant step. Each step forward creates a psychological 'win' that propels people to continue in that direction. A 'win' generates excitement, energy, and commitment" (Kouzes and Posner, 2007, p. 193).

Guskey has proposed several guidelines for "integrating innovations" that can create a "connectedness" between small-scale changes. These deal with goal and strategy compatibility, the recognition that no one innovation can do everything, and adaptability to local conditions (1990). He contends that, by using a set of innovations, far more improvement can occur in a shorter period of time than is usually the case when focusing on one or two major innovations. The PLC, the Model Schools, physical education, home economics, mathematics, and technology examples illustrate Guskey's strategy.

Finally, the mosaic strategy fits nicely into the process of evolutionary planning, derived by Louis and Miles from their study of five urban high schools implementing effective schools programs. In that process, small-scale innovations play a key role because there is more certainty that they will be implemented successfully, and that success increases motivation and stimulates further action (1990, p. 211).

Crafting needed change from a mosaic of innovations could generate the "excitement, energy, and commitment" uncovered by Kouses and Posner. A cascade of technological changes, over time, could have this psychological effect.

INNOVATION INVENTORIES AND
CATALOGS OF INNOVATIONS

Schools could annually survey their staffs to identify the kinds of innovations that have been implemented and those that have been discontinued. Technology advances in hardware and software are ready made for such an activity. Certainly the small-scale changes described in chapter 4 were not very visible even to immediate peers, much less to administrators. I discovered this when I shared my findings with the principals of Bromley and Mansfield and noted how surprised they were to hear about all the innovations effected by teachers beyond new courses (which they were aware of because they had to approve them).

The results of such a survey could provide a rich information base for discussion and insights about the "health" of the organization; the findings could serve as a motivator in terms of local achievement; and they could serve as stepping stones for the examination of goals and coherence of programs. But such an activity would require more transparency among staff and more cooperation than has been the case for most schools historically.

What to some people appear as minor or trivial accomplishments can be small wins of real importance to organization members. "Large-scale problems seem impenetrable whereas incremental steps are both doable and consistently rewarding" (Waterman, 1987, p. 261). In addition to conducting an internal inventory, schools could also conduct an external survey of possible innovations that would help them meet organizational needs, innovations that could form a mosaic.

The software available today, as we have seen, contains a wealth of curricular and instructional information. So, too, do professional journals in the various subject fields. Lack of information, ideas, and potential practices is no longer the problem; rather, the challenge comes from the sheer abundance of choices and the challenge of finding time to determine what is of value and of potential use, how to use an innovation, whether it can be joined with other innovations, and what would be a successful implementation strategy.

Indeed, as Fullan points out many times in his writings, the main problem public education faces is not resistance to change, but the presence of too many innovations that flood schools uncritically and superficially (1993, p. 23). The Internet can inject ideas into teachers' consciousness with a mouse click. Being swamped with ideas but lacking time—as we have seen in the discussion of site management—opens teachers to considerable professional frustration and stress.

I still remember the comment of one of my graduate students. "My cup is full. I wish that someone would turn off the spigot for a while so that I could think about what I'm doing and how to do it better." Administrators and teachers can easily feel almost psychically paralyzed by the overwhelming flow of information and innovations hitting their desks and screens.

As described in chapter 2, the What Works Clearinghouse is a prime source of well-developed, tested, and judged innovations. The ERIC system is another useful national source. Convention programs abound with descriptions and demonstrations of innovations. Joyce and Calhoun found that connecting educators to the professional knowledge base expands the possibilities for effective action (1996, p. 187).

Rosenholtz, whose study predated the Internet, asked the teachers of learning-enriched and learning-impoverished schools where they got new ideas. In the former schools, prime sources were peers, journals, conferences, and in-service programs and colleges courses (1989, pp, 96–99). These sources parallel the sources identified by Bromley and Mansfield teachers in chapter 4. Currently, the Internet and software add immeasurably to the information store.

Despite the availability of all this information, many educators remain unaware of innovations that could help them and their organizations. Too often, I have heard educators say, "I don't have time to read." What a damaging message for professionals to send to the public! I have never heard a dentist, doctor, or lawyer make such a statement. There will never be enough time; as professionals, we must schedule a few hours periodically to read and think about what is relevant to our work. Sarason asserts, "Reading is more than desirable, it is crucial" (1996, p. 369).

Granted, extensive professional reading is difficult to do during the press of the school year. But it must be done during the summer break. As study findings revealed, the "simple" act of reading by the principals and teachers of Bromley and Mansfield resulted in many dividends for their schools. The accountability squeeze pressing on schools in this new century dictates that educators can ill afford to be ignorant about issues and the innovative possibilities that might be beneficial to their classrooms and schools.

This environment also requires more openness to sharing with colleagues, more transparency in informing them what works and does not work in one's classroom. However, to what extent will the new practice of at least partially basing a teacher's salary on student performance erode this much-needed increase in professionalism?

PLANNING

The traditional framework of planning revolves around system and subsystem goals with subsequent organizational activities occurring in a sequential, highly structured, and quite predictable pattern. It represents the rationalistic perspective toward change discussed in chapter 3. As we saw in chapter 2, the change research has focused on planned approaches, so there is a rich literature available on the subject. Most of it examines what has not worked. Fullan's review of it led him to conclude, "The history of implementation research is not pleasant. It shows that planned change attempts rarely succeed as intended" (2007, p. 13).

Although research has not produced the kind of success that encourages us to place great credence in the activity, educators cannot say to their communities and boards that "we don't believe in planning." The challenge is to make planning work within the unique conditions of schools. The outcomes from all the research, as discussed in chapter 5, do not support the notion that being engaged in planning is "irrational" because the process rarely succeeds as intended.

In those pages, I discussed "arationality" and presented evidence that we are often driven by rational reasons other than the desire to attain organizational goals. Such reasons link integrally to attitudes, values, and feelings. Behavior is intentional but influenced considerably by affective factors. Waterman has recognized this fact in his study of the factors connected to renewal in the private sector. He concludes that planning may be important in itself because the process promotes communication, information sharing, and an atmosphere of "informed opportunism" and invention (1987, pp. 26–76). This idea connects nicely to PLCs.

Louis and Miles found from their study of five urban high schools that, in "evolutionary planning," a guiding premise needs to be "act first, then plan" (1990, p. 215). They talk about establishing "targets for change" that may evolve into "themes" that create an image of what outcomes successful change could lead to, a powerful motivator (pp. 206–208).

This approach to planning rests on the assumption that the internal and external organizational environments may be "chaotic" at times (p. 193), an observation that links with the organized anarchy and busy kitchen characteristics of schools. Their book, still highly relevant, is rich with detailed findings about another perspective on planning that can be useful to educators working in all levels and types of schools.

However, if educators engage in more formal planning, they must not let the process become an end in itself nor should they allow "one best way" mentality to dominate the steps they take. And given the turbulent/uncertain economic, political, cultural, and social environments surrounding schools, plan for the unexpected. Be fast afoot! Pay attention to the ten "do and don't" assumptions about planning that Fullan has extrapolated from the literature (2007, pp. 122–125). Some of these include the inevitability of disagreement and conflict, expect that they will need more time than they thought, and recognize that changing the culture of the organization may be the most important outcome of all.

TREND ANALYSES AND ISSUE IDENTIFICATION

Schools should not plan without looking seriously at the future, yet too seldom do they do this. Thus their planning activities have little meaning for participants because so often they are in the abstract. Instead, planning must connect to the local context and its impact on educators. Other students of schools have come to similar conclusions (Louis and Miles, 1990; Sarason, 1996, p. 379).

Rarely in my career did I encounter a school that built into its schedule a regular time to examine societal and educational trends and their implications for curriculum, instruction, learning, and the way "business" is conducted. Yet external changes swirl around us, as portrayed in chapter 1. Most schools have at least four to five contractual in-service days a year in their calendar. Some segment of them should be reserved for such an activity on some scheduled basis.

One way to begin to look at trends might be to first discuss local issues that reflect trends. Some districts use an annual survey of staff to identify key issues that will be addressed through staff development initiatives. These schools have planning teams composed of teachers, counselors, and special educators. Eventually, the outcomes from schools could feed into a district-level team. This would be a productive PLC activity.

Looking at trends can lead to the solution of immediate problems as well rather than expanding into a more long-term "futures" focus. But eventually, educators need to plan beyond the short term if their schools are to move beyond their current status. "An old [mental] map is useless when the terrain is new. Old beliefs cannot help in the tasks managers face today: managing the unknowable" (Stacey, 1992, pp. 3–4).

Trend analysis is a basic element of planning and can be initiated through "simple" traditional steps such as reading professional and popular journals, observing the local community and workplaces, and observing what is conveyed through the public media. And, of course, the Internet is a prime source of information.

DERIVED GOALS

As discussed in chapter 4, research shows that organizational goals, as currently used, are not very important factors in planning and changing in most schools. In addition to the literature cited there, Wagner, after conducting three field studies of schools undergoing extensive change, found that ". . . while most adults shared a commitment to educational change, they had never discussed *why* (emphasis in the original) we need fundamental educational reform" (1994, p. 251).

Louis and Miles came to similar conclusions after their study of urban high schools (1990, 204–206). Conley's analysis of the restructuring literature revealed the importance to educators of "agreed upon ends" for their schools. However, educators seldom identify them (1997, p. 451). We must do better at finding ways for goals to play a part in effecting needed changes. Why?

- By nature, we are goal-seeking, goal-motivated creatures. We do not want to live and work in an environment we perceive as directionless. If we feel that the system has no goals, then our personal goals become dominant, and these goals may or may not mesh with what the system is trying to accomplish in fulfilling its societal mission. There is a constant tension in organizations between personal and organizational goals.

- Goals can help to create a different future. If we just extrapolate from individual actions, then the chances are high that our future will be quite similar to our present—unless the organizational context orchestrates the movement of individual goals in a more common direction. "If the image of a potential future is convincing and rationally persuasive to men [people] in the present; the image may become part of the dynamics and motivation of present action" (Chin and Benne, 1976, p. 30).
- Goals focus the mission and vigor of an organization. As we saw in chapter 1, schools feel such intense pressure to assume so many tasks that they often lose their sense of direction. "Organizations have limited resources. Survival requires them to focus their resources on certain activities to the exclusion of others" (English and Larson, 1996, p. 42). Explicit goals would not automatically do this, but they could help greatly in keeping the school on course.
- As much of the research cited has demonstrated, just emphasizing small-scale, inside out innovation will probably not move a school rapidly in new directions. That did not happen at Bromley and Mansfield, and it seems to be a message from the historical analysis of Tyack and Cuban. Hence the notion of "top-down" and "bottom- up" change is stressed more and more in the literature. We know that top-down, "rationalistic" strategies in themselves are rarely successful, but it is unclear how to combine them effectively with bottom-up approaches described in this book (Fullan, 1994; 2007, p. 262–263). Goals, vision, and mission statements have a central role in this agenda.
- Finally, it is simply poor public relations for a school to have no functional, stated goals. Possessing goals is so imbedded in the traditional definition of an organization and in the public's understanding of what an organization is all about that it is, in reality, an article of faith. To respond to the questioner who asks, "What are your goals?" by replying, "We don't have any," is risky business, considering the vulnerability of schools to their external constituencies in this high-stakes accountability milieu.

So we must continue to search for useful ways to set goals and to use them. Although logic says that we should arrive at our goals before we act, we know, as described in chapters 4 and 5 and from studies just cited, that schools act for reasons other than ones consciously attached to organizational goals. Louis and Miles' ideas about "action before planning" and "vision building" (1990, pp. 199–238) and Elmore's discussion of professional development (2004, p. 97) tap into what people are doing *now*.

If we know the general direction in which we want to go, we may discover more if we start walking than if we spend the morning studying maps, listening to weather reports, and plotting out the precise route (Louis and Miles, 1990, p. 202).

Taking an "innovation inventory" would be another means to identify operational goals. What does what we're doing say about what we believe? How desirable is it for us to be guided by these goals rather than by others? The answers to questions such as these might help us develop vision and mission statements with real meaning, statements that will prove increasingly useful because they will help us to focus our attention and energy.

Such a procedure should avoid the possibility of "visions that blind," where bland statements imposed by leaders or generated hastily to meet a printing deadline fail to get organizational members invested in the future goals or to the work required to change current practices (Fullan, 1992).

IDEA FORUMS AND RESEARCH SEMINARS

As we have seen, schools need to create ways to step back, to pause, so they enable teachers and others to share ideas and discuss research of value to practice. Sarason asserts that the culture of schools has no means or traditions for doing this or for examining the fundamental questions about education (1996, p. 328). As seen in chapter 3, there are powerful norms within the organized anarchy and busy kitchens environs that impede such exchanging.

But the evidence presented earlier demonstrates that the motivation to be "enlightened" is a powerful stimulant to change. As this drive gathers momentum among several staff, their example could gradually bring others aboard. Norms would begin to shift. While reading itself is a prime source of new knowledge and ideas for change, discussing what has been read is a vital additional step to making the habit pay off for organizational improvement.

Consider, for example, a document that has stimulated such dialogue. In 1989, the National Council of Teachers of Mathematics published its "Curriculum and Evaluation Standards for School Mathematics." Many mathematics departments have used this excellent treatise to help examine their mathematics curriculum and sometimes to even adopt integrated mathematics curricula. The NCTM publication describes societal changes that demand significant alterations in the way mathematics is taught; its content; where that content should be placed in the curriculum; and what content should be learned by what groups of children and youth.

The latest version (2000), "Principles and Standards for School Mathematics," addresses curriculum, teaching, and assessment and is organized for K-2, 3–5, 6–8, and 9–12 structures, each level containing helpful examples (NCTM, 2000).

Educators need to alter their often indifferent attitudes toward research such as this and begin to value it as a vital tool for school improvement. While it is true that the sometimes inconclusive history of educational research has given practitioners little reason to place much faith in it as a tool for decision-making, research is changing for the better. Professional journals such as *Educational Leadership,* the *Phi Delta Kappan,* and others aimed at specific roles carry many articles with a theory-into-practice bent. So although good schools may have some skepticism about research, they are learning to value it nevertheless and find ways to discuss it and, in some instances, make decisions based on it.

An important accompanying benefit of forums and seminars is that they help to break down the separatist norms and interaction barriers that exist in most schools. New norms of collegiality, collaboration, and teamwork are not formed overnight; they must be achieved through a commitment to meet with peers; to expose one's ideas, values, attitudes, and feelings; to work through conflict; and to strive toward creating different expectations for and patterns of behavior. Forums and seminars are effective vehicles for staff development days and for PLCs.

ASSESSMENT DATA

In the years prior to NCLB, many schools spent considerable time and resources on standardized testing, yet many did not use the scores for much else than public relations. During my working years, I found it far too common to hear educators say:

> Yes, we gave the Metropolitan Achievement Tests this year as we have every year I have worked here, but teachers have yet to see the results. To my knowledge, they are somewhere in the principal's office. It's like they were dropped in a black hole.

It is highly unlikely that any current state or nationwide survey of educators would produce such a statement. Instead, the pressure of accountability has created what, at times, seems to be a data-obsessed environment. Educators are swamped with data, but have too little time to process it, think about it, and make decisions based on it. But try to justify that fact to school critics who rarely have regular contact with schools and classrooms.

Witness the statement by Bob Wise, former Democratic governor of West Virginia, now president of the Washington-based Alliance for Excellent Education. "Every decision needs to have data showing why it works and [sic] helping teachers inform their decisions with data that improves student learn-ing" (*Education Week,* June 2010, p. 7).

"Every decision"? It sounds so commonsensical to laypeople. One won-ders to what degree they act in such a premeditated manner in their places of employment! Such a fixation on data, as Hess points out, could put us in danger of becoming the "new stupid" relative to data compared to the "old stupid" where test results were too often shelved and not considered again.

Additionally, he says, "Because so few educators today are inclined to denounce data, there has been an unfortunate tendency to embrace glib new solutions rather than ask the simple question, 'What exactly does it mean to use data or research to inform decisions?'" (2009, p. 12).

Educators today, immersed in a sea of data, become "data rich, but infor-mation poor" (Ronka, D., Lachat, M.A., Slaughter, R., and Melzer, J., 2009, p. 18). They are often not well prepared through undergraduate or graduate programs to deal with this data glut. Local districts often lack the resources and in-service time to adequately re-educate staff in all the topics, nor do they have the funds to contract with the few outside resources that could provide such services. Almost always, it is a push for speed in this vital new aspect of school life, the "data dimension."

Yet it is absolutely essential for schools to identify and address assessment data to see what they say about different groups of learners and the programs they are in, about the characteristics of students who gain proficiency and those who do not, and about how teacher tests correlate with state tests and other measures used (Ronka, 2009. p. 19). It is also important to address questions relating to what data indicates about curriculum and instruction and the use of alternative assessments such as portfolios, demonstrations, and exhibits.

Yet all these data-related activities could place formidable additional time requirements on school staff. These are all tough and time-consuming tasks. Heavy lifting is required. Staff has to collaborate to develop responses to these kinds of questions. The PLC in some form could be an important vehicle for such dialogue. Love, Stiles, Mundry, and DiRanna provide an alternative for such collaboration with detailed guidelines for the formation of "data teams" and "data coaches" that provide leadership in this new reality of school life (2008). But this focus on data will surely undercut opportunities for what is required to effect successful large-scale change.

Mueller and Hovde revealed the challenges of utilizing data to increase student achievement when they analyzed results from three high schools that had implemented SchoolNet, an Internet-based system of products, support, and services focused on student data. The system is geared to track student performance and examine data at the organization, group, and individual levels. It aims to streamline and integrate existing data systems.

The research analyzed implementation over two school years, during which the school district provided considerable training and support before implementation and during use. Despite the groundwork and follow-up, however, teacher use varied, few changes in classroom practice could be attributed to the program, and program sustainability over time was questionable (2008, pp. 38–41). So policymakers promoting "data-driven" schools need to take note of what is required for eventual success, based on these results from a "best case" scenario.

SCHOOL REPORT CARDS

Just as we give report cards for student performance, educators can also issue "report cards" that inform their citizenry about school performance. Until the advent of NCLB in 2002, such reports were rare and were mostly voluntary. But now any district receiving Title I funds must issue "annual report cards" for district and school performance that show, at minimum, Annual Yearly Progress in English language arts and mathematics categorized by grades 3–5, 6–8, and 9–12. Whether they want to be or not, schools are now data-driven. The challenge is to not become data-obsessed.

Massachusetts now requires districts and schools to publish annual "School District Profiles" that contain the above information because such data

> . . . enables policymakers, parents, and the public to assess the effectiveness and monitor the improvement of all public schools and districts, hold school leaders accountable for that performance and improvement, and identify where state intervention is needed (MA DESE, 2010).

But districts and schools can go beyond test information to meet the goal of transparency. For example, in 1997, the Vermont legislature passed Act 60, the Equal Educational Opportunity Act, that focused on a new formula for school funding but also included a "quality and accountability" dimension. Beyond publishing standardized test scores, districts and schools were urged to volunteer "any other statistical information about the school and community it deems necessary to place student performance results in context" (VT. DOE: Act 60).

Vermont's Chittenden South Supervisory Union met the voluntary request by including, in addition to portrayals of test scores, information on student demographics, staff profiles, and detailed building-level budgets by programs

(2010). Each school also describes its needs and challenges and how it is responding to them. This public reporting is a very different practice from the ways that schools operated when I came to Vermont in 1968. The culture has been altered radically in all states by the squeeze of accountability.

CURRICULUM AUDITING AND MANAGEMENT

Curriculum auditing and management can stimulate school improvement, drawing partially on assessment data and report cards. They focus initially on what is going on *now* and are constructed around the premise that, before one can (or ought) to change, one must have a better understanding of present conditions. Auditing and management rely on the common, everyday activities, events, and infrastructure of schools for their implementation. Rarely does anything new have to be created to use their principles, concepts, practices, and processes.

No organization should function under conditions such as ones described once by one of my workshop participants, "Staff perform their assignments without a written curriculum guide, textbook sequence, departmental organization, grade level coordination, or planned communication among themselves." Today, these conditions set a school on the road to takeover or closure.

Auditing, as originally developed by English (1988) and honed further by Frase, English, and Poston (2000), is an adaptation of financial auditing and uses five broad standards relating to:

(1) Resources, programs, and personnel
(2) Goals and objectives
(3) Written plans and policies
(4) Use of program and student assessment data for adjusting, improving, or terminating programs
(5) Educational results and related costs

Curriculum management, a relative of auditing that focuses on curriculum practices, is structured around the key concepts of the written, taught, and assessed curricula; quality control of curriculum; factors in curriculum design and delivery; and curriculum alignment (English and Larson, 1996; English 2010). While excessive application of auditing and management practices can lead to a "hyper-rationalization" of change (described in chapter 2), each can be equally liberating in terms of helping to establish a sense of organizational control and direction.

FOOTINGS FOR CHANGE

Whether use of the "levers" results in real improvement depends heavily on the organizational conditions under which they are employed. Like the footings for a building, footings for change are critical to stability and organizational renewal, but it may be difficult to recognize their presence or absence. To determine such, one must be a good listener and observer.

ORGANIZATIONAL CLIMATE

One of the quickest routes to changing schools is to alter organizational climate. Climate is different from culture, which was discussed in chapter 3. Culture is comprised of the norms, beliefs, and values of people in (in this case) an organization that become the ". . . *shared orientations that hold the unit together and give it a distinctive identity* (emphasis in the original) (Hoy & Miskell, 1996, p. 129). These orientations are relatively enduring over time. Dufour, DuFour, and Eaker discuss extensively how to shape culture (2008, pp. 89–111). Culture changes slowly. This is a partial explanation for the enduring "regularities" of schooling that Sarason describes so perceptively (1996).

Climate, on the other hand, is analogous to the weather. It is "the situation or atmosphere that prevails at a particular time or place (Encarta Webster's Dictionary of the English Language, 2004). It is how the workplace is perceived by those who work there. Climate is comprised of human elements such as morale, trust, communications, participation in decision-making, relationships, and uses of power. Until a few years ago, Phi Delta Kappa offered instruments to assess climate. Its "Comprehensive Assessment of School Environments" (Howard & Keefe, 1991; Kelly, 1980) and "School Climate Profile" were very utilitarian (Howard, Howell, & Brainard, 1987).

A positive environment ". . . makes a school a place where both staff and students want to spend a substantial portion of their time; it is a good place to be" (Howard, Howell, & Brainard, 1987, p. 5). A distinguishing feature of good schools is the health of their organizational climates. That was true for Bromley and Mansfield and for other good schools portrayed in the literature cited earlier. Nieto, in her studies of high school teachers, found that ". . . an important condition that encourages teachers to remain in the profession is a climate of openness, shared decision-making, and collaboration in the school" (2009, p. 11).

A negative climate can sap employee (and student) attitudes, morale, and motivation, as well as interest in and willingness to change. It can sour parent and board attitudes about the school and its personnel. Reading graduate student papers, I encountered comments such as the following that illustrate how certain behaviors and attitudes (in this case, on the part of administrators) can affect climate.

- None of my administrators has ever asked what it is that I do, nor has anyone asked to see my curriculum notebook—and I've been in this school for ten years.
- I receive no verbal recognition, have little status in the organization, and have little chance for career advancement. I have no one to share my successes and problems with and work in a extremely isolated context.
- My supervisor doesn't believe in positive feedback. His motto is, "No news is good news."
- In eighteen years of teaching in three schools, no supervisor has ever visited my class, and, thus, I have never had another adult give me feedback about my work, pro or con.
- I taught for two years before I ever saw my superintendent (a district of less than 2,000 students). And when I did, he gave no indication that he recognized me, nor sent any signal that he cared to find out who I was.

I marvel at the resiliency of teachers in these situations. Despite the climate, they go about their work in a professional manner, motivated primarily by the psychic rewards discussed in chapters 4 and 5.

On the other hand, climates can change quickly. As a teacher put it in a workshop, "The atmosphere is 100 percent different than it was last year. Jim's already thanked me three times for something. I never got a thank you in ten years from the other guy."

Certainly, it is simplistic to think that all negative school climates can be modified magically by a few TLC comments from a principal. But the fact remains that administrators have a significant impact on climate. In good schools, administrators know that and behave accordingly. All people in the organization are treated with respect and care and are supported in their endeavors.

However, it would be a disservice to administrators to imply that they alone have the responsibility to make their organizations productive and enjoyable workplaces. All professionals have this responsibility. Unfortunately, as is true for most organizations, there is a small contingent of teachers in too many schools who behave in thoughtless and uncaring ways even when they are in a positive work environment.

They put down students and colleagues, are uncooperative with colleagues and supervisors, are lazy, are disinterested in research, never read a professional journal or book or belong to a professional organization, and seldom have a good thing to say about anything. These teachers have a negative impact on climate and are a drag on the organization's adaptability.

Here is a disheartening vignette. A new high school principal told me about his efforts to begin to get his school to examine itself. He asked his department chairs if they would read the NASSP *Breaking Ranks* report over the summer so it could be the base for mapping out an inservice strategy in the fall. Their response, "Are you kidding? We never do any school-related work in the summer!"

In 1987, a National Standards Board for Professional Teaching Standards was created for the purpose of enhancing the profession through a national certification program. In 1995, after years of field testing the standards and processes, the first group of teachers passed the rigorous assessments, designed largely by their peers (Buday & Kelly, 1996). In their schools, was this achievement applauded and celebrated? In some cases, yes; in some cases, no. In several instances, these teachers received cold shoulders from colleagues, derogatory comments, and even mailbox missives in the form of banana peels, coffee cups, and candy wrappers (Bradley, 1995).

I need not elaborate on the negative impact such unprofessional behavior has on a school and on other teachers. In addition to all the obvious effects, they also prevent the breaking down of the separatist norms that characterize the profession and inhibit larger-scale change. Such behaviors clearly undermine movement in the direction of establishing a PLC, for example. In many instances, one could contend that these behaviors are imbedded in the culture as well. As Nieto concluded from her research on teaching, not all teachers are excellent, some should never have entered the profession, and some should have left it long ago (2006, p. 10).

Finally, boards of education have a great impact on climate (as do the communities they represent). Their attitudes and behavior send messages that can either boost or undermine morale and motivation. For example, there are too many cases where principals do not supervise their staffs in a systematic way because their workloads prevent them from doing so. Their already hectic and stressed jobs (as seen by the literature reviewed in previous chapters) are made more so by being responsible, in many instances, for supervising—by themselves—thirty or forty teachers as well as other staff, such as counselors and special educators. In the private sector, the ratio of supervisors to supervisees historically has been half that.

On top of all this, they are responsible for endless lists of other routine tasks that range from bus supervision to building maintenance (as portrayed by the Principal's Plate, Figure 3.2), all the while attempting to deal with the sometimes interference of the boards in the management of the school. Every veteran administrator has such stories to tell!

It does not take extra dollars to change climate! As the above examples demonstrate, very "simple" acts can positively alter it, significant payoff in this accountability environment we inhabit. But in this environment, with its demand for immediate turnarounds, combined with increasing detrimental practices such as reductions-in-force and wage "givebacks," it is no easy task to maintain already positive working conditions in a high percentage of our schools. How depressing it is to read each day about official and unofficial negative practices that exert a counterproductive force on educational improvement!

PSYCHOLOGICAL CONTRACTS AND ORGANIZATIONAL LEARNING

The work climate contributes significantly to the "psychological contract" between employees and their organization. The notion of a psychological contract implies that there is an unwritten set of expectations operating at all times between every member of an organization and the various managers and others in that organization (Schein, 1980, p. 22).

Such contracts ebb and flow as employee and organization needs and conditions change; the necessarily dynamic contracts undergo continual renegotiation. The ability of an organization to adapt, to be innovative, and, ultimately to do a better job is dependent on the extent to which the system supports and encourages initiative and creative thinking (Schein, 1980, pp. 33–36).

Good schools establish and maintain positive contracts with their employees, thus fostering considerable small-scale change. This was the case with the pattern of innovation uncovered at Bromley and Mansfield. The climates in these schools were instrumental to the psychological contracts prevalent there. Teachers were empowered and motivated to be change agents.

According to Argyris and Schön, "Just as individuals are the agents of organizational action, so they are the agents for organizational learning" (1978, p. 19). Such learning occurs when educators see themselves as representatives of the school with a responsibility to be open to environmental signals that change may be needed; to respond to the signals and consider whether to make adjustments in behavior; and to restructure their learning theory to a new level of effectiveness (Argyris & Schön, pp. 17–29). Although idealistic, organizational learning becomes a key factor in system adaptability.

Existing evidence about good school climates indicates that they have great potential to become learning organizations, ones that are continually expanding their capacity to create their futures (Senge, 2006, p. 14). Teachers and administrators in such schools do not just talk about innovation but effect it. Strebel contends that positive "personal compacts" have a considerable impact on such innovation because, all too often, managers are unaware of the many ways in which the compacts could take on a negative cast instead (1996). Over time, these "ordinary" people could push their organizations to the level of system learning.

REFLECTIVE PRACTITIONERS AND ADULT LEARNERS

Because schools as organizations contain considerable uncertainty, instability, uniqueness, and ambiguity and value conflict, organizational learning depends upon professionals who, in their everyday activities, behave spontaneously and intuitively. They possess the qualities of knowing-in-action and even reflection-in-action (Schön, 1983, pp. 21–69).

When individuals who know-in-action confront situations that they perceive as normal, they can make judgments about quality without always being able to state explicit criteria and can apply skills to problem situations without always being able to state the rules and procedures. When individuals who reflect-in-action confront something out of the ordinary, they realize that old solutions may no longer work. They have to invent alternative solutions or perhaps experiment on the spot to find other solutions. These are the "cooks" in their "busy kitchens" (chapter 3). The concepts link with the discussion about "arational" behavior in chapter 5.

Technology is currently a prime example of this dynamic. As described in earlier chapters, the technology of this second decade of the 21st century is more complex and challenging than technology has ever been for educators. As the instructional technology specialist in my school district said in an interview, technology today demands *behavioral* change if it is to be fully utilized in the classroom (or if administrators are to use it in managing the organization). Fear of failing has to be overcome because the specter of failing in front of a class of "digital natives" is unnerving. Teachers need to take small steps so they can build confidence.

Although it is often difficult to distinguish clearly between knowing-in-action and reflection-in-action, the critical point is that well-prepared professionals possess the ability to make the adjustments necessary to meet new situations. Based on the study of Bromley and Mansfield and other related research on good schools where small wins are common, it appears that most educators in such schools are competent problem solvers and that most are close to being reflective practitioners who behave as innovators. If most of them did not behave this way, the organization would not be self-renewing.

During the interviews I conducted, teachers could readily discuss what they had done and why they had done it when faced with familiar and unfamiliar problem situations. However, they could not describe the spontaneous, intuitive thought processes underlying their actions. "Like knowing-in-action, reflection-in-action is a process we can deliver without being able to say why we are doing it" (Schön, 1987, p. 31). Sergiovanni, in applying the ideas of reflective practice to the role of the principal, comes to similar conclusions about this form of knowledge creation and use (1987, p. 567).

While it may not seem possible in the often untidy world of the school to teach employees how to be more reflective in practice, schools can nurture and support this behavior. By doing so, they will promote empowerment and thus use more fully the talents of their staffs. Such empowerment can lead to the initiation of small-scale innovations that can have a multiplier effect by increasing the competence of the staff as a whole. Competence builds efficacy; efficacy begets innovation, and innovation enlarges organizational capacity to change (March, 1981; Kouzes & Posner, 2007, pp. 188–215).

Good schools treat teachers and other employees as adult learners while recognizing that not everyone is at the same place on the maturity and competence scales. They recognize the reality of "readiness" among staff, which is ". . . the extent to which a follower demonstrates the ability and willingness to accomplish a specific task" (Hersey, Blanchard, & Johnson, 2001, p. 175). Good schools start with positive, theory Y assumptions about human nature rather than with negative, theory X assumptions that lead them to treat employees as children who need authoritarian administrators to direct and control their behavior (Hersey, Blanchard, & Johnson, 2001, pp. 67–70).

Good schools recognize and value their staffs as the instrumental change agents who deliver relevant and effective education to learners. They see teachers as highly capable, thoughtful individuals who appreciate the support they receive when they do a good job and when they innovate. Good schools treat teachers as professionals rather than as mere technicians plugged into classrooms in order to carry out hierarchical mandates.

To enhance professionalism, an old concept that is being dusted off for our new world of organizational life is that of "tribes," defined as any work group between 20 and 150 people that represents a social unit bigger than a group and smaller than a society (Logan, King, & Fischer-Wright, 2008, pp. 4; 24). The authors studied, over ten years through surveys and interviews, 24,000 people in two dozen private and public organizations to gain an understanding as to how leaders can work *with* (my emphasis) employees to "unstick" the organization and make it more effective through collaboration, reduction of stress, and an emphasis on having more fun (pp. 7–9).

Tribal Leadership examines five stages that employees can move through to progress from "despairing hostility" to "tribal pride." In today's school environments, these ideas could be most useful in changing organizational culture and climate and they connect neatly to the ideas of Kouzes and Posner on how to foster collaboration, leadership, trust, relationships, and a spirit of community for the long term (2007, pp. 221–351).

In good schools, administrators create a conscious agenda that fosters teacher development for the long term so that they become better, and a key to achieving that goal, according to Glickman, is to assist them in developing their ability to think abstractly. It is ". . . the ability to determine relationships, to make comparisons and contrasts between information and experience, and to use these to generate multiple possibilities in formulating a decision" (1990, pp. 60–61).

An abstract thinker and a reflective practitioner share the same definition: an independent change agent who can think and respond to problems rapidly and decisively and who sees being innovative as a major professional responsibility.

However, as Glickman contends, there are numerous factors in the school environment (similar to those described in chapter 3) that interfere with teachers who aim to become more effective in these regards. It is a formidable task for school leaders to intervene in order to alter those conditions and reshape the work environment into one that is more stimulating and growth-producing (1996, pp. 15–31).

Here I pause to insert a commonplace example of a "factor." I taught graduate courses for thirty years. I was continually impressed by the quality of the students I encountered. They were a great potential resource for their schools. Many of them paid for their education, and many received a stipend from their district. After a course was completed, I sometimes asked students when I saw them at a later date whether their supervisor (who approved the course) asked them to discuss the experience and to share thoughts about how learning outcomes from a fifteen-week investment could be useful locally.

Rarely did I hear, "Oh, yes, we got together. He was really interested in what I learned, and I'm to submit a list of ideas about next steps." How easy it would be for supervisors to do this—to send an important signal that employees are adult learners who have something to offer to the organization! In turn, the school would benefit by nurturing the development of more "idea champions" (as discussed in chapter 5).

If school leaders related to their employees in this way, then we would make an impact on one problem that is still all too prevalent in public education, the mindlessness depicted by Silberman in 1970 in *Crisis in the Classroom*. He defined it as "the failure or refusal to think seriously about educational purpose, the reluctance to question established practice" (p. 11). The quotations from students in classes and workshops cited in previous sections of this chapter attest to the continued existence of this distressing phenomenon in too many schools. As professionals, we have a responsibility to combat mindlessness, not to aid and abet it.

THE ADMINISTRATOR AS TEACHER

Throughout this book, the role of the principal has been highlighted as instrumental to school improvement. However, I have, at the same time, attempted to make clear that this person need not—and indeed should not and cannot—be the person on the fabled white horse leading the charge for virtually all change. "Leadership is not a solo act, it's a team effort" (Kouzes & Posner, 2007, p. 223). The role is too demanding and complex to "go it alone." Plus, the current trends toward site-based management, shared governance, and PLCs require an increased collaborative working environment.

Nevertheless, the principal, as previously cited literature demonstrates, has a significant impact on large- and small-scale innovation and on overall school improvement. In the portraits of Bromley and Mansfield, the principals were instructional leaders integral to the dynamics of change.

They worked hard to support their staffs and to find ways to release the creative energy that is present in most groups of teachers. They were successful at the task and verified a main thesis of Fiedler's approach to understanding leadership: the most important ingredient for successful leadership is leader-member relations (Fiedler & Chemers, 1984, p. 59). Other noted students of leadership have come to similar conclusions (e.g., Gardner, 1990, pp. 23–37). In addition, the principals recognized the need to individualize, as much as possible, the way that they related to and worked with their staffs—situational leadership in action (Hersey, Blanchard, & Johnson, 2001, pp. 171–203).

These men had worked out an approach to authority, power, and organizational control that led to a productive work environment and productive relationships among employees at all levels, from the custodians, bus drivers, and secretaries to teachers and fellow administrators. Bromley and Mansfield, as is the case for other good schools, had developed positive work-life conditions.

Finally, I would like to return to a book on management whose ideas have lingered with me over the years, Levinson's *The Exceptional Executive.* Levinson discusses an exciting metaphor for enriching the life of an administrator—the administrator as teacher, a person who attends to the ministration, maturation, and mastery needs of his employees.

> When the executive views his role as leadership-teaching, the essence of his task is to enhance the capabilities of each of his subordinates and to enable them to strengthen each other toward accomplishing their mutual goals and fulfilling their joint needs (1968, p. 171).

Gardner advocates for similar attention to this important dimension of leadership when he states, "The consideration leaders must never forget is that the key to renewal is the release of human energy and talent" (1990. p. 136). Evans, in an insightful book about the "human side" of schools, delves deeply into this connection between energy, talent, and innovation (1996).

As a principal said to me one day when I was visiting his school, "I have a great staff here. Often I have to put the brakes on them as I'm afraid they'll overdo it." He is well on his way to being an administrator-teacher.

PERSPECTIVES ON TIME

Organizational climate, psychological contracts, an environment for organizational learning, the role of educator as reflective practitioner and adult learner, and the administrator as teacher, all combine to create an organizational perspective on time.

Ringle and Savickas discuss the subjective time orientation of institutions and their employees, i.e., how they view and orient themselves in relation to the past, present, and future (1983, pp. 649–661).

They see these modalities as having different profiles in different organizations, as represented by Figure 8.1.

While a focus on the past, present, or future may change quickly, due to internal or external conditions—witness the relatively new "hard" forms of accountability now confronting schools—most organizations develop a "preferred" orientation that affects decision-making and innovation. Important to the development of that orientation are culture and climate.

If the past is dominant, administrators and staff will view themselves as protectors who ensure that what has worked will continue to steer present and future decisions. "The institution is a projectile from the past, and the administrator's job is to protect the original trajectory" (p. 652). Challenges to

Figure 8.1. Perspectives on Individual and Organizational Time

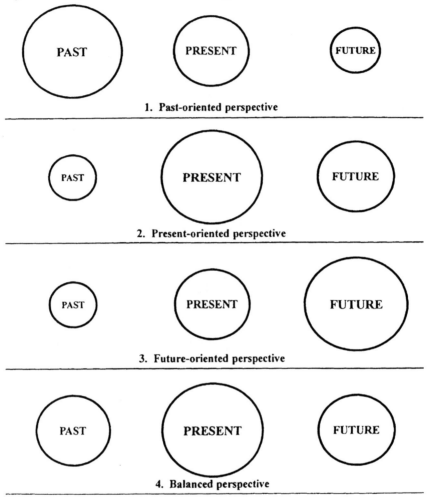

1. **Past-oriented perspective**

2. **Present-oriented perspective**

3. **Future-oriented perspective**

4. **Balanced perspective**

or even soft requests to discuss present practice will often be taken personally and dismissed summarily.

But the past has a flip side. We all have an investment in it. Few people react positively if the past is discounted because that action sends a strong negative message about one's contributions to it. Rarely is everything done in the past of little or no value; yet too many leaders, upon assuming a new job, forge ahead with no reference to the past, often deliberately advocating new directions that will roll back the past or at least ignore it.

But if the present dominates, the organization may feel rudderless, buffeted about by the latest fads, crises, and daily events, a dynamic that is more pronounced than ever in our schools today. It has not learned from past successes and mistakes, and it shows scant interest in the future. Few professionals, sadly, would have difficulty conjuring up examples of such organizations. If the future dominates, there may be such emphasis on what "should be" that worthy traditions and lessons from the past are ignored and present opportunities are missed, and employees are seen as idealists disconnected from the "real world."

What organizations need to strive for is a balance in perspectives so that there is a healthy mix of remembering the past, experiencing the present, and anticipating the future. No school today can afford to *not* create this balance. From my experience and research, I think that good schools have achieved such a balance and that the perspective on time that permeates organizations such as Bromley and Mansfield contributes in important ways to their ability to adapt. In this second decade of the 21st century, this professional and organizational trait will be critical for schools to remain vital societal institutions.

Concluding Comments

I have always liked the bumper sticker, "If you think education is expensive, try ignorance." One sentence states powerfully why we must improve public education.

Aside from being in the midst of the worst economic times since the Great Depression, we also find ourselves in the midst of a swirl of additional cultural, social, and political forces that are new in nature and intensity. In turn, we do not understand clearly their societal impact as well as their impact on public education.

Political debates are more uncompromising and acerbic than ever. Civility seems rare. In this climate, we find only a handful of politicians who step forth and speak up for our schools, the educators who staff them, and the school's instrumental role in building and sustaining a fair and just society. Rather, bashing schools is far easier. Educators feel beleaguered. It would be easy to lose heart.

The world appears topsy-turvy at times when we factor in events on the international front. Increasingly, we hear talk about the decline of the U.S. as a world power. Such talk fuels the anger running in our society. What we remember as the relatively placid, predictable, and thriving times of just a few decades ago have disappeared forever.

In addition, we must cope with the unprecedented new control role that states and the federal government wield in their relationship with local districts and schools. The accountability squeeze is here to stay. To outsiders, that may seem like a good thing. But to public educators, it does not seem so because accountability measures require them to do more with less, while expectations rise and consequences threaten them with school closure should they fail to achieve success.

Our federal secretary of education, Arne Duncan, says that, "Incremental change is not going to get us where we need to go" (cited in Friedman, 2010). Who would disagree? But he does not explain how thousands of good schools are to get there posthaste, given the realities of the Great Recession in which we are mired. Government again fails to educate its constituents and instead adds to the frustration and unhappiness of the citizenry with its schools. The gap between the rhetoric from political officials about public education and reality in the field is stark. Most distressing is that they do not seem to realize it.

The decades ahead present educators with a thicket of unclear paths. The media contributes to the unclearness by its mostly superficial reporting about schools that fails to educate the public in depth about these paths. We see instead the constantly blaring headlines about the dreadful condition of public education. Seldom does the media make the effort to distinguish between all the types of schools and settings in America and the full spectrum of successes and shortcomings they present.

This fall, filmmaker David Guggenheim had such a chance. But he chose to produce *Waiting for Superman* that focuses on big city schools that are severely underperforming, the lottery system for selecting students to attend charter schools instead, and the impact on students not selected who must remain in those schools. There is no question that ineffective city schools present our nation with a huge educational and moral problem.

But other than briefly describing some successful inner-city schools, the film makes no attempt to mention all the good local schools in our nation, the efforts they are making to provide an excellent education despite the constraints they face, and the high percentage of parents surveyed by Phi Delta Kappa who give high marks to their local school. The dramatic again subsumes the familiar. Yet critics have acclaimed the film.

Superficial reporting takes so little effort and creates such drama that reporting on school failure as endemic trumps reporting on the unique successes and challenges to success that characterize all human enterprises, including the most intense of these, educating our children and youth.

And, of course, how much more dramatic the failure seems when the media tosses in the usual comparison with other nations. In recent weeks, I have heard again the United States—with its greater than 300 million heterogeneous citizens, widespread poverty and homelessness, highly impacted urban areas, and a complex landscape of states, cities, and towns—juxtaposed with Finland.

Finland has a homogenous population of five million people, it has no poverty or inner-city slums, and it has a "cradle to grave" social system so no one is hungry, lacks a warm bed, or worries about health care. Its citizens greatly value education, and teaching is a prestigious profession. In Finland, teachers do not have to appeal to the public for paper, pencils, pens, and software, as they often do here as seen in chapter 2.

McKinsey and Co. reported recently on its study of teacher recruitment in the fourteen top-performing nations on international exams. Singapore, Finland, and South Korea draw 100 percent of their teachers from the top third of the academic pool. But only 23 percent of U.S. teachers come from the top third. And in Finland, the process to become a teacher is extremely competitive with only one in ten applicants accepted into a preparation program (Heitin, 2010).

Is it any wonder that student achievement in the usual tested subjects might be significantly higher in Finland, where it is a given that an excellent teacher is the key to student learning (as our politicians are prone to declare)? I have taught graduate education in Finland during three summers and have observed its schools firsthand, so I know that the media demonstrate great irresponsibility when it trumpets the U.S–Finland comparison without explaining why there are such differences in student achievement. And, to be sure, the next comparison will be with nations like Singapore, South Korea, and Japan.

Hence, I have concluded, after being immersed in media reports about public education for the past year, that much of the time the media, especially at the national and state levels, is no supporter of public education. Not only does it provoke anger and disenchantment, but it receives aid and comfort from too many of our politicians.

I have also concluded that many people in the media (publishers, editors, and reporters) are content—"satisficed" as discussed in chapter 3—to choose superficial coverage of schools rather than scrupulous and thorough coverage that explains to the various communities across the country the particular conditions schools face today and the particular American influences that affect them. After all, the media may assume—as do many outside the daily work of public education—"We have all been through school so why explain something that citizens already know a lot about?"

Therefore, I have a far-out wish. I wish that all media pundits and reporters, all critics, all legislators, all the executive branch, all foundation officials, and all state and federal department of education staff would, with some orientation and a reading of this book or other related literature, be assigned to prepare for at least a week of teaching at the elementary, middle, or high school level.

During their teaching stint, they would be required to: engage all their students in learning; maintain a stimulating, controlled classroom; attend all meetings before, during, and after school; monitor the lunchroom, playground, or hallways; deal correctly with bullying and sexual harassment; return parent phone calls and e-mail promptly and with equanimity; respond to and grade each day's written or other produced work; attend the school play; coach a club . . . and do these and countless other human-related activities while maintaining healthy relationships with family, friends, and self.

At the end of the assignment, they would report to the public and to legislative bodies what they learned from their total immersion experience and what that experience tells them about educational improvement, reform, or whatever one chooses to call it. Hopefully, this time in the field would enlarge their perceptions about public education and help them to acquire further understanding and empathy before making judgments, enacting legislation, or engaging in change endeavors.

Without such immersion, however, these constituencies and other societal groups—such as the PTAs, the Rotary, and other clubs—will very likely continue to send conflicting signals about expectations to those committed to public education. No wonder educators have difficulty deciding to which signals they should respond, the yellow, red, or green? How to respond can baffle the most discerning professional.

How easy for any school then, to become, in Rosenholtz's terms, a "stuck" rather than "moving" organization (1991, p. 149). "Stuck" schools avoid risks and proceed with great caution, the yellow and red lights being their guideposts. The "moving" schools recognize the challenges, take risks, grow, and move forward. The green light is their guidepost. They are "persistent innovators" (March, 1994, p. 34). A key to school improvement is increasing the capacity of districts and local schools to be persistent innovators.

Sufficient financial resources, a highly educated staff, an ongoing and well-supported staff development program, time for staff planning, engaged students, and an involved and supportive community, these are a few of the ideal major components of capacity that are linked to innovation. Capacity is rooted in context, as we have seen in research cited throughout this book.

As you have noted from that research, we need to recognize and work with these broad factors in order to marshal political support for increasing capacity in the vast complexity of cities and towns across America's landscape. "Lack of capacity (as discussed in chapter 2) is the Achilles heel of accountability." Given the economic state of the country, enhancing national educational capacity is one of the central challenges of our time

The focus of this book has been on "small wins"—a strategy for change that can work *now* in all schools, even those short on the capacity scale. But clearly we also need, in most situations, a serious rethinking about existing curriculum and the very nature of instruction, combined with a comprehensive knowledge about how change occurs, if we are to truly reform and perhaps restructure public education to address the needs of 21st-century learners and our 21st-century society.

This level of change is the real improvement discussed by Elmore, who distinguishes between it and incremental change. "Improvement equals increased quality and performance over time" (2004, p. 221). How can we build on successful small-scale change to accomplish this goal?

Additionally, education requires, despite the contentions of the no-tax advocates, an infusion of substantial dollars—to name just one factor—to underwrite such an effort. But, rather than wait years for them to be forthcoming, we must forge ahead, taking other workable approaches that may not fit the textbook prescriptions for more orderly, planned, and farsighted change. Small wins are a key to adaptability and to continuous organizational renewal. It is very possible to combine them with elements of site-based management already existing in most schools to move forward and not stagnate at the local level.

Yes, as difficult as it will be, we must see instead what is problematic as an opportunity and thus move into the future with a confident rather than timorous air. "In accepting uncertainty, we unlock school reform and enter a new phase of professionalism" (Glickman, 1987, p. 122). By doing so, we will also have influence over policymakers and communities and a rightful and needed leadership role for administrators, teachers, counselors, special educators, and other persons involved each day in public education.

Society must not slough off its absolutely central responsibilities to support public education. Educators must work diligently with their constituents for its renewal and perhaps even restructuring. Our survival as a vibrant, humane, and powerful nation depends on the quality of the education provided to our children and youth.

In the Introduction, I list several themes that permeate this book and demonstrate how they mesh with the cultural perspective on organizations and change. Let us revisit them.

- Organizations are always changing but usually in routine, fairly unnoticed ways rather than in dramatic, grand ways.
- Change is usually effected by ordinary people doing ordinary things in a competent way.
- Routine organizational processes are often key levers for improvement.
- Change is often unpredictable and not well understood.
- Organizational adaptation is an interplay of rationality and foolishness, of cognition and affect.
- Small wins can set in motion a process for continued small wins, a process that strengthens organizational capacity and ability to solve larger-scale problems.

"Think big, and start small." "Be an idealist without illusions." These admonitions should be posted above all our doors. *Changing Schools from the Inside Out: Small Wins in Hard Times* presents an effective approach to improvement, an approach that can draw and build on the wealth of energy and inventiveness in our schools. But there is no magic in it. It is incremental and evolutionary, requiring the support and industry of all the parties that have an investment in public education in America.

Bibliography

American Institutes for Research. (2006, August). *Evaluation of the Bill and Melinda Gates Foundation's high school grants initiative: 2000–2005.* Washington, DC.

Argyris, C., & Schön, D. A. (1978). *Organizational learning: A theory in action perspective.* Reading, MA: Addison-Wesley.

Aston, P. T., & Webb, R. B. (1986). *Making a difference: Teachers' sense of efficacy.* New York: Longman.

Barnet, B. G., & Whitaker, K. S. (1996). *Restructuring for student learning.* Lancaster, PA: Technomic.

Barnett, H. G. (1953). *Innovation: The basis of cultural change.* New York: McGraw-Hill.

Barth, R. S. (1990). *Improving schools from within.* San Francisco, CA: Jossey-Bass.

Benne, K. D., Bennis, W. G., & Chin, R. (1976). Planned change in America. In W. G. Bennis, K. D. Benne, & R. Chin (Eds.), *The planning of change* (3rd ed.) (pp. 13–45). New York: Holt, Rinehart, & Winston.

Berends, M., Bodilly, S. J., & Kirby, S. N. (2002). *Facing the challenge of whole school reform: New American schools after a decade.* Santa Monica, CA: RAND.

Berliner, D. C. (1984). The half-full glass: A review of research on teaching. In P. L. Hosford (Ed.), *Using what we know about teaching* (pp. 51–84). Alexandria, VA: Association for Supervision and Curriculum Development.

Berman, P. (1981). Educational change: An implementation paradigm. In R. Lehming & M. Kane (Eds.), *Improving schools: Using what we know* (pp. 253–286). Beverly Hills, CA: SAGE.

Berman, P., & McLaughlin, M. W. (1978). *Federal programs supporting educational change, Vol. VIII: Implementing and sustaining innovations.* Santa Monica, CA: The Rand Corporation.

Bidwell, C. E. (1965). The school as a formal organization. In J. G. March (Ed.), *Handbook of organizations* (pp. 972–1022). Chicago, IL: Rand McNally.

Block, P. (1987). *The empowered manager: Positive political skills at work.* San Francisco, CA: Jossey-Bass.

Bloom, B. S. (1980). The new direction in education research: Alterable variables. *Phi Delta Kappan, 61*(6), 382–385.

Bolman, L. G., & Deal, T. E. (1991). *Reframing organizations.* San Francisco, CA: Jossey-Bass.

Bonsting, J. J. (1992). *Schools of quality.* Alexandria, VA: Association for Supervision and Curriculum Development.

Bossert, S. T., Dwyer, D. C., Rowen, B., & Lee, G. Y. (1982). The instructional management role of the principal. *Educational Administration Quarterly, 28*(3), 34–64.

Boyer, E. L. (1983). *High school: A report on secondary education in America.* New York: Harper & Row.

Bradley, A. (1990). In Rochester, skepticism, confusion greets news of 'revolutionary' pact. *Education Week, 10*(4), 1, 13.

Bradley, A. (1995). What price success? *Education Week, 15*(12), 1, 8–9.

Brookhart, S. (2009). The many meanings of multiple measures. *Educational Leadership, 67*(3), 6–12.

Buday, M. C., & Kelly, J. A. (1996). "National certification and the teaching profession's commitment to quality assurance," *Phi Delta Kappan, 78*(3): 215–219.

Burlington Free Press. (2010, April 20). Retrieved from http://www.burlingtonfreepress.com/fdcp.

Burrell, J. (2009, September 24). Teens texting, and the sleep connection. *Cape Cod Times*, p. C2.

Bushaw, W. J., & Lopez, S. J. (2010). Highlights of the 2010 Phi Delta Kappa/Gallup poll. *Phi Delta Kappan, 92* (1), 9–26.

Calhoun, E., & Allen, L. (1996). The action network: Action research on action research. In B. Joyce & E. Calhoun (Eds.). *Learning experiences in school renewal* (pp. 137–174). Eugene: ERIC Clearinghouse on Educational Management, University of Oregon.

Callahan, R. (1962). *Education and the cult of efficiency.* Chicago, IL: The University of Chicago Press.

Calmes, J. (2010, March 17). Deficit hawk returns, much to his party's dismay. *New York Times.* Retrieved from http://www.nytimes.com.

Cape Cod Times. (2002, March 9). Dear Ann Landers, p. C5.

Cape Cod Times. (2010, February 16). Teen wins round in Facebook suit. p. A4.

Carlson, R. V. (1996). *Reframing and reform.* White Plains, NY: Longman.

Carlson, R. V., & Awkerman, G. (Eds.) (1991). *Educational planning: Concepts, strategies, practices.* New York: Longman.

Carnegie Forum on Education and the Economy. (1986). *A nation prepared: Teachers for the 21st Century.* New York: Carnegie Corporation.

Carnegie Foundation for the Advancement of Teaching. (1988). *Teacher involvement in decision making: A state-by-state profile.* New York: Carnegie Corporation.

Carroll, D. T. (1983). A disappointing search for excellence. *Harvard Business Review, 61*(6), 78–79, 82–83.

Cassidy T. (1996, February 18). Penmanship signing off. *Boston Globe*, pp. 1, 14.

Center for Comprehensive School Reform and Improvement (2010). Retrieved from http://www.centerforcsri.org.

Chase, B. (1997). Sleeping with the enemy? *NEA Today, 15*(6), p. 2.

Chia, T. (2010, February 15). Outlook is grim for the public schools. *Boston Globe*, p. A2.

Chien-Kenney, L. (1994). Negotiating the challenge of outcome-based education. *The School Administrator, 51*(8), 8–19.

Chin, R., & Benne, K. D. (1976). General strategies for effecting changes in human systems. In W. G. Bennis, K. D. Benne, R. Chin, & K. E. Corey (Eds.), *The planning of change* (3rd ed.) (pp. 22–45). New York: Holt, Rinehart, and Winston.

Chittenden South Supervisory Union. School report, 2009–2010. Shelburne, VT. Retrieved from http://www.cssu.org.

Christensen, C. M., Horn, M. B., & Johnson, C. W. (2008). *Disrupting class: How disruptive innovation will change the way the world learns.* New York: McGraw Hill.

Christensen, S. (1979). Decision making and socialization. In J. G. March & J. P. Olsen (Eds.), *Ambiguity and choice in organizations* (2nd ed.) (pp. 351–396). Bergen, Norway: Universitetsforlaget.

Clark, D. L., & McKibbin, S. (1982). From orthodoxy to pluralism: New views of school administration. *Phi Delta Kappan, 63*(10), 669–672.

Clifford, S. (2010, August 15). Scissors, glue, pencils? Check. Cleaning spray? *New York Times*. Retrieved from http://www.nytimes.com.

Clune, W. H., & White, P. A. (1988). *School-based management.* New Brunswick, NJ: Rutgers, The State University of New Jersey, Center for Policy Research in Education.

Cohen, M. (1989, September 28). Bennett says U.S. governors agree on keeping drugs out of schools. *Boston Globe*, p. 18.

Cohen, M. D., March, J. G., & Olsen, J. P. (1972). A garbage can model of organizational choice. *Administrative Science Quarterly, 17*(1), 1–25.

Cohen, M.D., March, J. G., & Olsen, J. P. (1979). People, problems, solutions, and the ambiguity of relevance. In J. G. March & J. P. Olsen (Eds.), *Ambiguity and choice in organizations* (2nd ed.) (pp. 24–37). Bergen, Norway: Universitetsforlaget.

Cohen, R.M. (1995). *Understanding how school change really happens: Reform at Brookville High.* Thousand Oaks, CA: Corwin Press.

Conant, J. B. (1959). *The American high school today.* New York: McGraw-Hill.

Conant, J. B. (1967). *The comprehensive high school.* New York: McGraw-Hill.

Conley, D. T. (1997). *Roadmap to restructuring* (2nd ed.). Eugene: ERIC Clearinghouse on Educational Management, University of Oregon.

Corbett, H. D. (1982). Principals' contributions to maintaining change. *Phi Delta Kappan, 64*(3), 190–192.

Cresap, McCormick, & Paget. (1984). *Teacher incentives: A tool for effective management.* Reston, VA: National Association of Secondary School Principals.

Cruz, G. (2010, February 22). A quick fix for bad schools. *Time,* 85–87.

Cuban L. (1982). Persistent instruction: The high school classroom, 1900—1980. *Phi Delta Kappan, 64*(2), 113–118.

Cuban, L. (1984). *How teachers taught: Constancy and change in American classrooms, 1890–1980.* New York: Longman.

Cuban, L. (1986). Persistent instruction: Another look at constancy in the classroom. *Phi Delta Kappan, 68*(1), 7–11.

Cuban, L. (1988a). A fundamental puzzle of school reform. *Phi Delta Kappan, 69*(5), 341–344.

Cuban, L. (1988b). Why do some reforms persist? *Educational Administration Quarterly, 24*(3), 329–335.

Cuban, L. (1990a). Reforming again, again, and again. *Education Researcher, 19*(1), 3–13.

Cuban, L. (1990b). What I learned from what I had forgotten about teaching: Notes from a professor. *Phi Delta Kappan, 71*(6), 479–482.

Cuban, L. (2003). *Why is it so hard to get good schools?* New York: Teachers College Press.

Cuban, L. (2008). The perennial reform: Fixing school time. *Phi Delta Kappan, 90*(4), 240–250.

Cusick, P. A. (1983). *The equalitarian ideal and the American high school.* New York: Longman.

Daft, R. L., & Becker, S. W. (1978). *Innovation in organizations: Innovation adoption in school organizations.* New York: Elsevier.

Darling-Hammond, L. (1993). Reframing the school reform agenda. *Phi Delta Kappan, 74*(10), 753–761.

Darling-Hammond, L. (1997). *The right to learn.* San Francisco, CA: Jossey-Bass.

David, J. L. (1989). Synthesis of research on school-based management. *Educational Leadership, 46*(8), 45–53.

Davis, A., & Felknor, C. (1994). The demise of performance-based graduation in Littleton. *Educational Leadership, 51*(6), 64–65.

DeGersdorff, S. (2009). Is a private school education still worth it? *Boston Magazine, 9*(47), 64–73.

Dewey, J. (1946). *Problems of men.* New York: Philosophical Library.

Diegmueller, K. (1995). Struggling for standards. An *Education Week* special report, 1–70.

Digest of Education Statistics (2010). National Center for Educational Statistics. Retrieved from http://www.nces.ed.gov/ccd/pdf.

Digital Nation. (2010, February 3). *Frontline* television episode. Public Broadcasting System.

Dillon, S. (2010b, April 5). States skeptical about 'race to top' school aid contest. *New York Times.* Retrieved from http://www.nytimes.com.

Dillon, S. (2010a, September 1). Method to grade teachers provokes battles. *New York Times.* Retrieved from http://www.nytimes.com.

DuFour, R., DuFour, R., & Eaker, R. (Eds.). (2005). *On common ground: The power of professional learning communities.* Bloomington, IN: National Educational Service.

DuFour, R., Dufour, R., & Eaker, R. (2008). *Revisiting professional learning communities at work.* Bloomington, IN: Solution Tree Press.

Dufour, R., Dufour, R., Eaker, R., & Karhanek, G. (2004). *Whatever it takes: How professional learning communities respond when kids don't learn.* Bloomington, IN: Solution Tree Press.

Dwyer, D. C., Lee, G. V., Rowan, B., & Bossert, S. T. (1983). *Five principals in action: Perspectives on instructional management.* San Francisco, CA: Far West Laboratory for Educational Research and Development.

Eckholm, E. (2010, November 7). In efforts to end bullying, some see agenda. *New York Times.* Retrieved from http://www.nytimes.com.

Education Week. (1994). Summary of the improving America's schools act 14(10), 18–19.

Education Week. (1997). Quality counts: A report card on the condition of public education in the 50 states (Special Supplement, January 22).

Education Week. (2007) Ready for what? Preparing students for college, careers, and life after high school 40(26).

Education Week (2010). Quality counts 17(29), 39–41.

Education Week. (2010) Diplomas count: Graduation by the numbers 34(29)

Educational Leadership. (1983). 41(3), 3–36.

Egan, G. (1985). *Change agent skills in helping and human service settings.* Monterey, CA: Brooks/Cole.

Ellis, A. K., & Fouts, J. T. (1994). *Research on school restructuring.* Princeton Junction, NJ: Eye on Education.

Elmore, R. F. (2004). *School reform from the inside out.* Cambridge, MA: Harvard Education Press.

Elmore, R. F. (2009). The problem of capacity in the (re) design of educational accountability systems. In M. A. Robell & J. R. Wolff (Eds.) *NCLB at the crossroads: Reshaping the federal effort to close the achievement gap* (pp. 230–245). New York: Teachers College Press.

Elmore, R. F., & McLaughlin, M. W. (1988). *Steady work: Policy, practice, and the reform of American education.* Santa Monica, CA: The Rand Corporation.

English, F. W. (1988). *Curriculum auditing.* Lancaster, PA: Technomic.

English, F. W., & Larson, R. L. (1996). *Curriculum management for educational and social service organizations* (2nd ed.). Springfield, IL: Charles C. Thomas.

English, F. (2010). *Deciding what to teach and test: Developing, aligning, and leading the curriculum* (3rd ed.). Thousand Oaks, CA: Corwin Press.

Etzioni, A. (1989). Humble decision making. *Harvard Business Review, 89*(4), 122–126.

Evans, P. M. (2003, February). A principal's dilemma: Theory and reality of school redesign. *Phi Delta Kappan, 84*(6), 424–437.

Evans, R. (1996). *The human side of change.* San Francisco, CA: Jossey-Bass.

Fiedler, F. E., & Chemers, M. M. (1984). *Improving leadership effectiveness: The leader match concept* (2nd ed.). New York: John Wiley.

Finn, C. (2008, March 30). 5 myths about no child left behind. *Washington Post.* Retrieved from http://www.washingtonpost.com.

Firestone, W. A., & Corbett, H. D. (1988). Planned organizational change. In N. Boyan (Ed.), *Handbook of research in educational administration* (pp. 321–340). New York: Longman.

Fouts and Associates. (2006). *Leading the conversion process: Lessons learned and recommendations for converting to small learning communities.* Prepared for the Bill and Melinda Gates Foundation. Tucson, AZ.

Frase, L. E., English, F. W., & Poston, W. K., Jr. (Eds.). (2000). *The curriculum management audit: Improving school quality.* Lanham, MD: Rowman & Littlefield.

Freed, C. W., & Ketchem, M. E. (1986). *Teacher paperwork study: Type, time, and difficulty.* Dover, DE: Department of Public Instruction.

Friedman, T. L. (2005). *The world is flat.* New York: Farrar, Straus and Giroux.

Friedman. T. L. (2010, November 21). Teaching for America. *New York Times.* Retrieved from http: //www. nytimes.com.

Fullan, M. (1991). *The new meaning of educational change* (2nd ed.). New York: Columbia University, Teachers College Press.

Fullan, M. (1993). *Change forces.* London: The Falmer Press.

Fullan, M. (2007). *The new meaning of educational change* (4th ed.). New York: Teachers College Press.

Fullan, M. (Ed.). (2009). *The challenge of change: Start school improvement now!* Thousand Oaks, CA: Corwin.

Fullan, M. G. (1992). Visions that blind. *Educational Leadership 49*(5), 10–11.

Fullan, M. G. (1994). Coordinating top-down and bottom-up strategies for educational reform. In R. F. Elmore and S. H. Fuhrman (Eds.), *The governance of curriculum* (pp. 186–202). Alexandria, VA: Association for Supervision and Curriculum Development.

Fullan, M. G., & Miles, M. B. (1992). Getting reform right: What works and what doesn't. *Phi Delta Kappan, 73*(10), 745–752.

Futrell, M. H. (1989). Mission not accomplished: Education reform in retrospect. *Phi Delta Kappan, 71*(1), 9–14.

Gardner, J.W. (1965). *Self renewal.* New York: Harper Colophon.

Gardner, J. W. (1990). *On leadership.* New York: The Free Press.

Garmston, R., & Wellman, B. (1995). Adaptive schools in a quantum universe. *Educational Leadership, 52*(7), 6–12.

Gates, B. (2009). *Annual letter.* Seattle: Bill & Melinda Gates Foundation. Retrieved from http://www.gatesfoundation.org/annual-letter.

Gavin, R. (2010, August 25). With stimulus fading, economy must find its way. *Boston Globe*, B7, 11.

General Assembly of the State of Vermont. (1990). No. 230. An act relating to reforms in special education. Retrieved from http://www.education.vermont.gov.

Gewertz, C. (2007). Soft skills in big demand. *Education Week, 40*(26), 25–27.

Gewertz, C. (2008). States press ahead on 21st century skills. *Education Week, 8*(28), 21, 23.

Giles, C., & Hargreaves, A. (2006). The sustainability of innovative schools as learning organizations and professional learning communities during standardized reform. *Educational Administration Quarterly, 1*(42), 124–156.

Gleibermann, E. (2007). Even 100 hours a week leave children behind. *Phi Delta Kappan, 6*(88), 455–459.

Gleick, J. (1987). *Chaos: Making a new science.* New York: Penguin Books.

Glickman, C. D. (1987). Unlocking school reform: Uncertainty as a condition of professionalism. *Phi Delta Kappan, 69*(2), 120–122.

Glickman, C. D. (1990). Pushing school reform to the edge: The seven ironies of school empowerment. *Phi Delta Kappan, 72*(1), 68–75.

Glickman, C.D. (1993). *Renewing America's schools.* San Francisco, CA: Jossey-Bass.

Glickman, C. D., Gordon, S. P., & Ross-Gordon, J. M. (1995). *Supervision of instruction: A developmental approach* (3rd ed.). Boston, MA: Allyn and Bacon.

Goldin, C., & Katz, L. F. (2008). *The race between education and technology.* Cambridge, MA: The Belknap Press of the Harvard University Press.

Goodlad, J. I. (1984). *A place called school.* New York: McGraw-Hill.

Gottfredson, G. D., & Hybl, L. G. (1987). *An analytical description of the school principal's job.* Baltimore, MD: The Johns Hopkins University, Center for Research on Elementary and Middle Schools.

Grant, G. (1988). *The world we created at Hamilton High.* Cambridge, MA: Harvard University Press.

Green, E. (2010, March 7). Can good teaching be learned? *The New York Times Magazine,* 30–37; 44–46.

Growing Up Online. (2008, June 20). *Frontline* television episode. Public Broadcasting System.

Guskey, T. R. (1985). Staff development and teacher change. *Educational Leadership, 42*(7), 57–60.

Guskey, T. R. (1990). Integrating innovations. *Education Leadership, 47*(5), 11–15.

Hall, G. E., George, A. A., & Rutherford, W. L. (1979). *Measuring stages of concern about the innovation: A manual for use of the SoC questionnaire.* Austin, TX: The University of Texas, Research and Development Center for Teacher Education.

Hall, G. E., & Hord, S. M. (1987). *Change in schools: Facilitating the process.* Albany, NY: SUNY Press.

Hall, G. E., & Rutherford, W. L. (1990). Stages of concern. Paper presented at the annual meeting of the American Education Research Association. Boston, MA.

Hallinger, P., & Heck, R. H. (1996). Reassessing the principal's role in school effectiveness: A review of empirical research, 1980–1995. *Educational Administration Quarterly, 32*(1), 5–44.

Hargreaves, A. (1994). *Changing teachers, changing times.* New York: Teachers College Press.

Hargreaves, A. (2003). *Teaching in the knowledge society: Education in the age of insecurity.* New York: Teachers College Press.

Hargreaves, A., Earl, L., Moore, S., & Manning, S. (2001). *Learning to change: Teaching beyond subjects and standards.* San Francisco, CA: Jossey-Bass.

Hargreaves, A., & Goodson, I. (2006). Educational change over time? The sustainability and non-sustainability of three decades of secondary school change and continuity. *Educational Administration Quarterly, 1*(42), 3–41.

Hawley, W. D. (1988). Missing pieces of the educational reform agenda: Or, why the first and second waves may miss the boat. *Educational Administration Quarterly, 24*(4), 416–437.

Heitin, L. (2010). U.S. found to recruit fewer teachers from top ranks. *Education Week, 30*(8), 7.

Henry, Jules. (1963). *Culture against man.* New York: Vintage Books.

Herbert, B. (2009, January 13). Where the money is. *New York Times.* Retrieved from http://www.nytimes.com.

Hersey, P., Blanchard, K. H., & Johnson, D. E. (2001). *Management of organizational behavior: Leading human resources* (8th ed.). Upper Saddle River, NJ: Prentice-Hall.

Hess, F. M. (2009). The new stupid. *Educational Leadership, 4*(66), 12–17.

Horace. (1990). *The coalition of essential schools.* Providence, RI: Brown University.

Hord, S. M. (1991). *Personal communication.*

Hord, S. M., Rutherford, W. L., Huling-Austin, L., & Hall, G. E. (1987). *Taking charge of change.* Alexandria, VA: Association for Supervision and Curriculum Development.

House, E. R. (1981). Three perspectives on innovation. In R. Lehming and M. Kane (Eds.), *Improving schools: Using what we know* (pp. 17–41). Beverly Hills, CA: SAGE.

Howard, E., Howell, B., & Brainard, E. (1987). *Handbook for conducting school climate improvement projects.* Bloomington, IN: Phi Delta Kappa.

Howard, E. R., & Keefe, J. W. (1991). *The CASE-IMS school improvement process.* Reston, VA. National Association of Secondary School Principals.

Hoy, W. K., & Miskel, C. G. (1996). *Educational administration: Theory, research, and practice* (5th ed.). New York: McGraw-Hill.

Huberman, A. M., & Miles, M. B. (1984). *Innovation up close.* New York: Plenum Press.

Huberman, M. (1983). Recipes for busy kitchens. *Knowledge: Creation, diffusion, utilization, 4*(4), 478–511.

Jackson, P. W. (1968). *Life in classrooms.* Chicago, IL: Holt, Rinehart, & Winston.

Jacobson, D. (2010). Coherent instructional improvement and PLCs: Is it possible to do both? *Phi Delta Kappan, 6*(91), 38–45.

Johnson, L. B. (1965, January 13). Message to congress on education. *New York Times*, p. A20.

Johnson, S. M. (1990). *Teachers at work.* New York: Basic Books.

Johnson, S. M., & Boles, K. C. (1994). The role of teachers in school reform. In S. A. Mohrman, P. Wohlstetter, & Associates (Eds.), *School-based management* (pp. 109–137). San Francisco, CA: Jossey-Bass.

Joyce, B., & Calhoun, E. (Eds.) (1996). *Learning experiences in school renewal.* Eugene, OR: University of Oregon, Clearinghouse on Educational Management.

Kanter, R. M. (1983). *The change masters.* New York: Simon & Schuster.

Kantrowitz, B., & Mathews, J. (2007, May 28). The principal principle. *Newsweek,* 44–54.

Katz, D., & Kahn, R. L. (1978). *The social psychology of organizations* (2nd ed.). New York: John Wiley & Sons.

Keefe, J. W., & Amenta, R. B. (2005). Whatever happened to the Model School Project? *Phi Delta Kappan, 7*(86), 536–544.

Kelley, E. A. (1980). *Improving school climate.* Reston, VA: National Association of Secondary School Principals.

Kirst, M. K. (1982). How to improve schools without spending more money. *Phi Delta Kappan, 64*(1), 6–8.

Klein, A. (2009). New ESEA may sport initiatives. *Education Week, 14*(29), 1, 17.

Kottkamp, R. B., Provenzo, E. F., & Cohn, M. M. (1986). Stability and change in a profession: Two decades of teacher attitudes, 1964–1984. *Phi Delta Kappan, 67(8),* 559–567.

Kouzes, J. M., & Posner, B. Z. (2007). *The leadership challenge* (3rd ed.). San Francisco, CA: Jossey-Bass.

Krugman, P. (2009). *The return of depression era economics and the crisis of 2008.* (2nd ed.) New York: W. W. Norton & Co.

Kuttner, R. (2010, November 5). Cheap money won't fix this economy. *Boston Globe*, p. A11.

Larson, R. L. (1988). Change process' and 'change variables.' In R. A. Gorton, G. T. Schneider, & J. C. Fisher (Eds.), *Encyclopedia of school administration and supervision* (pp. 52–55). Phoenix: Oryx Press.

Larson, R. L. (1991). Small is beautiful: Innovation from the inside out. *Phi Delta Kappan, 72*(7), 550–554.

Lawrence-Turner, J. (2010, January 4). Spokane area teachers quietly add to classroom funding. *Seattle Times.* Retrieved from http://www.seattletimes.nwsource.com.

Lebaton, S. (2009, September 16). Fed chief says recession is 'very likely' over. *New York Times.* Retrieved from http://www.nytimes.com.

Lessinger, L. (1970). *Every kid a winner: Accountability in education.* Palo Alto, CA: Science Research Associates.

Levinson, H. (1968). *The exceptional executive: A psychological conception.* New York: New American Library.

Lewin, T. (2010, January 20). If your kids are awake, they're probably online. *New York Times.* Retrieved from http://www.nytimes.com.

Lewis, A. (1989). *Restructuring America's schools.* Arlington, VA: American Association of School Administrators.

Lieberman, A., & Miller, L. (1984). *Teachers, their world, and their work*. Alexandria, VA: Association for Supervision and Curriculum Development.

Lightfoot, S. L. (1983). *The good high school*. New York: Basic Books.

Lincoln, Y. S., & Guba, E. G. (1985). *Naturalistic inquiry*. Beverly Hills, CA: SAGE.

Linn, R. (2009). Improving the accountability provision of NCLB. In M. A. Robell & J. R. Wolff (Eds.), *NCLB at the crossroads: Reshaping the federal effort to close the achievement gap (pp. 163–197)*. New York: Teachers College Press.

Lipsitz, J. (1984). *Successful schools for young adolescents*. New Brunswick, NJ: Transaction Books.

Logan, D., King, J., & Fischer-Wright, H. (2008). *Tribal leadership: Leveraging natural groups to build a thriving organization*. New York: HarperBusiness.

Lortie, D. C. (1969). The balance of control and autonomy in elementary school teaching. In A. Etzioni (Ed.), *The semi-professions and their organization* (pp. 1–53). New York: The Free Press.

Lortie, D. C. (1975). *Schoolteacher: A sociological study*. Chicago, IL: The University of Chicago Press.

Loucks, S. F., Newlove, B. W., & Hall, G. E. (1975). *Measuring levels of use of the innovation: A manual for trainers, interviewers, and raters*. Austin, TX: The University of Texas, Research and Development Center for Teacher Education.

Loucks, S. F., & Zacchei, D. A. (1983). Applying our findings to today's innovations. *Educational Leadership, 41*(3), 28–31.

Loucks-Horsley, S., & Hergert, L. F. (1985). *An action guide to school improvement*. Alexandria, VA: Association for Supervision and Curriculum Development.

Louis, K. S., & Miles, M. B. (1990). *Improving the urban high school: What works and why*. New York: Teachers College Press, Columbia University.

Love, N., Stiles, K. E., Mundry, S., & Ranna, K. (2008). *The data coach's guide to improving learning for all students*. Thousand Oaks, CA: Corwin Press.

Lovett, I. (2010, November 10). Teacher's death exposes tensions in Los Angeles. *New York Times*. Retrieved from http://www.nytimes.com.

MA Department of Elementary and Secondary Education. (2008). *Ready for 21st century success. Boston, MA*.

MA Department of Elementary and Secondary Education (MADESE). (2010). *School redesign: Expanding learning time to support student success*. Retrieved from http://www.doe.mass.edu/research/reports/legistative.

MacQuarrie, B. (2010a, January 19). Patrick trumpets education legislation. *Boston Globe*, pp. B1, 3.

MacQuarrie, B. (2010b, March 4). Teacher firings ripple past Central Falls borders. *Boston Globe*, A1, 10.

MacQuarrie, B. (2010c, May 18). R.I. teachers subdued after agreement. *Boston Globe*, B1, 6.

Maeroff, G. I. (1988). *The empowerment of teachers*. New York: Teachers College Press.

Manasse, A. L. (1985). Improving conditions for principal effectiveness: Policy implications of research. *The Elementary School Journal, 85*(3), 439–463.

Manno, B. V. (1995). The new school wars: Battle over outcome-based education. *Phi Delta Kappan, 76*(9), 720–726.

March, J. G. (1981). Footnotes to organizational change. *Administrative Science Quarterly, 26,* 563–577.

March, J. G. (1983). How we talk and how we act: Administrative theory and administrative life. In T. Sergiovanni & J. J. Corbally (Eds.), *Leadership and organizational culture: New perspectives on administrative theory and practice* (pp. 18–35). Urbana: University of Illinois Press.

March, J. G. (1994). *A primer on decision making.* New York: The Free Press.

March, J. G., & Olsen, J. P. (1979). *Ambiguity and choice in organizations.* Bergen, Norway: Universitetsforlaget.

March, J. G., & Olsen, J. P. (1986). Garbage can models of decision making in organizations. In J. G. March and R. Weissinger-Baylon (Eds.), *Ambiguity and command: organizational perspectives on military decision making* (pp. 11–35). Cambridge, MA: Harvard Business School Press.

March, J. G., & Simon, H. A. (1958). *Organizations.* New York: John Wiley & Sons.

Marsh, D. D. (1994). Change in schools: Lessons from the literature. In S. A. Mohrman, P. Wohlstetter, & Associates (Eds.), *School-based management* (pp. 215–251). San Francisco, CA: Jossey-Bass.

Marshall, S. P. (1995). The vision, meaning and language of educational transformation. *The School Administrator, 52*(1), 8–15.

Martin, W. J., & Willower, D. T. (1981). The managerial behavior of high school principals. *Educational Administration Quarterly, 17*(1), 69–90.

Marzano, R. (2003). *What works in schools: Translating theory into action.* Alexandria, VA: Association for Supervising and Curriculum Development.

Massachusetts Department of Elementary & Secondary Education. (2010). Retrieved from http://madese/schooldistrictprofiles/accountability.

Maxwell, L. A. (2010). Turnaround team racing summer's clock. *Education Week, 37*(29), 1, 24, 25.

McAvoy, B. (1987). Everyday acts: How principals influence development of their staffs. *Educational Leadership, 44*(5), 73–77.

McCabe, K. (2010, January 24). Teen's suicide prompts a look at bullying. *Boston Globe*, pp. B1, 4.

McDonald, J. P., Klein, E. J., & Riordan, M. (2009). *Going to scale with new school designs.* New York: Teacher College Press.

McDonnell, L. M. (1994). *Policymakers' views of student assessment.* Los Angeles: University of California, Center for the Study of Evaluation, technical report.

McDonnell, L. M., & Elmore, R. F. (1987). Getting the job done: Alternative policy instruments. *Evaluation and Policy Analysis, 9*(2), 133–152.

McLuhan, M., & Fiore, Q. (1967). *The medium is the massage.* New York: Bantam Books.

McLaughlin, M. W., & Talbert, J. E. (2001). *Professional community and the work of high school teaching.* Chicago, IL: The University of Chicago Press.

McNeal, M. (2009b). Tight leash likely on turnaround aid. *Education Week, 2*(29), 1, 20–21.

McNeal, M. (2009a). Starting gun sounds for 'race to the top.' *Education Week, 12*(29), 1, 18–19.

Mead, M. (1970). *Culture and commitment.* Garden City, NY: Natural History Press.

Mehegan, D. (2009, January 19). "Cursive, foiled again." *Boston Globe,* pp. G14–15.

Miles, M. B. (Ed.) (1964). *Innovation in education.* New York: Teachers College Press.

Miles, M. B. (1973). Planned change and organizational health: Figure and ground. In M. M. Milstein & J. A. Belasko (Eds.), *Educational administration and the behavioral sciences: A systems perspective* (pp. 429–456). Boston, MA: Allyn & Bacon.

Miles, M. B. (1980). School innovation from the ground up: Some dilemmas. *New York University Education Quarterly, 11*(2), 2–9.

Miles, M. B. (1981). Mapping the common properties of schools. In R. Lehming, and M. Kane, (Eds.), *Improving schools: Using what we know* (pp. 42–114). Beverly Hills, CA: SAGE.

Miles, M. B.(1983). Unraveling the mystery of institutionalization. *Educational Leadership, 41*(3), 14–19.

Miller, S. J., Hickson, D. J., & Wilson, D. C. (1996). Decision-making in organizations. In S. R. Clegg, C. Hardy, and W. R. Nord (Eds.), *Handbook of organization studies* (pp. 293–312). London: Sage.

Mintzberg, H. (1973). *The nature of managerial work.* New York: Harper & Row.

Mohrman, S. A. (1994). High-involvement management in the private sector. In S. A. Mohrman, P. Wohlstetter, & Associates (Eds.), *School-based management* (pp. 25–52). San Francisco, CA: Jossey-Bass.

Mosberg, S. (1996). *How money matters to school performance.* Portland, OR: Northwest Regional Educational Laboratory

Moss, J. (Fall 2010). Modern age: How a new generation of young principals is handling the job. *The Magazine of the Harvard Graduate School of Education, 1,* (LIV), 30–35.

Moynihan, D. P. (1993, Winter). Defining deviancy down. *American Scholar.* Retrieved from http://www2.sunysuffolk.edu/formans/definingdeviancy.

Mueller, J. A., & Hovdes, K. H. (2008). Theme and variations in the enactment of reform: Case studies. In J. A. Supovitz & E. H. Weinbaum (Eds.), *The implementation gap: Understanding reform in high schools* (pp. 21–45). New York: Teachers College Press.

Muncey, D. E., & McQuillan, P. J. (1996). *Reform and resistance in schools and classrooms.* New Haven, CT: Yale University Press.

NAASP Bulletin. (1977). 61(412), entire issue.

National Association of Secondary School Principals. (2004). *Breaking ranks II: Strategies for leading high school reform.* Reston, VA.

National Board for Professional Teaching Standards. (2010). Retrieved from http://www.nbpts.org/about_us.

National Commission on Excellence in Education. (1983). *A nation at risk: The imperative for educational reform.* Washington, DC: U.S. Government Printing Office.

National Council of Teachers of Mathematics. (2000). *Principles and standards for school mathematics.* Retrieved from http://standards.nctm.org.

National Governors' Association. (1990). National goals statement. *Education Week, 9*(24), 16–17.

National Tax Journal. (2004, September 1). Is no child left behind an un (or under) funded federal mandate? Evidence from Texas. Retrieved from http://www. goliath.ecnext.com/com2/gi.

Neill, M. (2003). Leaving children behind: How no child left behind will fail our children. *Phi Delta Kappan, 3*(85), 225–228.

Newmann, F. (Ed.) (1992). *Student engagement and achievement in American secondary schools.* New York: Teachers College Press.

Newmann, F. M. & Associates. (1996). *Authentic achievement: Restructuring schools for intellectual quality.* San Francisco, CA: Jossey-Bass.

Newmann, F. M., & Wehlage, G. G. (1995). *Successful school restructuring.* Alexandria, VA: Association for Supervision and Curriculum Development.

Nieto, S. (2003). *What keeps teachers going?* New York: Teachers College Press.

Nieto, S. (2005). *Why we teach.* New York: Teachers College Press.

Nieto, S. (2009). From surviving to thriving. *Educational Leadership, 5*(66), 8–13.

Nixon, R. (1971, January 22). *Message to congress.* Retrieved from http://www. millercenter.org/scripps/archieve/speeches.

Nixon, R. (1972, January 20). *Message to congress.* Retrieved from http://millercenter. org/scripps/archieve/speeches.

North Central Regional Educational Laboratory. (2000*). Critical issue report 2000: Implementing site-based management to support student achievement.* Retrieved from http://ncrel.org/sdrs/areas/issues.

Ogawa, R. T., & White, P. A. (1994). School-based management: An overview. In S. A. Mohrman, P. Wohlstetter, & Associates (Eds.), *School-based management* (pp. 53–80). San Francisco, CA: Jossey-Bass.

Ogden, E. H., & Germinario, V. (1995). *The nation's best schools' blueprints for excellence.* Volume 2: Middle and secondary schools. Lancaster, PA: Technomic.

Olson, L. (1990). N. G. A. lists strategies for achieving national goals. *Education Week, 9*(40), 7.

Olson, L. (2004). Taking root. *Education Week, 15*(24), S1–S7.

Olson, L., & Miller, J. A. (1991). The education president at midterm: Mismatch between rhetoric, results? *Education Week, 10*(16), 1, 30–31.

O'Neil, J. (1995). Finding time to learn. *Educational Leadership, 53*(3), 11–15.

O'Neil, J. (1996). New options, old concerns. *Educational Leadership, 54*(2), 6–8.

Orlosky, D., & Smith, B. O. (1972). Educational change: Its origins and characteristics. *Phi Delta Kappan, 53*(7), 412–414.

Ortutay, B. (2009, June 16). In the Facebook age, families spend less time together. *Boston Globe,* p. A4.

Packard, J. S., Carlson, R. O., Charters, W. W. Jr., Moser, R. A., & Schmuck, P. A. (1976). *Governance and task interdependence in schools: Final report of a longitudinal study.* Eugene, OR: University of Oregon, Center for Educational Policy and Management.

Packer, J. (2007). The NEA supports substantial overhaul, not repeal, of NCLB. *Phi Delta Kappan, 4*(89), 265–269.

Palfrey, J., & Gasser, U. (2008). *Born digital: Understanding the first generation of digital natives.* New York: Basic Books.

Palonsky, S. B. (1986). *900 shows a year.* New York: Random House.

Passow, A. H. (1989). Present and future directions in school reform. In T. J. Sergiovanni & J. H. Moore (Eds.), *Schooling for tomorrow* (pp. 13–39). Boston: Allyn & Bacon.

Pellegrin, R. J. (1976). Schools as work organizations. In R. Dubin (Ed.), *Handbook of work, organizations, and society* (pp. 343–374). Chicago, IL: Rand McNally.

Pellicer, L. L., Anderson, L. N., Keefe, J. W., Kelley, E. A., & McCleary, L. E. (1988). *High school leaders and their schools—Volume I.* Reston, VA: National Association of Secondary School Principals.

Pellicer, L. L., Anderson, L. N., Keefe, J. W., Kelley, E. A., & McCleary, L. E. (1990). *High school leaders and their schools—Volume II.* Reston, VA: National Association of Secondary School Principals.

Peters, T. J., & Waterman, R. H. (1982). *In search of excellence: Lessons from America's best run companies.* New York: Harper & Row.

Peterson, P. E. (2010). *Saving schools: From Horace Mann to virtual learning.* Cambridge, MA: The Belknap Press of Harvard University.

Philips, K. (2002). *Wealth and democracy.* New York: Broadway Books.

Pink, D. (2006). *A whole new mind.* New York: Riverhead Books.

Pitsch, M. (1994). With students' aid, Clinton signs goals 2000. *Education Week 13*(28), 1, 21.

Powell, A. G., Farrar, E., & Cohen, D. K. (1985). *The shopping mall high school: Winners and losers in the educational marketplace.* Boston, MA: Houghton Mifflin.

Purkey, S. C., Rutter, R. A., & Newmann, F. M. (1986). U.S. high school improvement programs: A profile from the high school and beyond supplemental survey. *Metropolitan Education, 3*, 59–91.

Rasky, S. F. (1990, October 30). Substantial power on spending is shifted from Congress to Bush. *New York Times,* 1, 22.

Rauch, J. (1999). *Government's end: Why Washington stopped working.* New York: Public Affairs.

Rauth, M. (1990). Exploring heresy in collective bargaining with school restructuring. *Phi Delta Kappan, 71*(10), 781–784.

Ravitch, D. (1983). *The troubled crusade: American education, 1945–1980.* New York: Basic Books.

Ravitch, D. (2010). *The death and life of the great American school system.* New York: Basic Books.

Reavis, C., & Griffith, H. (1992). *Restructuring schools.* Lancaster, PA: Technomic.

Ringle, P. M., & Savickas, M. L. (1983). Administrative leadership: Planning and time perspectives. *Journal of Higher Education, 54*(6), 649–661.

Ripley, A. (2008, December 8). Can she save our schools? *Time,* 36–44.

Ripley, A. (2010, September 20). A call to action for public schools. *Time,* 32–42.

Robelan, E. W. (2010). Spending by education philanthropies drops. *Education Week, 18*(29), 1, 12–13.

Rogers, E. M. (1983). *Diffusion of innovations* (3rd ed.). New York: The Free Press.

Rogers, E. M., & Rogers, R. A. (1976). *Communication in organizations.* New York: The Free Press.

Ronka, D., Lachat, M. A., Slaughter, R., & Meltzer, J. (December 2008/January 2009). Answering the questions that count. *Educational Leadership, (4)66,* 18–24.

Rosenholtz, S. J. (1991). *Teachers' workplace.* New York: Teachers College Press.

Ross, D. (Ed.) (1958). *Administration for adaptability.* New York: Metropolitan School Study Council, Columbia University.

Rutherford, W. L., & Huling-Austin, L. (1984). Changes in high schools: What is happening—what is wanted. Paper presented at the annual meeting of the American Educational Research Association, New Orleans, LA.

Salganik, L. H. (1995). Why testing reforms are so popular and how they are changing education. *Phi Delta Kappan, 66*(9), 607–610.

Saltzman, J. (2010, May 4). Antibully law may face free speech challenges. *Boston Globe,* pp. A1, 9.

Sarason, S. (1996). *"Revisiting" the culture of the school and the problem of change.* New York: Teachers College Press.

Sarason, S. B. (1983). *Schooling in America: Scapegoat and salvation.* New York: The Free Press.

Sarason, S. B. (1990). *The coming failure of education reform.* San Francisco, CA: Jossey-Bass.

Sawchuk, S. (2010c). AFT chief promises due-process reform. *Education Week, 18*(29), 1, 11.

Sawchuk, S. (2010b). Recession drives states to rethink policies on National-Board Teachers. *Education Week, 21*(29), 1, 13.

Sawchuk, S. (2010a). States rush to adopt common standards as RTT contest ends. *Education Week, 37*(29), 6.

Sawchuk, S. (2010d). NEA, AFT choose divergent paths on Obama goals. *Education Week, 1*(30), 1, 18–19.

Schein, E. H. (1980). *Organizational psychology* (3rd ed.). Englewood Cliffs, NJ: Prentice-Hall.

Schmuck, R. A., & Runkel, P. J. (1994). *The handbook of organizational development in schools and colleges.* (4th ed.). Prospect Heights, IL: Waveland Press.

Schön, D. A. (1983). *The reflective practitioner.* New York: Basic Books.

Schön, D. A. (1987). *Educating the reflective practitioner.* San Francisco, CA: Jossey-Bass.

Schworm, P. (2010, April 30). State bill targeting bullying approved. *Boston Globe,* pp. A1, 6.

Senge, P. (2006). The *fifth discipline: The art and practice of the learning organization* (2nd ed.). New York: A Currency Book published by Doublday.

Sergiovanni, T. J. (1987). *The principalship: A reflective practice perspective.* Boston, MA: Allyn & Bacon.

Shinn, D. (personal communication). Council for Exceptional Children, February 12, 2010.

Sieber, S. D. (1981). Knowledge utilization in public education: Incentives and disincentives. In R. Lehming and M. Kane (Eds.), *Improving schools: Using what we know* (pp. 115–167). Beverly Hills, CA: SAGE.

Silberman, C. (1970). *Crisis in the classroom*. New York: Random House.

Silverman, J. (2006, September 3). Small schools movement hits some bumps. *Boston Globe*, p. A21.

Sizer, T. R. (1984). *Horace's compromise: The dilemma of the American high school*. Boston, MA: Houghton Mifflin.

Sizer, T. R. (1992). *Horace's school: Redesigning the American high school*. Boston, MA: Houghton Mifflin.

Sizer, T. R. (1996). *Horace's hope*. Boston, MA: Houghton Mifflin.

Slevin, C. (2010, June 12). In bold move, Colorado alters teacher tenure rules. *Yahoo! News*. Retrieved from http://www.news.yahoo.com.

Smith, L. M., Kleine, P. F., Prunty, J. J., & Dwyer, D. C. (1986). *Educational innovators: Then and now*. New York: The Falmer Press.

Smith, L. M., Prunty, J. J., Dwyer, D. C., & Kleine, P. F. (1987). *The fate of an innovative school*. New York: The Falmer Press.

Smith, L. M., Dwyer, D. C., Prunty, J. J., & Kleine, P. F. (1988). *Innovation and change in schooling: History, politics, and agency*. New York: The Falmer Press.

Spady, W. (1997). *Paradigm lost: Reclaiming America's educational future*. Arlington, VA: American Association of School Administrators.

Spady, W. (2001). *Beyond counterfeit reforms*. Lanham, MD: The Scarecrow Press.

Stacey, R. D. (1992). *Managing the unknowable*. San Francisco, CA: Jossey-Bass.

Stiggins, R. J. (1995). Assessment literacy for the 21st century. *Phi Delta Kappan, 77*(3), 238–245.

Stone, B. (2009, August 10). Breakfast can wait. The day's first stop is online. *New York Times*. Retrieved from http://www.nytimes.com.

Strebel, P. (1996). Why do employees resist change? *Harvard Business Review 74*(3), 86–92.

Stringfield, S., Ross, S., & Smith, L. (Eds.). (1996). *Bold plans for school restructuring*. Mahwah, NJ: Lawrence Earlbaum.

Supovitz, J. A. (2008). Implementation as iterative refraction. In J. A. Supovitz & E. H. Weinbaum (Eds.), *The implementation gap: Understanding reform in high schools* (pp. 151–172). New York: Teachers College Press.

Supovitz, J. A., & Weinbaum, E. H. (Eds.). (2008). *The implementation gap: Understanding reform in high schools*. New York: Teachers College Press.

The New York Times. (2010, June 14). Editorial, Washington's teacher's contract. Retrieved from http://www.nytimes.com/opinion.

The New York Times. (2010, August 12). Editorial, When the fed speaks. Retrieved from http://nytimes.com.

The Week. (2009, January 23). Only in America. 13.

Timar, T. (1989). The politics of school restructuring. *Phi Delta Kappan, 71*(4), 265–275.

Timar, T. B., & Kirp, D. L. (1989). Educational reform in the 1980s: Lesson from the states. *Phi Delta Kappan, 70*(7), 504–511.

Toffler, A. (1970). *Future shock*. New York: Bantam Books.

Toffler, A. (1980). *The third wave*. New York: Bantam Books.

Toffler, A. (1990). *Powershift*. New York: Bantam Books.

Trump, J. L. (1959). *Images of the future*. Washington, DC: National Association of Secondary School Principals.

Trump, J. L. (1977). *A school for everyone*. Reston, VA: National Association of Secondary School Principals.

Trump, J. L., & Baynham, D. (1961). *Focus on change: Guide to betters schools*. Chicago, IL: Rand McNally.

Trump, J. L., & Georgiades, W. (1970). Doing better with what you have. *The Bulletin of the National Association of Secondary School Principals, 54*(346), 106–133.

Trump, J. L., & Georgiades, W. (1977). What happened and what did not happen in the Model Schools Project. *The Bulletin of the National Association of Secondary School Principals, 61*(409), 72–79.

Tuthill, D. (1990). Expanding the union contract: One teacher's perspective. *Phi Delta Kappan, 71*(10), 775–780.

Tyack, D. (1990). Restructuring in historical perspective: Tinkering toward utopia. *Teachers College Record, 92*(2), 170–191.

Tyack, D., & Cuban, L. (1995). *Tinkering toward utopia: A century of public school reform*. Cambridge, MA: Harvard University Press.

Tye, K. A., & Tye, B. B. (1984). Teacher isolation and school reform. *Phi Delta Kappan, 65*(5), 319–322.

U.S. Department of Education. (1991). *America 2000: An education strategy*. Washington, DC.

U.S. News & World Report. (2010, January). Will School Reform Fail? pp. 25–51.

Vaznis, J. (2010a, March 30). Bay state loses first round of grants for education. *Boston Globe*. pp. A1, 9.

Vaznis, L. (2010b, November 9). Boston rethinking small-school experiment. *Boston Globe*, pp. 1, A9.

Vaznis, J., & Levenson. (2010, August 25). Mass. wins $250m for schools. *Boston Globe*, pp. A1, 8.

Vermont Department of Education. (2010). Act 60: The Equal Educational Opportunity Act. Retrieved from http://www.vtdoe/schooldatareports/accountabilitydata.

Viadero, D. (1995). Mixed record for Coalition schools is seen. *Education Week, 15*(9), 1, 12–13.

Viadero, D. (2009a). 'Scientifically based' giving way to 'development' innovation. *Education Week, 19*(28), 1, 11.

Viadero, D. (2009b). Sizer's legacy seen in appeal of personalized high schools. *Education Week, 9*(29), 1, 12–13.

Viadero, D. (2010). Ravitch lays out change of heart on earlier ideas. *Education Week, 24*(29), 1, 14–15.

Wagner, T. (1994). *How schools change: Lesson from three communities.* Boston, MA: Beacon Press

Wagner, T. (2008). *The global achievement gap.* New York: Basic Books.

Waller, W. (1965). *The sociology of teaching.* New York: John Wiley.

Walton, M. (1986). *The Deming management method.* New York: Perigee Books.

Walton, M. (1990). *Deming management at work.* New York: G. P. Putnam's Sons.

Wasley, P., Hampel, R., & Clark, R. (1997). The puzzle of whole school change. *Phi Delta Kappan, 78*(9), 690–697.

Wasley, P. A. (1994). *Stirring the chalkdust.* New York: Teachers College Press.

Waterman, R. H., Jr. (1987). *The renewal factor.* New York: Bantam Books.

Watts, G. D., & McClure, R. M. (1990). Expanding the contract to revolutionize school renewal. *Phi Delta Kappan, 71*(10), 765–774.

Weick, K. E. (1976). Educational organizations as loosely coupled systems. *Administrative Science Quarterly, 21,* 1–19.

Weick, K. E. (1982). Management of organizational change among loosely coupled elements. In P. S. Goodman & Associates, (Eds.), *Change in organizations: New perspectives on theory, research, and practice* (pp. 375–408). San Francisco, CA: Jossey-Bass.

Weick K. E. (1984). Small wins: Redefining the scale of social problems. *American Psychologist, 39*(1), 40–49.

Weick, K. E. (1985). Sources of order in unorganized systems: Themes in recent organizational theory. In Y. S. Lincoln, (Ed.), *Organizational theory and inquiry: The paradigm revolution* (pp. 106–136). Beverly Hills, CA: SAGE.

Weick, K. E. (1995). *Sensemaking in organizations.* Thousand Oaks, CA: SAGE.

Wells, A. (2009). Our children's burden. In M. A. Robell & J. R. Wolff (Eds)., *NCLB at the crossroads: Reshaping the federal effort to close the achievement gap* (pp. 1–40), New York: Teachers College Press.

What Works Cleaning House. (2010). Institute for Education Science. Retrieved from http://www.ies.ed.gov/ncee/wwc.

Wheatley, M. J. (1992). *Leadership and the new science.* San Francisco, CA: Berrett-Koehler.

Wikipedia. (2009, November 18). *Coalition of essential schools.* Retrieved from http://en.wikipedia.org.

Williams, J. (2009, July 25). Administration launches school reform contest. *Boston Globe,* p. A2.

Wilson, B. L., & Corcoran, T. B. (1988). *Successful secondary schools.* Philadelphia, PA: The Falmer Press.

Wise, A. E. (1979). *Legislated learning.* Berkeley, CA: University of California Press.

Wise A. E. (1988). Legislated learning revisited. *Phi Delta Kappan, 69*(5), 329–333.

Wohlstetter, P. (1995). Getting school-based management right. *Phi Delta Kappan, 77*(1), 22–26.

Wohlstetter, P., & Mohrman, S. A. (1994a). Conclusion: New directions for school-based management. In S. A. Mohrman, P. Wohlstetter, & Associates (Eds.), *School-based management* (pp. 269–286). San Francisco, CA: Jossey-Bass.

Wohlstetter, P., & Mohrman, S. A. (1994b). *School-based management: Promise and process*. CPRE finance briefs. New Brunswick, NJ: Rutgers, The State University of New Jersey.

Wolcott, H. F. (1977). *Teachers versus technocrats*. Eugene, OR: University of Oregon, Center for Educational Policy and Management. (Republished in 2003 by Rowman & Littlefield, Summit, PA.)

Yen, H. (2009, December 16). Popularity of text messaging is edging out cell phone calls. *Boston Globe*, p. A5.

Zaltman, G., Duncan, R., & Holbek, J. (1973). *Innovation and organization*. New York: John Wiley.

Note: Those readers interested in a detailed description of the research methodology used in the study of the Bromley and Mansfield schools should contact rlarson89@cape.com

Index

About the Author

Robert Larson is a professor emeritus of education at the University of Vermont, College of Education and Social Services. For thirty one years, he taught graduate courses in curriculum management, effecting and managing change, organizational leadership, research methods, supervision, and staff evaluation and development. He conducted several field studies about change and innovation in high schools, the outcomes used in his writing and in his courses to ensure the relevance of theory to practice.

Dr. Larson has been a high school teacher and administrative intern with the National Association of Secondary School Principals' Ford Foundation Program. During his years in Vermont, he served on committees of the Vermont Principals' Association, the NASSP, and the National Council of Professors of Educational Administration. He was also a member of the American Association of School Administrators and a presenter for AASA, NASSP, and Phi Delta Kappa in-service institutes.

CPSIA information can be obtained at www.ICGtesting.com
263562BV00002B/1/P